THE WAR THAT MADE THE MIDDLE EAST

The War That Made the Middle East

WORLD WAR I AND THE END OF THE OTTOMAN EMPIRE

MUSTAFA AKSAKAL

PRINCETON UNIVERSITY PRESS
PRINCETON & OXFORD

Published by Princeton University Press
41 William Street, Princeton, New Jersey 08540
99 Banbury Road, Oxford OX2 6JX

press.princeton.edu

GPSR Authorized Representative: Easy Access System Europe - Mustamäe tee 50, 10621 Tallinn, Estonia, gpsr.requests@easproject.com

ISBN 978-0-691-26249-9
ISBN (e-book) 978-0-691-26251-2

Library of Congress Control Number: 2025941930

British Library Cataloging-in-Publication Data is available

Editorial: Priya Nelson and Emma Wagh
Production Editorial: Kathleen Cioffi
Jacket Design: Chris Ferrante
Production: Erin Suydam
Publicity: Alyssa Sanford and Kathryn Stevens
Copyeditor: Irina du Quenoy

Jacket image: Ruins of Gaza at the time of the Great Attack, April 1917. Courtesy of Library of Congress Prints and Photographs Division, Washington, D.C.

This book has been composed in Minion Pro and Universe

Printed in the United States of America

10 9 8 7 6 5 4 3 2 1

CONTENTS

ILLUSTRATIONS

Maps

Figures

Tables

ACKNOWLEDGMENTS

I GREW up in Germany and Turkey and have lived my adult life in the United States. All three places, in different ways, feel like home. All three places have dark histories of state-orchestrated mass killing. Much of this book was written steps from the Potomac River, named after a people whose presence has been all but erased in the contemporary neighborhoods that now line its banks. The histories of all three of my "home countries" have been closely intertwined with violence and atrocities against civilians, a circumstance that should not be attributed to coincidence. Rather it suggests that such violence is common to many states and societies and that all of them harbor the capacity for destroying human life on a massive scale. It also suggests that most, perhaps all, modern identities, in one way or another, are linked to communal trauma and state violence, whether on the receiving or the inflicting end, and often both. If that's true, then all of us living in modern times, in one way or another, are part of this human drama. This book takes up one facet of that history. It is both particular and universal.

While writing this book I have incurred a great debt of gratitude to many colleagues, students, archivists, librarians, friends, and family. Here I can acknowledge only a small number of them. I am grateful to Margaret Lavinia Anderson and M. Şükrü Hanioğlu, whose wisdom and knowledge have guided me since my student days long ago. I am grateful for their erudition as much as for their sound advice and kindness. Elizabeth F. Thompson has been an indefatigable sounding board and source of inspiration over many years. It has been a privilege to draw on the sage counsel and support of Ronald Grigor Suny. Dominique Reill, Aimee Genell, Max Friedman, and Osama Abi-Mershed shared invaluable feedback on late iterations of the manuscript. Without them I might have abandoned this project altogether. Aviel Roshwald and James Sheehan read early drafts of the manuscript and saved me from multiple wrong turns. I thank Graham Pitts for sharing with me an important set of French archival documents. Over the years, I have benefited from the insight and generosity of a great many colleagues and friends: Yiğit Akın, Cemil Aydın, Oliver Bast, Lâle Can, Mary Elisabeth Cox, Santanu Das, Selim Deringil, Lerna Ekmekçioğlu, Michael Gavlak, Robert Geraci, Robert Gerwarth, Peter Holquist, Hilmar Kaiser, Hasan Kayalı, Hans-Lukas Kieser, Nora Lessersohn, Eric Lohr, Wolfgang P. Mueller, William Mulligan, Nilay Özok-Gündoğan, Andrew Patrick, Zozan Pehlivan, Graham Pitts, Michael Reynolds, Sophie De Schaepdrijver, Leonard Smith, Nader Sohrabi, Hew Strachan, James Tallon, Salim Tamari, Melanie Tanielian, Gizem Tongo, Jonathan Wyrtzen, Yücel Yanıkdağ, İpek Yosmaoğlu, and Erik Jan Zürcher.

At Georgetown University, my academic home, I am grateful for the support of many wonderful colleagues: Osama Abi-Mershed, Fida Adely, Gábor Ágoston, Rochelle Davis, Maurice Jackson, John McNeill, Aviel Roshwald, Joseph Sassoon, Nefertiti Takla, and Judith Tucker. I have benefited greatly from the manuscript workshop organized by John McNeill and the invaluable comments offered by its participants: Osama Abi-Mershed, Gábor Ágoston, Carol Benedict, Ananya Chakravarty, Elizabeth Cross, Michael David-Fox, Charles King, Eric Lohr, Meredith McKittrick, Aviel Roshwald, and James Shedel. Our PhD students at Georgetown, both current and former, have been a constant source of inspiration: Önder Eren Akgül, Sopanit (Dede) Angsusingha, Diogo Bercito, Kate Dannies, Nicholas Danforth, Fatma Esen, Laura Goffman, Benan Grams, Idun Hauge, Stefan Hock, Ben Jones, Armen Manuk-Khaloyan, Jackson Perry, Juan Ramirez, Samar Saeed, Patrick Schilling, Yasser Sultan, Mary Tezak, Diana Yayloyan, and Yinan Zhang. A special thank you to the students in my First-Year Proseminar on the end of the First World War in the Middle East. I am grateful to the undergraduate research assistants I had the privilege of mentoring and who contributed to this project in numerous ways: Reilly Barry, Harrison Goohs, Irmak Şensöz, and Mohamed Meshal. At Georgetown's Lauinger Library, Brenda Bickett, Scott Taylor, and Ryan Zohar have been indispensable. I have been incredibly fortunate to enjoy the support of many institutions, including the National Endowment for the Humanities, the Institute for Advanced Study at Princeton, the American Council of Learned Societies, the Harry Frank Guggenheim Foundation, the Library of Congress, and Princeton University's Firestone Library. I could not have hoped for a more supportive editorial team than Priya Nelson and Emma Wagh.

Finally, I thank my family—Clara, Gabe, Miles, Kristen, Özgür, Yeşim, Yeliz, Aylin, Handan, Zeynep, Ekin, Peter, Bassam, Naila, and Ziad—for all their love and encouragement. Writing this book has been a truly collaborative effort, though its shortcomings of course are all mine.

THE WAR THAT MADE THE MIDDLE EAST

Introduction

HISTORY AS A MINEFIELD

AROUND THREE o'clock in the afternoon on Tuesday, October 19, 1920, in the small village of Çay, near Gallipoli, a seven-year-old boy named Ferhad ran up to his friends, gesturing with excitement about an artillery shell he had found in the local cemetery. Ferhad could not speak (he is described as *dilsiz*, or "tongueless," in Ottoman Turkish), but fragmentary records in the Ottoman archives in Istanbul allow us to hear his historical voice nonetheless, if only for a moment. The shell, and perhaps Ferhad's disability, were remnants of the First World War. Eight children followed Ferhad to examine the shell. Seventeen-year-old İsmail, the son of Ali of Lemnos, had brought along an axe. İsmail stood over the shell and struck it. The resulting explosion killed him in an instant, along with Hüseyin, the son of Mehmed, and seriously injured several of their friends. İsmail and Hüseyin had survived the First World War, but two years after the armistice, it killed them just the same.[1]

The years 1914–1918 claimed at least two and a half million Ottoman lives, or about 10 percent of the empire's entire population. Only Serbia suffered a higher civilian death rate. The war set ablaze the empire's social fabric and gave birth to radically new political identities. It put into motion developments that have shaped the former Ottoman lands—"the Middle East," as we know it today—for over a century. Much of the history of this period remains buried under the debris of war, and it continues to be a political minefield no less explosive than the shell that killed the two curious boys that afternoon in the cemetery at Çay.[2]

In 1914 the Ottoman government took the empire to war in order to "save our people and our homeland."[3] But over the next four years that same government killed more of its citizens—men, women, and children—than enemy guns. It allowed hundreds of thousands of people to starve to death, lost perhaps as many as a million men in uniform, and surrendered more than half of its territory. The First World War put an end to a state that, although it had suffered a series of defeats in the two years immediately preceding the war, had governed vast territories and diverse populations for over six centuries. Why was the First World War in the Ottoman Empire so destructive? This book seeks to answer that question and proposes a new interpretation of the war years.

One of the most enduring ideas about the Ottoman Empire is that it was destroyed by the storms of nationalist and separatist movements that swept the world in the nineteenth century. This understanding is often accompanied by a powerful but misleading image of the Ottoman Empire as the "Sick Man of Europe," a state that collapsed in on itself at the end of the war. Another entrenched narrative is that of the empire's inevitable decline, a view that takes the Ottomans' dissolution for granted and renders its demise a logical conclusion to a long history.

Such depictions of the empire served many political agendas, and they continue to do so today, explaining, in part, why they have proved so enduring both in the popular imagination and in much of the scholarship outside of the academic field of Ottoman studies. In the nineteenth century, the imagery of a declining, decrepit empire provided the basis for legitimizing Great Power intervention; the image of the empire's impending implosion could justify military occupation, annexation, and even colonial rule. It also made possible European denial of responsibility for altering the place of Christians and Jews in the empire, indeed, for endangering their membership in a multireligious, multiethnic, and multilingual polity. European powers could make such denials even as they framed such interventions as benefiting the populations they occupied.

The understanding of the empire as sick did not only serve European political agendas. In due course, the same Orientalist imagery of a failing empire proved useful to the state-building and nation-making projects that replaced it after the First World War. The new states defined themselves with their own, national images promising a safe and bright future that set them apart from those of the Ottoman past. It is crucial not to succumb to the temptation of viewing the empire through religious or ethnonational blocks, however. Such blocks first crystallized and later were consolidated only *after* the First World War. In other words, they were molded in the crucible of the war itself, born in blood. They were a product, not a cause, of the empire's dissolution.

This book turns those old images on their head. It begins with the observation that the Ottoman Empire was a vital political community in 1914. In Salim Tamari's words, referring to the experience in Ottoman Palestine, "four miserable years of tyranny" in the First World War "erased four centuries of a rich and complex Ottoman patrimony."[4] The many memoirs of those who lived through this period echo Tamari's words. One such example comes from Demetrios Theodore, or Dimitri, as he was known. Dimitri was born in 1904 in Maden, a small town in eastern Anatolia. It was the home of some five hundred Greek Orthodox families and an even larger Armenian Christian population. Greek Orthodox himself, Dimitri recalled that the "spirit of friendship and co-operation in a social order where both the Greeks and the Turks had found their respective places and were learning to live together in harmony was torpedoed during the four years [of] war."[5] Dimitri's memories suggest a profound breakdown in intercommunal relations during the war years. Indeed, the scholar Nicholas Doumanis has noted that so abrupt was the shift in intercommunal relations that recollections of coexistence such as Dimitri's, despite their frequency, have been largely dismissed as nostalgia, treated as a romanticization of a past that, given the bloodshed with which the empire ended, could not have existed.[6]

It is important to situate the First World War in the Middle East within its Ottoman context. The Ottoman government's participation in the war marked a new phase in the empire's 1908 Revolution, a revolution that had

FIGURE 1. Original Caption: "Raft of sheep or goat skin holding Turks and Armenians. Euphrates River, 1903." *Source*: Shishmanian Collection, box 3. Hoover Library and Archives, Stanford University

sidelined the sultan and initiated empire-wide elections to a parliament in Istanbul. Those elections brought to power a revolutionary organization, the Ottoman Committee of Union and Progress, or the "Unionists."[7] It was this revolutionary organization that conducted the Ottoman state's policies in the First World War.

The Unionists' revolution had both a foreign and a domestic side. At home, the objective was to remove the authoritarian power of the long-reigning sultan, Abdülhamid II (r. 1876–1909), to promote economic development, and to foster and modernize the unity of the empire's diverse population and thereby secure the empire's territorial integrity. On the international stage, the Unionists were fighting European imperialism. They saw themselves as defending the country against the daily injustices the Great Powers were inflicting on the empire. They called out the hypocrisy of the Great Powers' claims of acting in the name of free trade, freedom, and civilization.

If the First World War was central to the making of the Middle East, however, then the Ottoman Empire was just as central to the making of the conflict. Europe's six Great Powers—Austria-Hungary, Germany, Great Britain, France, Italy, and Russia—exercised their dominance in the Ottoman Empire through a variety of political and legal instruments, ranging from informal rule to financial control to outright military occupation and colonization. France ruled Algeria (since 1830) as a colony and Tunis (since 1881) as a protectorate. Britain governed Cyprus (1878) as a protectorate and occupied Egypt-Sudan (since 1882). Britain also signed treaties with several leading families in the Gulf region, promising them virtual independence from Istanbul.[8] Austria-Hungary occupied the provinces of Bosnia and Herzegovina in 1878 and annexed them in 1908.[9] Russia occupied and annexed the eastern Anatolian territories of Ardahan, Batum, and Kars in 1878, supported independence movements in southeastern Europe (the Balkans), and claimed Istanbul/Constantinople and the Straits waterway as a Russian manifest destiny that would give the tsar's navy access to the warm waters of the Mediterranean. Italy occupied Ottoman provinces in North Africa (Tripolitania, or Libya) and the Dodecanese Islands in 1911 and 1912. Though not under European colonial rule according to international law, much of Ottoman territory was effectively subject to Great Power rule.

Moreover, by 1912, the Ottomans' neighbors Iran and Morocco were divided into spheres of influence, while Afghanistan had fallen to British hegemony already in the late nineteenth century.[10] By 1914 the Ottoman Empire was one of a small number of states in Africa and Asia that, even if deeply circumscribed, could claim to possess a degree of sovereignty.

To avoid war between themselves, the Great Powers formed a loose international association styled as the Concert of Europe, which allowed them to coordinate their interests and delineate areas of influence around the globe. As the Great Powers laid claim to various parts of the world, they used diplomacy and the expanding body of international law—which they themselves wrote—to manage what they referred to as the "balance of powers." In the nineteenth century, international law, though not unchallenged, served to facilitate the relations among the expanding, imperial powers of Western Europe, the United States, and Japan.[11]

By 1914 the Ottoman Empire had confronted the destabilizing arrival of European and American missionaries, merchants, diplomats, and soldiers for over a century. But the experience of suffering under colonialism and oppression was not only an international story. Populations inside the Ottoman Empire—from Diyarbekir in the Ottoman East to Basra in the Gulf, and from Aleppo and Beirut to Mecca and Yemen—could view the Unionist government in Istanbul not as liberators but as subjugators. Much like modern states elsewhere, Ottoman governments in the nineteenth century pursued a capacious control over populations and natural resources. Unsurprisingly, as the state extended its reach, political elites, landowners, tribal chieftains, local communities, women, and workers demanded political freedoms, legal rights, and participatory government.[12]

Thus, in the nineteenth century the Ottoman state found itself under increasing colonial pressure. Foreign powers ruled some of its territories, exercised legal jurisdiction over a considerable segment of the population, dictated the hiring and firing of high-ranking officials, collected directly the profits from products such as salt and tobacco, set import and export tariffs, and could even determine where Ottoman companies could and could not construct railways (e.g., they were prevented from doing so near the Russian border). At the same time, the Ottoman state's aggressive drive for modernizing its realm and centralizing its control over it had its own colonial effects.[13] As in Egypt or China, modern state-building in the Ottoman Empire converged with struggles to keep European (and United States) imperialism out. In the effort to escape foreign control, states all around the world sought to monopolize their domestic resources. In the process, they endeavored to push their legal and physical control into every nook and cranny of society, right up to the edge of its territorial borders. Census counts, military conscription regimes, mandatory education, and new communication and transportation technologies became key instruments in that pursuit. This form of anti-colonial state-building, intended to keep foreign powers out, could produce in turn its own breed of colonialism.[14] While the Unionists saw themselves as taking up arms against foreign control, inside the empire opposition groups fought their own anti-colonial cause against the very same Unionists.[15] The Ottoman state, first under Sultan Abdülhamid II and then under the Unionists, took the war to its own communities before taking it to the Great Powers. It was this dynamic—the interplay of war, historical memory, and Unionist decision-making—that destroyed the empire in the years of the First World War.

A crucial characteristic of the Ottoman Empire, then, was the presence of a double, or twofold anti-colonialism, but it was not unique to the Ottomans. In China, internal anti-colonialists aimed to overthrow Manchu rule, while external anti-colonialists targeted foreign control, leading to revolution in China in 1911.[16] In Egypt, Colonel Ahmed Urabi led a movement in 1881 against both the khedive in Cairo and British influence. In Iran, revolutionaries established a parliament and a constitution in 1905, challenging both the power of the shah and foreign interests. The Ottoman First World War represented a moment in a longer history that reached back to the first half of the nineteenth century, and it continues to shape the region in important ways today. As in China and elsewhere, Ottoman state and society were "navigating semi-colonialism" in their own vernacular ways.[17] In this respect, for the people of the Eastern Mediterranean and North Africa, the First World War neither began nor ended in the twentieth century.

In the second half of the nineteenth century, the sultan's authoritarianism gave rise to a revolutionary age and political dissent across the empire and beyond. Members of the opposition, often collectively called "the Young Turks," forged their movement from places such as Geneva, Paris, and British-held Cairo.[18] On July 23, 1908, at long last, the Ottoman Constitutional Revolution generated a moment of euphoria and hope across the country. It provided for empire-wide elections and the formation of the first parliament since 1878, ushering in an Ottoman Spring. "The country at once sprang to life," reported a young Russian correspondent in *Pravda*, Leon Trotsky, in December 1908.[19]

Across the empire, Ottoman citizens from all walks of life, men and women, girls and boys, members of the empire's various religious communities and social classes, celebrated the promises of the newly proclaimed constitution. The revolution attracted broad popular support for participatory politics and affirmed hopes in the empire's political viability.[20] Speakers at mass rallies invoked the French Revolution. Flags and postcards, many of them multilingual in the various languages of the empire, extolled the revolutionary virtues of freedom, equality, brotherhood, and justice.[21]

Deputies elected to the parliament—Muslims, Christians, and Jews—hailed from all parts of the empire. A multitude of new parties, associations, and publications advocated unity and conciliation among the empire's ethnic groups under the banner of "Ottomanism."[22] One such organization, the Ottoman Democratic Party, proclaimed that "today the government of Turkey [*Türkiye hükümeti*] and the Ottoman nation consist of Turkish, Arab, Albanian, Kurdish, Armenian, Greek Orthodox [*Rum*], Jewish, Bulgarian, and many other different elements. All elements are in unity and alliance with each other."[23] Unionists and the Armenian Revolutionary Federation, the largest Armenian political organization in the prerevolutionary era, worked together closely in the aftermath of the 1908 Revolution, at least initially.[24] For the first time in thirty years, there would be empire-wide elections to send representatives to the Assembly of Deputies, the lower house of parliament, known as the Meclis-i Mebusan.[25] Winds of democracy, it seemed, had swept away the sultan's police state.

Fulfilling the promises of the revolution, unsurprisingly, proved to be a highly contentious process. Hundreds of publications and public fora exercised their newfound freedoms of speech and association. They fueled the campaigns of new political parties and prominent individuals. Electioneering spoke to the needs of constituents, but it could also generate identitarian politics as parties and candidates sought to distinguish themselves from competitors. As in any election, parties and candidates appealed to voters by making claims to offer them true representation, or at least better representation, than their rivals.[26] Representative politics could be simultaneously inclusive and divisive.

For most people around the world in 1914, the words "the Middle East" would not have meant very much. Its cognate siblings, "the Near East" and "the Far East," had been in use as geographical descriptors for several decades, but "the Middle East" as a phrase to designate the territories of the Ottoman Empire came into common usage only in the years immediately following the First World War, and then primarily in diplomatic parlance. All three "Easts"—Near, Middle, and Far—reflected a division of the world that made sense only when gazing out the windows of the British Foreign Office in London. The labels were imposed by outsiders, and even today the designation "the Middle East" has "few claimants" from within the region itself.[27] The region's renaming from the Ottoman Empire to the Middle East, however, was an act not only of Eurocentrism but also of erasure. It hid from memory the existence of social and political institutions that had fostered relatively stable relations over a vast and diverse geographical region for centuries.

Notably, the empire's inability to resist the concerted military prowess of the European Great Powers in the nineteenth century has been equated to the empire's wholescale dysfunctionality. The fact that the empire was outgunned, however, did not mean it had run its course. To the contrary, it retained cultural and political vibrancy despite its military weakness. For the sake of argument, if the Ottoman Empire could not stand up to the combined forces of Great Power armies, neither could, say, Switzerland or Spain in the early twentieth century, though they were never put to the test in the same way. What we do know is that Italy's invasion of Ottoman Libya in October 1911, despite its brutality, elicited a rather different response from the Great Powers than the violation of Belgian neutrality in August 1914.

Be that as it may, this book takes seriously the empire's potential viability that was destroyed in the First World War. A different future for the empire was also on the table, one that kept alive and extended the empire's history of a multiethnic and multireligious society. That potential, too, was a principal casualty of the war. It spelled disaster for the people of the Ottoman Empire during the conflict and, arguably, ever since. The empire before 1914 was not "a multicultural paradise," as one scholar has reminded us (and no place could have been described as such in the early twentieth century).[28] But its dissolution in 1923 did not put an end to the problems facing the people of the region. While there is no place for nostalgia—after all, the empire treated its people with so much violence—it is doubtful whether the states that replaced it resolved the challenges that confronted the people of the Ottoman Empire in 1914. The new states, too, proved largely unable to foster domestic peace, forge fair and representative government, deliver economic prosperity, and stay out of military conflict. Ethnic and religious difference, for one, remained a central feature of politics, and, in this respect at least, the empire arguably proved more capable in managing diverse populations than the states that took its place. If there can be no nostalgia for the empire, then neither can there be triumphalism over the arrival of the nation-states. Both state forms engendered mass violence.

Today, beyond a small group of specialists, the war as *experienced* in the Ottoman Empire remains largely unknown. In most Western histories, the war is typically portrayed as a peripheral stage on which the main actors were outsiders: Germans declaring jihad, Australians and New Zealanders perishing on the Gallipoli Peninsula, Sykes and Picot divvying up the Arab lands (into future British and French "mandates"), T. E. Lawrence lighting the spark for the so-called Arab Revolt, and Lord Balfour pledging British support for "the establishment in Palestine of a national home for the Jewish people."[29] In the commonly accepted Western narrative, the one aspect of the war in which Ottomans themselves played an active role is the Armenian *Aghet* ("The Catastrophe") or the *Medz Yeghern* ("The Great Crime"), known to historians (although not to most Turks) as the Armenian Genocide. And yet, all of these wartime events—significant as they are—too often appear as separate dramas, isolated from each other rather than part of a single Ottoman story.[30] The empire, however, was at war as a whole, against the world and against itself.

For the people of the empire, disparate experiences of the war produced disparate legacies and memories. In the new ethnonational limbs of the old multiethnic empire, an imperial past became repackaged as national memory: the history of the empire became remembered as the history of the nation. For Armenians, the memory of the imperial past became subsumed under the great national trauma of genocide. For the empire's

Arab lands, the war was overshadowed by the era of Anglo-French colonial rule. For Kurds and Palestinians, in Kurdistan and Palestine, the war came to signify the birth of their statelessness. Amid these tragedies, for Turks, the war became remembered as a national triumph: the Ottomans lost an empire, the Turks won a nation.

On October 29, 1914, in the dark of night, a small fleet of German and Ottoman ships crossed the Black Sea, converged on several Russian port cities—Novorossiysk, Odessa, and Sevastopol—and, without a declaration of war, opened fire. They sank the gunboat *Kubanetz* and the minelayer *Pruth* and took three Russian officers and eighty-three members of the crew prisoner. Interior Minister Talat—perhaps the single most powerful Ottoman wartime figure—then claimed, falsely, that Russia had shot first. "The lying is excellent," a German officer who participated in the raid recorded in his diary.[31]

The Ottoman government's exit from the war was equally stealthy. Four years later, almost to the day, on November 1, 1918, Talat and several other strongmen who had conducted the war, climbed quietly aboard the German torpedo boat *R01*, which sped north from Istanbul into the Black Sea. Talat and his comrades' plan, on reaching Odessa, was to disembark "incognito," as the report—marked "to be destroyed"—indicated.[32] The Ottoman leaders, once all-powerful, had become fugitives.

Huddled together on the deck of the *R01*, Talat and the top brass of the Ottoman wartime government—War Minister Enver, Fourth Army Commander Cemal, Trabzon's Governor Azmi, Police Chief Bedri, the intelligence operative Dr. Bahaeddin Şakir, the Committee of Union and Progress party secretary Midhat Şükrü, and the chief of its Central Committee, Dr. Nazım—contemplated their next move. Enver favored joining Bolshevik revolutionaries in Central Asia.[33] Talat urged a period of hiding in Europe, waiting for tempers to cool and dust to settle: "Justified or not," he growled, public sentiment stood against them, and they now faced arrest and trial for their wartime policies, including, according to the Entente (the governments of Britain, France, and Russia), the crime

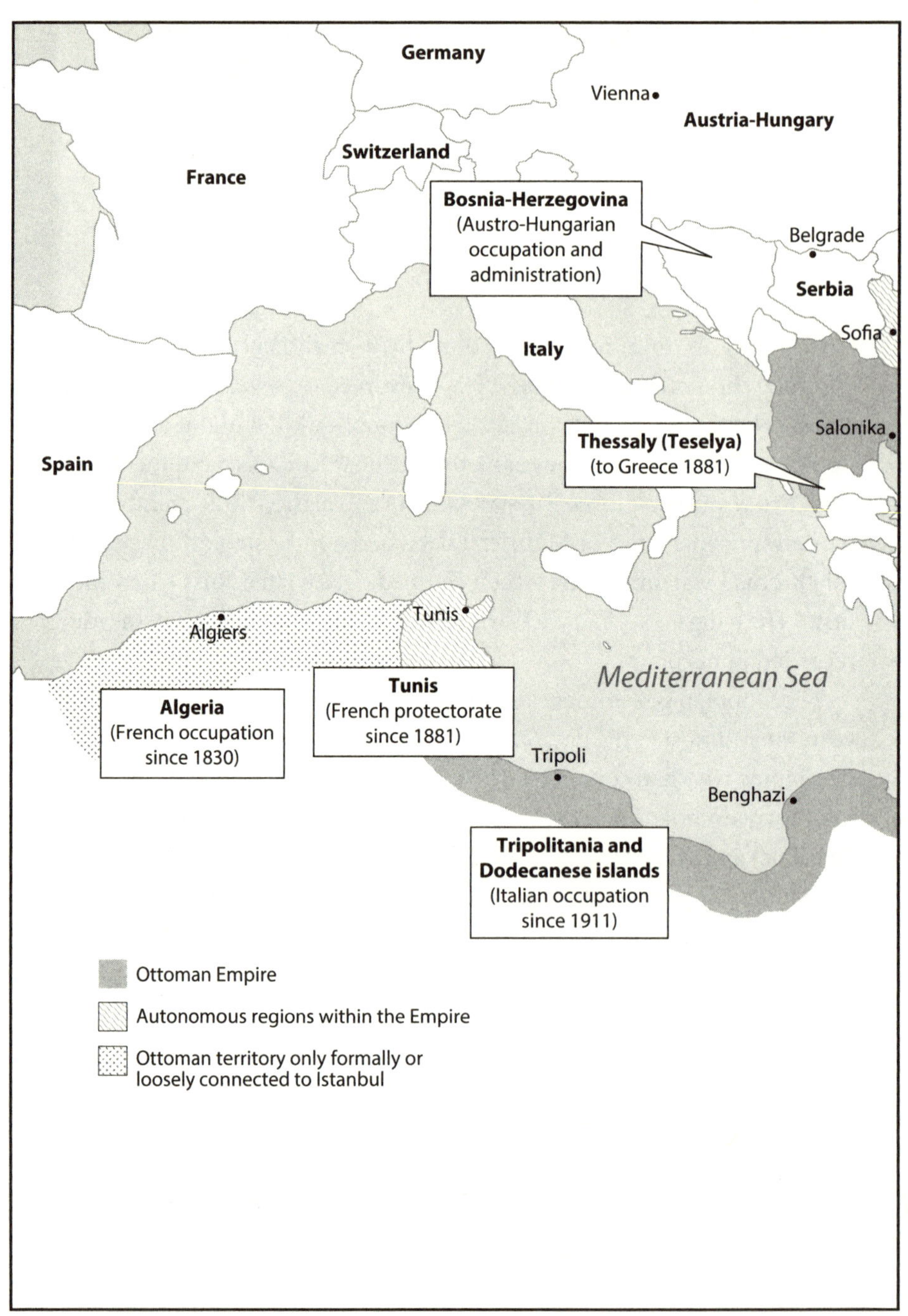

MAP 1. The Ottoman Empire, 1878.

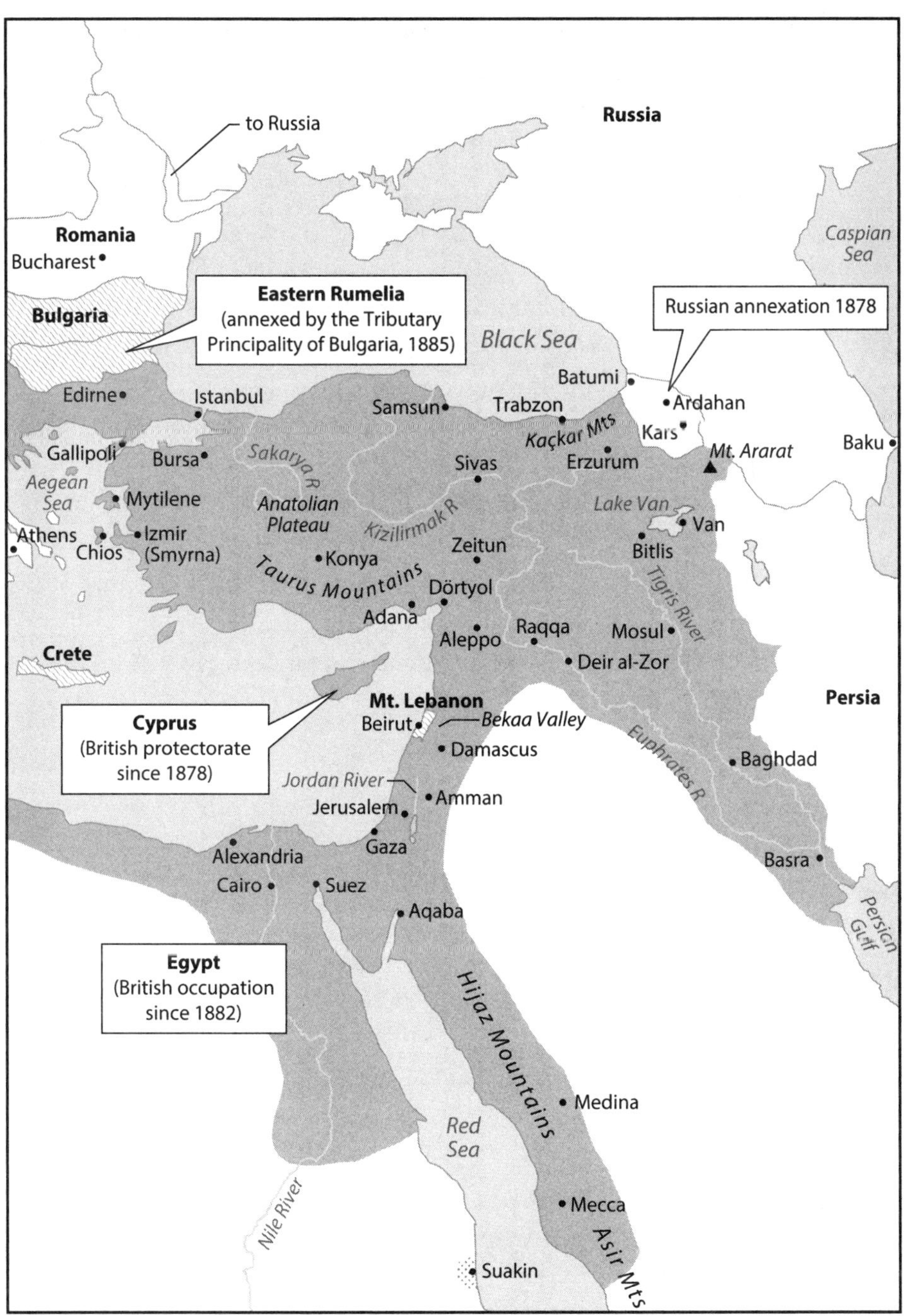

Russia
to Russia
Romania
Bucharest
Bulgaria
Eastern Rumelia
(annexed by the Tributary
Principality of Bulgaria, 1885)
Black Sea
Caspian Sea
Russian annexation 1878
Batumi
Ardahan
Kars
Mt. Ararat
Baku
Edirne
Istanbul
Samsun
Trabzon
Kaçkar Mts
Erzurum
Gallipoli
Bursa
Sakarya R
Sivas
Aegean Sea
Mytilene
Anatolian Plateau
Kizilirmak R
Lake Van
Van
Athens
Chios
Izmir
(Smyrna)
Konya
Zeitun
Bitlis
Taurus Mountains
Dörtyol
Tigris River
Adana
Aleppo
Raqqa
Mosul
Crete
Deir al-Zor
Persia
Cyprus
(British protectorate
since 1878)
Mt. Lebanon
Beirut
Bekaa Valley
Damascus
Euphrates R
Baghdad
Jordan River
Amman
Jerusalem
Gaza
Alexandria
Basra
Cairo
Suez
Aqaba
Persian Gulf
Egypt
(British occupation
since 1882)
Hijaz Mountains
Medina
Red Sea
Mecca
Nile River
Asir Mts
Suakin

of "killing the empire's Armenian population."[34] Most of the men, and some of their wives, found temporary refuge in Berlin.

The book is divided into six chapters. Chapter 1 tells the story of the Unionists' fight for sovereignty and the Ottoman Empire's entangled place in the global colonial order. Chapter 2 examines the social fissures that began bursting inside the empire, first slowly in 1914 and then rapidly under the weight of global war. Chapter 3 provides an overview of the Ottoman army's first major campaigns—the first an offensive into the Russian Caucasus, the second an attempted push across the Suez Canal into Egypt—and the domestic consequences of the failure of both. Chapter 4 explores the diminishing availability of food in the empire and the making of famine in Beirut and Mount Lebanon. Chapter 5 begins with the first military deportations of Ottoman Armenians that morphed into the categorical and violent uprooting of the empire's entire civilian Christian Armenian population. Chapter 6 follows the thickening of opposition groups that sought to resist the heavy hand of Unionist rule.

It is to the war that destroyed the Ottoman Empire and gave rise to "the Middle East" that we now turn.

1

An Empire's Revolutionary War

OVER A century after they took place, the events that led to the Ottoman participation in the First World War continue to be deeply misunderstood, in large part because the governments of the Entente, the war's victors, wanted them to be. Following the assassination of the Habsburg crown prince at Sarajevo on June 28, 1914, Ottoman leaders sought to leverage the ensuing crisis to their advantage. Lining up behind one of the two sides in the conflict, they believed, would allow them to reap short- and long-term benefits. They saw an alliance with a European state as a means to halt the Great Powers' massive, century-long assault on Ottoman territories and institutions. To Ottoman leaders in Istanbul, war in 1914 appeared as an escape route from European imperial rule.

This chapter explores the global context shaping that vision of war as opportunity. Ottoman leaders hoped to end the Great Powers' financial control over the empire and to improve its precarious economic footing. The loss of financial independence over the course of the nineteenth century meant that Ottoman sovereignty, while formally intact, was severely diminished by 1914. When the six European Great Powers cooperated in managing their interests in Ottoman lands, Ottoman officials could do little to push back, either militarily or by invoking international law. The absence of international partners had resulted in the loss of large swaths of territory and the consequent arrival of millions of refugees from these lands.

Four months passed between the assassination at Sarajevo and the Ottoman entry into the war on October 29, 1914. Over the course of those four months, the Ottoman government under the Unionists repeatedly sought alliances with the powers of the Entente—Britain, France, and Russia. Such an alliance, they hoped, would stop the territorial losses the empire had suffered and pave the way for ending the Great Powers' financial control. But the Unionists quickly recognized that even when faced with the possibility of global war and the greatest military conflict since the Napoleonic Wars, the Entente powers had no interest in an alliance with Istanbul. Taking on the Ottoman Empire as a partner, no matter how useful in summer 1914, ran contrary to their long-term objectives in the Eastern Mediterranean.

Nor was the Entente eager to go to war with the Ottomans. Open hostility against Istanbul was to be avoided. Britain ruled over millions of Muslims in Egypt and India, and officials in London feared an attack against the Ottoman state, whose head carried the title of sultan-caliph, would alienate the British Empire's Muslims. The Ottomans must "be compelled to strike the first blow," instructed Herbert Kitchener, in charge of British military policy in 1914.[1] Kitchener insisted that in the unfolding war the Ottomans be cast as the aggressor. At the end of October 1914, the Unionists, for their own reasons, obliged.

The Unionists on the World Stage

Following the 1908 Ottoman Revolution, the Unionists sought to defend their borders and shore up their sovereignty by diplomatic means, in the hopes that signing agreements with European powers would knit the empire into international society. They especially sought cooperation with the powers of the Entente, who, more so than Germany or Austria-Hungary, posed direct threats to Ottoman sovereignty. The Ottoman government proposed alliances to Britain in 1909, 1911, and 1913. It broached alliance talks with Russia in May 1914 and a friendship agreement with France in July. These proposals were rejected on the grounds that the empire's alliance with any one member of the Great Powers would attract the combined wrath of rival members and risk war.[2]

The Unionists' efforts to engage the Entente after 1908 never enjoyed a great chance of success. Sir Edward Grey, Britain's secretary of state for foreign affairs, worried about the effects a functioning constitutional model in the Ottoman Empire would have on British subjects elsewhere, especially in Egypt and India. Grey was eager to see Ottoman constitutionalism fail and the Unionist government collapse, viewing representative government in the Ottoman Empire—one that delivered on its promises—as potentially disastrous for London. A week after Sultan Abdülhamid II reinstated the constitution, Grey observed:

> If Turkey really establishes a Constitution and keeps it on its feet, and becomes strong herself, the consequences will reach further than any of us can yet foresee. The effect in Egypt will be tremendous, and will make itself felt in India. Hitherto whenever we have had Mahometan [i.e., Muslim] subjects, we have been able to tell them that the subjects in the countries ruled by the head of their religion were under a despotism which was not a benevolent one; while our Mahometan subjects were under a despotism which was benevolent. . . . But if Turkey now establishes a Parliament and improves her government, the demand for a Constitution in Egypt will gain great force, and our power of resisting the demand will be very much diminished. If, when there is a Turkish Constitution in good working order and things are going well in Turkey, we are engaged in suppressing by force and shooting a rising in Egypt of people who demand a Constitution, too, the position will be very awkward. It would never do for us to get into conflict on the subject of Egypt, not with the Turkish Government, but the feelings of the Turkish people.[3]

These remarks were not unconsidered but characteristic of Grey's thinking. "I am more interested in that," he wrote about the Ottoman Revolution, "than in anything that has happened while I have been in office." Grey believed "change in Turkey is pregnant with consequences."[4] Some thirty years earlier, when Grey was a university student, the British government brutally suppressed the Urabi Revolt in Egypt. In 1881 Colonel Ahmad Urabi and his followers had demanded representative government, challenging Egypt's British-appointed ruler. The London Foreign Office responded by destroying much of the port of Alexandria. British forces then incarcerated the revolutionaries and set up an occupation that would go on for decades.[5] The British Foreign Office was not in the habit of welcoming constitutional movements around the world.

The political dangers that Ottoman constitutionalism posed to British imperial rule were not the only reason Grey kept the Unionists at a distance. He wished not to alienate Britain's ally, Russia. Grey instructed his ambassador in Istanbul that "we must not give Russia the impression that we are reverting to the old policy of supporting Turkey as a barrier against her."[6] This had been London's policy until the 1870s. For Grey in 1914, the principal plank of British foreign policy was cooperation with Russia: what mattered was achieving "repose on our Indian frontier," referring to the border Britain and Russia shared in Central Asia.[7] Grey was willing, when necessary, to trade Ottoman territory—Istanbul and the Straits—for peace of mind in India. He was certain that opposing Russia and defending Ottoman integrity did not serve British interests, a sea change in British foreign policy.[8]

Between 1908 and 1914, the British government signed several important agreements with the Unionists to make official what was theirs already, especially concerning territorial disputes in the Arabian Peninsula and the Gulf. By 1914 Britain had seized and occupied several strategic Ottoman territories: the port city of Aden in the Red Sea, the major Mediterranean island of Cyprus, and, of course, Egypt. London had also signed treaties with local leaders in the Gulf and maintained a military presence in southern Iran. In other words, the British Empire controlled land and sea from the Eastern Mediterranean and Egypt all the way to India.[9]

For the people of the Ottoman Empire, the euphoria of new freedoms sparked by the 1908 Revolution dissipated amid a series of unnerving events. On October 5, the autonomous government of the province of Bulgaria proclaimed its independence from the empire. The next day, Austria-Hungary announced it was formally annexing Bosnia and Herzegovina, the two Ottoman provinces it had occupied since 1878. Then, the following day, October 7, it was Crete's turn; after some two centuries of Ottoman rule over the island, Cretan leaders declared the island's exit from the empire and its unification with the Kingdom of Greece.[10]

These moves elicited strong reactions from the Ottoman public. Crete's Muslim population had been expelled en masse from the island in 1897.

In hundreds of demonstrations, crowds protested Crete's unification with Greece. The protests, many led by Muslim Cretans expelled from the island, unfolded across the empire.[11] In Jerusalem, children delivered speeches demanding the island must stay Ottoman.[12] Protesters also called for the boycotting of Habsburg businesses and products. Austria-Hungary was a major producer of goods sold on the Ottoman market, including the fez, the ubiquitous headgear worn by the empire's men. As part of the boycott, men publicly destroyed their Habsburg-made fezzes in mock ceremonies.[13]

Women authors expressed their outrage in the press. Fatma Aliye, the esteemed feminist writer, encouraged readers to buy domestically. As the threefold fiasco by the Ottomans' Balkan neighbors coincided with Ramadan, the Islamic month of fasting, she urged women to do their Ramadan shopping in goods made at home, to buy products from Aleppo, Damascus, Hama, and Hereke.[14]

For now, the Unionists continued to pursue close ties with the Entente powers. They invited a team of British naval experts to reform the work of the Ottoman navy. Similarly, they called on the French army to send officers for the training of the empire's gendarmerie force. These European officers remained in the empire until the outbreak of war in 1914, but their presence bore little fruit for the Unionists in cultivating close relations with the Entente.

Starting in September 1911, Italian forces invaded Tripolitania (Ottoman Libya) and occupied a chain of islands in the Aegean Sea, the Dodecanese. Ottoman diplomats quickly made appeals to international law for support in London and Paris, but such pleas were brushed aside. In the decades following the Risorgimento, Italy's unification in 1861, the new Italian kingdom embarked on an ambitious program of empire-building; empire abroad was to serve national consolidation in the peninsula at home. Italy pursued the construction of the Suez Canal as one of its major imperial projects, and it sought colonial possessions in the Red Sea and North Africa, where tens of thousands of Italian migrants, many from Sicily, had already settled in search of better fortunes. When France preemptively occupied Tunis in 1881, before Italy could make a move, Italian imperialists set their eyes on Tripolitania. In 1911 Ottoman hopes that the

Great Powers would restrain Italy and its brutal occupation came to nothing.[15]

While the legality of Italy's aggression mattered little to the Great Powers, what did garner attention was the Ottomans' closing of the Straits for the duration of the conflict. The waterway linked Russian port cities on the Black Sea to the Mediterranean. It was the route through which Russia shipped a whopping 50 percent of its exports, including 90 percent of its exported grains. The temporary closure of the Straits illustrated urgently the importance of the entire Constantinople region for Saint Petersburg and its Entente allies.

The following year, the Balkan Wars once again demonstrated to the Unionists that in times of international crisis they could hardly count on Great Power support, even when international law appeared to be on their side. In October 1912, when war in southeastern Europe seemed imminent between the Ottoman Empire and the Balkan alliance—Bulgaria, Greece, Montenegro, and Serbia—the Great Powers attempted to prevent conflict. Anticipating Ottoman gains, they announced they would not recognize any territorial changes resulting from the war. When the Balkan states emerged victorious, however, in a war marked by massive atrocities against civilians on all sides, the Great Powers ignored their previous statement and confirmed the Balkan states' conquests. In the First Balkan War, the Ottoman state lost over two-thirds of its territories in southeastern Europe. In the war's aftermath, the Great Powers awarded two key islands in the Aegean Sea—Mytilene (*Midilli*, in Ottoman Turkish) and Chios (*Sakız*)—just miles off the Anatolian coast, to Greece. As the islands' inhabitants were primarily Greek-speaking and Greek Orthodox in religion, by assigning the islands to Athens the Great Powers were endorsing notions of ethnonational homogeneity.

For the Unionists, it became clear that adopting constitutionalism in 1908 was not enough to make friends or to find a secure place in the European state system. Instead, the empire's international isolation and vulnerability continued unabated.

The effects of the First Balkan War of 1912 were just as profound as had been those of the Ottoman-Russian War of 1877–1878. Both conflicts resulted in the loss of territory and touched off an influx of hundreds of thousands of Muslim refugees into the still-independent Ottoman core.

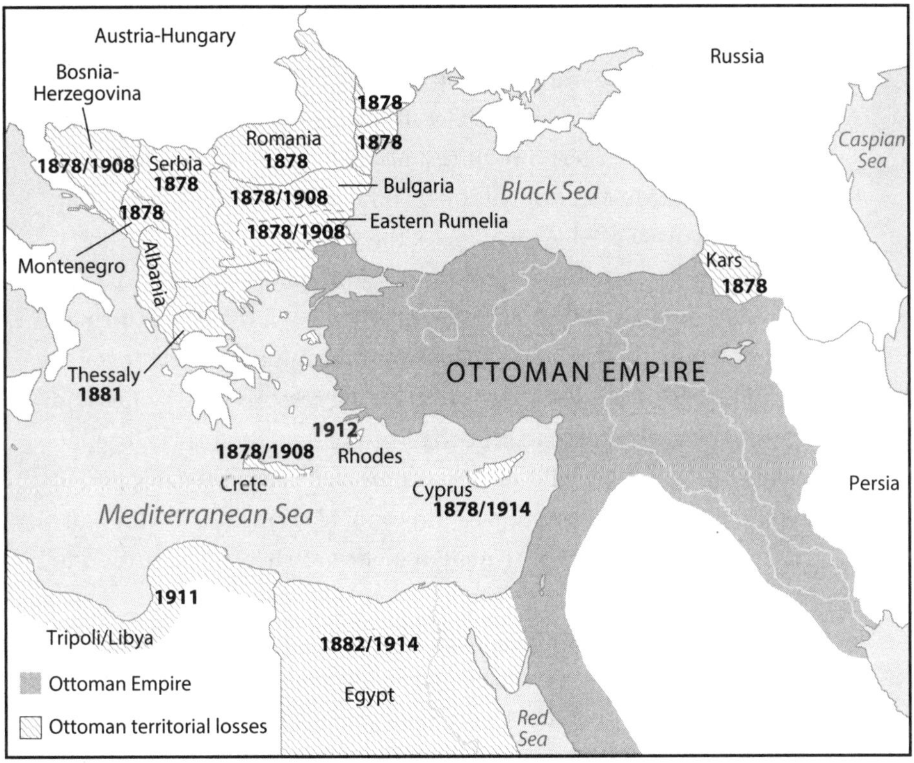

MAP 2. The Ottoman Empire, 1913.

FIGURE 2. Muslim refugee family arriving in the Ottoman Empire in the aftermath of the First Balkan War of 1912. *Source*: Cornelius Van H. Engert Papers, box 12, folder 65, Lauinger Library, Booth Special Collections, Georgetown University

In the aftermath of both wars, with the empire's foundations still shaking, Armenian leaders appealed to the Great Powers for international oversight of the empire's eastern provinces, home to large Armenian Christian and Kurdish Muslim populations. Following the First Balkan War, Catholikos Kevork V of All Armenians of the Armenian Apostolic Church at Etchmiadzin (then in Russia, present-day Armenia), appointed the distinguished Armenian leader Boghos Nubar to head the newly formed Armenian National Delegation. The delegation's mission was to travel to Europe and "present the need for implementing reforms in Armenia, and plead with them to intervene on behalf of the Armenians."[16] Ottoman Armenians had suffered land dispossession and had been subjected to mass violence against them in 1895 and 1909. Having failed to find justice in Ottoman courts, the Armenian National Delegation turned to European support.

Unsurprisingly, the Unionists, politically, opposed Boghos Nubar's mission. Emotionally, they resented it. Following the 1908 Revolution, the Unionists had sought to address Armenian grievances over land disputes that dated back to the Hamidian period, but the effort yielded little success.[17] In contrast, Boghos Nubar's mission in Europe bore fruit quickly. The Great Powers announced a plan to install European governors over six provinces in eastern Anatolia, home to large Armenian Christian and Kurdish Muslim populations. The proposal came on the heels of the Italian occupation of Tripolitania and the bloody territorial losses in the Balkans. To some, the plan appeared to establish yet another European sphere of influence or even outright colonization. Fearing the worst required no wild stretch of the imagination, of course; much of the world was under European control already. In response to the Great Powers' plan for eastern Anatolia, the Unionists made a surprising counterproposal. They suggested organizing the entire empire, not just the Armenian-Kurdish regions, into six districts, with British officials assigned to each one of them. The counterproposal may seem odd, given the Ottoman government's desire to shed the empire of foreign control, not deepen it. The calculation behind the Unionists' counterproposal, however, was to prevent a special status for Christian populations alone. The government hoped to bring in exclusively British officials rather than those of any other state, especially Russia. The plan demonstrates the Unionists' attempt to work with the Entente—at least Britain and France—and not against it. The Great Powers dismissed the plan without much ado, and eventually the Unionists had no choice but to sign a reform program drafted by the Russian government, the Armenian Reform Agreement.[18]

Signed on February 8, 1914, the agreement divided the empire's eastern Anatolian provinces into two zones, each overseen by a European inspector-general.[19] The Great Powers appointed the Norwegian military officer Major Nikolai Hoff as the inspector-general to the northern zone and the Dutchman Louis Constant Westenenk, a former colonial officer who had spent much of his career in Indonesia, to the southern one. In late February the Russian ambassador, Mikhail Giers, and the Armenian patriarch in Istanbul, Zaven Der Yeghiayan, exchanged visits congratulating each other on the agreement. On those occasions, Giers "urged" the patriarch "to send people to Europe to meet with the new Inspectors General and to win them over to the Armenian cause."[20] When the inspectors arrived in the Ottoman capital, it "occasioned great joy in Armenian circles," Patriarch Zaven later recalled in his memoirs.[21] But he also believed, not incorrectly, that the Unionists were enraged by this Armenian action for allowing themselves to become "the tool of foreign states."[22]

The new initiative for European direct intervention launched by Catholikos Kevork V came at a moment of deep political and military crisis for the Unionists. Historians have emphasized the grave psychological impact the First Balkan War exercised on Ottoman society: the atrocities committed against Muslim civilians in the Balkans, the resulting refugee emergency, and the loss of much of the empire's territories and populations in southeastern Europe.[23]

The British ambassador at the time, Louis Mallet, was highly critical of the Armenian Reform Agreement. He gave the project little chance for success and considered it "a farce to talk of Armenian reforms" given the Ottomans' economic situation.[24] Although hardly a friend of the Unionists, Mallet could at times be clear-eyed: all the Great Powers "profess to wish the maintenance of Turkey's integrity," but "no one ever thinks of this in practice." Rather, he felt, "All the Powers including ourselves are trying hard to get what they can out of Turkey."[25] In fact, Foreign Secretary

Grey was eager to see the Unionist government collapse.[26] The foreign ministries of the Great Powers were actively jockeying for their share of Ottoman lands and assets long before the outbreak of the First World War.[27]

Ambassador Mallet informed his own government that the Unionists were doing all they could to improve their financial situation, and that, in fact, War Minister Enver had reduced the war budget from nine to six million Ottoman pounds. In March 1914, Mallet reminded his boss, Foreign Secretary Grey, that the Unionists were looking to England for support in the form of a loan and that they had been very friendly, and that it would be good if Grey could, on occasion, demonstrate a measure of goodwill: "I venture to think that it is worth making this effort and that we now have a position which we had six years ago," referring back to 1908 and the reinstatement of the constitution.[28] Grey was not to be moved.

Moreover, the French government in the nineteenth century had shifted its imperial strategy in many parts of the world from direct military occupation to a "conquest by money" and "investment colonization," to, in other words, arrangements and treaties of financial control (with Algeria becoming the principal exception).[29] Mallet suggested that if the British government did not provide a loan to Istanbul, then such loans might come from Paris: "In thinking over the various ways in which we could help to preserve the independence and integrity of Turkey, financial assistance is the first thing which occurs to one, as Turkey's independence is a vanishing quantity before the advance of the French Financiers!"[30] Grey was not worried about such a scenario. Instead, he showed the ambassador a memorandum that outlined the divvying up of Ottoman assets, including railway lines and potential oil fields. Grey also noted the carved out shares that would go to France and Germany in such a division.[31] The foreign secretary had no interest in providing financial support to Istanbul, not least because he was fully aware that Russia strongly opposed both British and French loans to the Unionists.[32]

In fact, Grey believed the Unionists should be grateful to the London government. Grey had mediated between Russia and Germany in the recent Liman von Sanders Crisis, which broke out when Berlin installed a military mission under a high-ranking German officer in the Ottoman capital. Grey noted that without "our refusal to precipitate a crisis over the German command, the Russians would have been in Armenia by now, and the disintegration of Asiatic Turkey would have begun."[33] And if that process were to start, Grey scoffed, Germany would hardly attempt to stop it: "For the Germans are not going to fight Russia to defend Turkey, they are going to claim their share if disintegration begins."[34] Indeed, Sergey Sazonov, the Russian foreign minister, proposed the occupation of Erzurum once again in spring 1914. And the German emperor, Kaiser Wilhelm II, maintained that Ottoman partition had, in fact, commenced already.[35] The comments by the British foreign secretary and the German emperor underscored the precarity of Ottoman existence during the prewar years.

Grey was not wrong about Berlin's intentions. The well-informed and well-connected Habsburg military attaché, Joseph Pomiankowski, remarked that "everything I saw and heard indicated that the Germans—although they of course never admitted this openly—pursued the gradual control of the entire Turkish territory in the form of a protectorate or as the result of a political treaty."[36] Unlike Pomiankowski, we now have access to Berlin's internal correspondence that confirms his impression, if perhaps only for certain parts of the empire's territories. On July 28, 1913—exactly one year prior to Vienna's declaration of war on Serbia—German secretary for foreign affairs Gottlieb von Jagow declared that "we have only a single interest in Turkey: that it will survive in Asia long enough until we will have consolidated ourselves there in our zones of activity [*Arbeitszonen*] and have become prepared for annexation."[37] Jagow's opining in the uncertain aftermath of the Balkan Wars should not be read as a concrete plan but as an outlook contingent on future developments. And without the personal intervention of Kaiser Wilhelm II, the German-Ottoman alliance of August 2, 1914, as we shall see, may never have materialized.

Given the Unionists' experience with Great Power imperialism, it is hardly surprising that by 1913, Ottoman newspapers could declare that "our honor and our people's dignity cannot be preserved by those old books of international law, but only by war."[38] Violence, the paper claimed, could only be met with violence. By the time of the First World War, the Ottoman Empire's leading scholar of international law and diplomatic history, Ahmed Salaheddin, professor at the Law Faculty at Istanbul University (Darülfünun), opened his account of the Balkan Wars with an image of Otto von Bismarck and a quotation from the German chancellor's famous speech: "The great questions of the time will not be resolved by parliamentary speeches and majority decisions, but by iron and blood." Bismarck's assertion dated back to 1862, and Bismarck was dead, but the statement was alive and reflected the views of many Ottomans on international relations in 1914. Having come out on the losing side of negotiations with European imperialists for a century, Ottomans could see Bismarck's point.[39] They could also see that they lacked the "iron" half of Bismarck's formula and that therefore they needed to secure an alliance with at least one of the Great Powers.

"Ottoman Money Must Stay in Ottoman Hands"

In the aftermath of the 1908 Revolution, Ottoman newspapers and books argued that foreign businesses and their governments were strangling the empire's economy.[40] In particular, writers took aim at the special commercial and legal rights held by foreign citizens, known as the Capitulations. For many, the Capitulations represented a double standard that epitomized the central obstacles to the empire's prosperity. The press depicted the Capitulations as a form of colonialism that was putting local enterprises out of business and eroding Ottoman sovereignty by the day.[41] "We must throw off these chains of oppression that Europe has laid around our neck," a prominent publication proclaimed. Like so many books and news articles, it declared that "the termination of the Capitulations is an absolute must."[42] The Capitulations, the author argued, stood in violation of international law. No state, he insisted, had the right to impose its own rules within the sovereign borders of another state against its will.[43]

Advertisements appearing in such publications showcased domestic products and called on readers to buy "Ottoman." Articles and images challenged foreign businesses like the Swiss food company Nestlé and the US sewing giant Singer. They mobilized a reservoir of resentment of foreign influence and control.[44] "Ottoman Money Must Stay in Ottoman Hands" became a mantra in the popular press.[45]

Foreign observers, too, could recognize the Capitulations as tying Ottoman hands and preventing the country's economic progress. It was hard to miss. A long-time British official in Istanbul saw eye-to-eye with Ottoman critics of the Capitulations as predatory. In his words, the Capitulations so limited the Ottoman state that any "political and administrative reforms" were rendered "an impossibility."[46] Another prominent financial expert referred to the Capitulations as the foremost "Obstacles to Reform in Turkey."[47] Fixing the empire's finances, they acknowledged, was not simply a matter of domestic discipline.

Although their origins reached back hundreds of years, the Capitulations of the nineteenth and twentieth centuries were distinct in both character and volume from earlier iterations. During the fifteenth and sixteenth centuries, the sultan had bestowed trading rights on companies and merchant communities to facilitate the flow and ease of international trade. The Ottoman state understood such rights not as entitlements but as privileges that could be revoked, at least in theory, at any time.[48] Granting self-governing rights and certain tax exemptions to merchant companies was in keeping with the Ottoman (and pre-Ottoman) practice of allowing various groups and bodies, whether guild and trade associations or ethnic and religious communities, to regulate and govern themselves. But in 1825 the British government unilaterally transferred such commercial privileges enjoyed by the British Levant Company to itself.[49] Other European powers followed suit, and what previously had been privileges granted to foreign merchants and companies turned into rights issued to and backed by European states. Similar unilateral acts of arrogation by European powers occurred in the same year in Algeria, Egypt, Iran, Morocco, Tripoli, and Tunisia, followed by China in 1833, Siam (Thailand) in 1855, Japan in 1856, Madagascar in 1865, Samoa and Tonga in 1879, Korea in 1883, Congo in 1884, and in Zanzibar in 1886. Often the practice of extraterritorial rights ended with formal outright European occupation and the setting up of colonial rule, or, in some cases, a protectorate.[50] In this way, Capitulations became a pervasive tool of British and French imperial expansion around the globe.[51]

European legal scholars and the governments who backed them justified their claims to extraterritorial rights on the grounds that African and Asian states lacked unified legal systems. In other words, because they encountered a system of legal pluralism in Ottoman lands, European states maintained they had no choice but to bring their own laws along with them. Foreign powers established their own network of courts and judges, governed by dozens of consuls dotting the empire. In response, states such as the Ottoman Empire, Iran, and China embarked on massive legal projects of codifying laws and centralizing their legal institutions. The Ottoman government launched all-out efforts to abolish extraterritorial rights in 1862, 1867, 1871, 1881, and 1913/14.[52]

In the Ottoman realm and elsewhere around the globe, the campaigns of rulers to establish a single, unified legal system often meant eliminating legal authorities not under the direct control of the central state. Thus, the sweeping Ottoman reforms of the nineteenth century—known as the *tanzimat*, or "putting into order"—sought to revise, standardize, and expand the Ottoman state's legal presence in every corner of the empire. The state's declaration of the legal equality of all Ottoman subjects regardless of religion or ethnicity, enshrined in the two major *tanzimat* reform decrees of 1839 and 1856, reflected the attempt to replace a world of legal pluralism with a centrally controlled and monolithic one. Unsurprisingly, the state's centralization of the legal system sparked resistance throughout the empire. And, ironically, after having insisted on the elimination of legal pluralism, European powers throughout the nineteenth and twentieth centuries intervened to protect the rights of the empire's Christian communities.[53]

With respect to trade, across the globe, including in Europe, the proliferation of British manufactured goods displaced local production and caused economic dislocation. For a while, leading Ottoman economists such as Sakızlı Ohannes adhered to the free-market theories of Adam Smith and opposed protective measures.[54] In 1838, in exchange for British military support against Egypt, the sultan signed the Anglo-Ottoman Commercial Treaty (*Baltalimanı Ticaret Konvansiyonu*). That treaty further opened Ottoman markets to British businesses and put domestic manufacturers at a steep disadvantage. Nearly 80 percent of all manufactured cotton textiles in the empire were now being imported.[55] During the Crimean War, in which the empire found itself on the same side as Britain and France, the treasury took out its first foreign loans in 1854 and 1855.[56] The purpose behind these was the immediate financing of the military. At this point, by granting these loans Britain and France were fortifying their Ottoman ally against their Russian rival. Subsequently Ottoman rulers pursued similar loans in the attempt to raise their military capacity to the level of the major European armies. But much of the money was used to purchase foreign arms rather than to enable the empire to manufacture their own. Whereas in the early nineteenth century the military mainly used domestically manufactured arms, by the First World War most of the equipment was foreign built.[57] The empire possessed a foundry for cannons and its own munitions and gunpowder factory, but Ottoman industry produced little iron or steel.[58]

By 1875 the government was unable to meet interest payments on foreign loans. Following the war with Russia in 1877–1878, it agreed to the installation in Istanbul of a foreign collecting agency, the Ottoman Public Debt Administration. Substantial tax revenues such as those from salt and tobacco production now went directly to this international institution, which in turn passed the funds on to the empire's creditors. Greece's capture of the city of Salonika in the First Balkan War in 1912, moreover, meant the loss of the empire's most advanced industrial center, further weakening Ottoman economic foundations. Over half of the country's textile factories were located in the city and its environs.[59] In the attempt to keep European armies out, the state had become dependent on European banks in the span of just a few decades. By 1914 roughly one-third of revenues went directly to the Ottoman Public Debt Administration. By then, the institution had become "a state within a state," a bureaucracy of some five thousand employees.[60] It exercised not only financial control over the empire but also confined Ottoman political independence.[61] The chain of lending and indebtedness followed by the loss of economic and political dependence was an all-too-common experience of many states throughout the nineteenth-century global economy.[62]

Ottoman businesses and the state did not observe these developments as uninvolved bystanders, however, but sought actively to use them to their advantage. From the 1880s onward government agencies invested heavily in expanding the empire's transportation infrastructure, its schools at all levels, and in new agricultural methods and technology, including a massive irrigation project in the Konya plain.[63] In 1914, 63 percent of foreign investment streamed into railway construction. Tax revenue collected along the Anatolian Railway line doubled over the twenty-year period between 1889 and 1909. In the same years, some sixty million mulberry trees were planted in the hope of raising state revenue from silk. Roughly one-quarter of Ottoman wines were exported during this period, including to France, where some Ottoman wines were good enough to compete with French wines. When the French government raised protective import duties on Ottoman wines, this trade fell.[64] Much of the new revenue went directly to the Public Debt Administration and the repayment of loans.

An international company that controlled the production and sale of tobacco, the Tobacco Régie, established in 1883, locked up a thirty-year tobacco monopoly. The company's "infamous" collection agents frequently resorted to violence and antagonized the empire's tobacco growers. The Régie and its practices were widely seen "as a symbol of Western imperialism and exploitation."[65] Upon its founding, the Tobacco Régie shut down hundreds of privately run tobacco factories. Between 1881 and 1914, the Régie became a key source of foreign investment into the empire.[66] In Iran, a similar tobacco monopoly resulted in major protests in 1891. Exploitative lending, debt administrations, and régies became common instruments in the global toolkit of British and French informal imperial control.[67]

Over time, the international debt regime in the empire sparked deep popular resentment. Following the 1908 Revolution, a boycott movement denounced the Capitulations. Protest rallies mobilized feelings of economic hardship and foreign oppression and brought large segments of society into the streets. Newspapers decried the foreign exploitation of Ottoman workers and pointed to the ways in which imported goods undermined domestic production and the well-being of all Ottomans. The boycott movement called for full sovereignty and the end of European financial control.

The need to absorb millions of refugees added to the country's dire economic conditions. In the decades leading up to the First World War, the number of Muslim refugees from the Balkans and the Caucasus skyrocketed, increasing the Muslim population of Anatolia by some 40 percent between the 1860s and 1880s alone.[68] In January 1913 the popular social commentator İbrahim Hilmi estimated that about 80 percent of the empire's population was living in poverty.[69]

Hence, the late Ottoman period was shaped by military defeat, shifting boundaries, and the arrival of millions of refugees in the empire.[70] Yet the loss of territories and the influx of refugees were not only economic issues. Gory images and descriptions of atrocities committed against Ottoman Muslims filled the pages of publications, including schoolbooks, across the empire. Mediha, a twelve-year-old schoolgirl in the Black Sea city of Trabzon who kept a diary throughout the First World War, was overcome by panic when she first heard the news of the outbreak of war in Europe in 1914. She imagined the arrival of Russian troops in her hometown and could not get the "Balkan atrocities [*Rumeli mezalimi*]" out of her head. Unable to sleep, she sat up through the night until dawn, "covered in sweat, my entire body shivering and shaking."[71]

It was not only foreign intrusions into Ottoman life that engendered a storm of resentment and backlash against the Great Powers. The persecution of Muslims beyond Ottoman borders and in territories lost generated feelings of existential crisis. Rural populations, whose exposure to news reporting or large-scale boycotts and demonstrations may have been limited, experienced the empire's geopolitical frailties through waves of refugees arriving in the countryside for over half a century. From the late eighteenth century to 1900, over two million Russian Muslims, mostly from the Caucasus, were either expelled from their homes or killed.[72] In total, some five million refugees arrived in the Ottoman Empire over the course of the century prior to the First World War. These new Ottomans altered the empire's demographic composition; they were a living manifestation of the existential threat facing the empire.[73]

In the aftermath of the Balkan Wars, the empire experienced yet another wave of refugees, bringing with them eye-witness accounts of ethnic cleansing. Some 177,352 Muslim refugees arrived in the empire from southeastern Europe in 1912 and 1913, a number that rose to about 640,000 refugees by the end of the First World War.[74] From the 1850s to 1914, refugees formed over eleven hundred new villages in central and western Anatolia, the Syrian coast, and Iraq.[75] Many of the Unionist leaders themselves came from refugee families, making them "children of the borderlands."[76] These experiences of expulsion imbued leaders like Talat and Enver with profound feelings of injustice.[77]

The boycotts protesting the Balkan states and the Capitulations did not remain confined to foreign businesses, however. Soon, protesters targeted stores owned by the empire's Christian and Jewish populations, as these came to be regarded as profiting from European interests. The boycotts politicized society; they moved men, women, and children to action, and they identified common goals and enemies. The boycott movement united rural and urban populations, peasants and professionals, in a lived experience of collective anti-imperial action. Ottoman anti-imperialism, therefore, was not a solely intellectual or discursive one. The boycott movement provided the Unionist government with a reservoir of popular emotion it could tap into for political support in different parts of the empire.[78] Newspapers debated extensively the "economic war" that was being waged in Beirut, while "boycott societies" sprang up in major cities and towns across the empire.[79]

By 1910 boycott societies had placed signs on stores owned by Greek Orthodox Ottomans and posted guards outside these businesses, admonishing Muslims against patronizing Christian-owned stores. As publications reported atrocities committed against Crete's Muslims, some called for the expulsion of Izmir's Greek Orthodox population.[80]

It is important to note that the boycotts following the 1908 Revolution were not orchestrated by the government. Concerned about having to pay compensation, government officials opposed the boycotting of foreign businesses. The government's stance changed in 1913, following the Unionists' return to power in January. At that point, an official at the War Ministry penned a popular pamphlet, with the title *To Muslims and Turks*, describing in glowing terms the "economic and commercial revolution" he claimed was underway. The pamphlet insisted that the "economic revolution" was the daily talk in every Muslim home. It asked readers—and listeners, as popular texts were often read aloud publicly in tea houses and reading rooms—to take an oath pledging to never again shop in Christian-owned stores.[81] In the months leading up to war in 1914, physical attacks on stores selling European goods were not uncommon. The press spoke widely about the "economic war [*iktisadî harb*]" and the "economic holy war [*iktisadî cihad*]" being waged.[82]

And yet, broadly speaking, the Unionists' economic policies focused on strengthening ties with Western European businesses and investors. They were eager to get rid of the Capitulations and modestly raise tariffs so as to protect domestic manufactures, but they were far from seeking to cut off commercial links. Ironically, with the new liberalism that followed the 1908 Revolution came a rise in foreign economic activity inside the empire. It also brought with it an increased role for Ottoman subjects who worked with such foreign companies and as a result also enjoyed the privileges granted by the Capitulations regime. Unsurprisingly, the number of foreign stock companies and the volume of foreign capital inside the empire rose sharply during the years 1908–1913. Only when the empire entered the First World War were the privileges of foreign companies formally ended. A temporary law adopted on December 13, 1914, nationalized foreign-operated ports, dockyards, and railways in Aydın, Kasaba, Mudanya, and Syria.[83]

If the economic cost of the Capitulations was high, its social cost may have been even higher, as it pitted Muslim and Christian populations against each other. It was not true, as some claimed after the war, that the majority of non-Muslims and non-Turks secretly supported or were loyal to European states. The lives of so many Ottomans vividly illustrate this point. Hovhannes Cherishian was an Armenian Christian shoemaker in Maraş, the town in which he was born in 1886. His father had run a barbershop there together with a Turkish Muslim partner for decades. The intimate space of the barbershop had brought together Christians and Muslims. Reflecting on his life in Maraş, Cherishian remembered one of his bishop's Sunday sermons. On that morning in church, the bishop admonished those Armenians who were "pro-West." Armenians had been living under Ottoman rule for centuries, the bishop reminded his congregation. If "we had submitted to any Western power for even one hundred or one hundred and fifty years, the name of Armenians or of Armenia would not last upon the face of the earth." The bishop blamed European missionaries for dividing the Armenian community by converting members of the Armenian church to Catholicism and Protestantism, a common complaint that went back to the nineteenth century.[84] In his recollections, Cherishian also recounted his time serving in the Ottoman army. In 1910 he had proudly joined and served for four years, even though he could have opted out of ever putting on a uniform. In his unit of 225 enlisted men, 38, or over 16 percent, were fellow Armenians. Inspired by the 1908 Revolution, many young men from across the empire, like Cherishian himself, had rallied to the Ottoman flag, not shunned it.[85]

If the Unionists made terminating the Capitulations a major demand of both alliance blocks following the assassination of Franz Ferdinand, however, neither of the two sides was willing to accept this proposition.

Cornered: How the Entente Repeatedly Rejected Ottoman Offers for Alliance

On July 28, 1914, one month to the day after the Sarajevo assassination, Austria-Hungary declared war on Serbia. The governor of Edirne (Adrianople) province, located in the empire's northwestern corner bordering Bulgaria and Greece, followed the news nervously. His agents reported intense military preparations just across the border. The governor dispatched an urgent telegram to Interior Minister Talat in the capital. He wanted to know: Was another war coming? The two were old friends, and the governor reminded Talat of what needed no reminding, that Edirne's wounds from the recent Balkan Wars were still raw, still bloodied. Talat sought to put his friend at ease: "My brother," he wrote, "we are working day and night to protect ourselves from harm and to take advantage of the situation to the best of our abilities."[86] Talat could not know what the following weeks would bring, but he added, "This war will not remain local but spread."[87] He was right. As for shielding the empire "from harm," events would prove Talat tragically, catastrophically, wrong.

Edirne's safety and well-being was a deeply personal matter for Talat. He had been born there in 1874. Just before his birth, his father's family had arrived in Edirne city as refugees. They and their entire Muslim village had been driven out from lands that now belonged to Bulgaria. Just a few years later, during the Russo-Ottoman war of 1877–1878, Talat's family once again became refugees, this time fleeing Edirne for Istanbul.[88] Those experiences formed some of Talat's earliest childhood memories. As an adult, in 1912, during the First Balkan War, Talat witnessed Bulgarian troops capture Edirne after a suffocating siege and occupy the city for some four months. In that conflict, Talat put on a uniform and went to the frontlines, enlisting as a volunteer. In the end, Edirne's permanent loss was narrowly averted. But that war, too, forced hundreds of thousands of Muslims to seek refuge in the empire. Images of Muslim refugees from his childhood and those from more recent conflicts mixed and resonated deeply with Talat. The story of the refugee was the story of his family.[89]

By the time Talat and the Edirne governor were discussing the outbreak of war, on July 28, British officials had confiscated two Ottoman warships whose construction was being completed in British dockyards.[90] Two days later, the Unionists received notice that the ships would not be forthcoming.[91] The ships had been paid for, in part, through small individual contributions from Ottomans of all ranks of society who believed their united effort could save the empire. The confiscation, therefore, was a blow not only to the strength of the Ottoman navy but also to the morale of a great number of ordinary citizens.[92] Mediha, the schoolgirl diarist in Trabzon, recorded her sadness about what the loss of the ships meant for the country. "All our hopes and expectations disappeared. Not only all Ottomans, but all Muslims [worldwide] were waiting impatiently to welcome our beloved ships, our only hope."[93] Greece and Russia, two powers that had no desire to see the Ottoman navy strengthened, had objected to the sale of the British ships for months, long before the outbreak of war in July 1914.[94]

The story of the two ships was emblematic of the Ottomans' vulnerability on the international stage. In the aftermath of the 1908 Revolution and over the course of seventy-two hours, as we have seen, Bosnia and Herzegovina, Bulgaria, and Crete, all cast off Ottoman sovereignty. In the following weeks and months, disappointment over these losses gave rise to the formation of aid societies and patriotic associations. Among the most prominent of these was the Ottoman National Navy Society (Osmanlı Donanma-i Milliye Cemiyeti). The society quickly grew into a popular civic organization attracting hundreds of thousands of followers through festivities and fundraisers for the Ottoman navy. It set up collection boxes in public squares where young and old were encouraged to make their donation. Those who contributed five gold lira were awarded a medal that could be pinned and worn on one's lapel or shirt; those donating over five hundred lira were recognized with a gold medal. The society believed that the presence of a dreadnought-class Ottoman battleship would galvanize the empire's subjects living along distant coasts into a spirit of patriotic unity. It viewed the Ottoman navy as being in direct competition with that of Greece in the Aegean Sea, the Italian navy in the Mediterranean, and the Russian navy in the Black Sea. Following the overthrow of Sultan Abdülhamid II and his exile to Salonika, the new revolutionary government under the Unionists donated the former sultan's jewels to the society.[95] In April 1911, the Navy Ministry, supported by the society's funds and momentum, contracted for a dreadnought-class warship to be built in the British docks of Vickers Limited. Shortly thereafter, it placed another order with Armstrong Whitworth & Company for a major battleship that was being constructed for Brazil but whose contract had been canceled. The Vickers ship, the *Reşadiye*—named in honor of the new sultan, Mehmed Reşad V (r.1909–1918), was to be launched on September 3, 1913. By one account, rather than the traditional bottle of champagne, the ship, destined for a Muslim power, was put to sea by a bottle of rose water. Still, at the meal that followed, champagne, wine, and cognac seem to have flowed freely. The *Reşadiye*'s ceremonial launch was filmed and the triumph shown to schoolchildren in various towns and cities of the empire.[96] The delivery of both ships, however, was delayed, and it was *Sultan Osman I*, the ship originally contracted for Brazil, that was scheduled to be ready first. The *Reşadiye* would be ready only in August. Winston Churchill, First Lord of the Admiralty, had expressed his reservations about selling the ships to Istanbul as early as 1912.

Alarmed by the British government's confiscation of the ships, War Minister Enver turned to the Central Powers. He requested their navies send ships, of any kind, to Istanbul. Specifically, Enver asked for the ships

SMS *Goeben* and SMS *Breslau*, a request the German emperor, Kaiser Wilhelm II, approved personally.[97]

Back on land, the Unionists signed a secret alliance with Germany in the early morning hours of August 2. They promised Berlin immediate battle action, but they had no intention of jumping into the fray. With a Great Power alliance in hand, they hoped to sit *on* the alliance and to sit *out* the war. From the Unionists' perspective, the alliance was a long-term, postwar instrument that split the six European Powers and that, in peacetime, would provide the empire with international support. Grand Vizier Said Halim and War Minister Enver had conducted the negotiations with Berlin. Interior Minister Talat and Speaker of the Assembly of Deputies Halil were also privy to the talks. Finance Minister Cavid and Navy Minister Cemal learned of the alliance only on the morning of August 2. Cavid recorded in his diary that he opposed the alliance. He told Talat that if Russia invaded the Ottoman Empire, Germany would not lift a finger on the Ottomans' behalf.[98]

Despite the signing of the German alliance, the Unionists' top brass—Grand Vizier Said Halim, War Minister Enver, Interior Minister Talat, Navy Minister Cemal, and Finance Minister Cavid—continued their search for an alliance with the Entente. On August 5, with the two German ships still anchored and hiding near the Southern Dardanelles, Enver proposed a military alliance to Russia. Meeting with General Leontiev, the military attaché at the Russian embassy, Enver suggested a treaty "for a period of 5 or 10 years."[99] That same day, Giers suggested to his government in Saint Petersburg that the Ottoman Empire be kept neutral until "that point in time when circumstances permit our own firm entrance into the Straits."[100] Enver told Leontiev and Ambassador Giers that the Ottoman government was ready to send home the entire German contingent that was then in the Ottoman Empire. As war minister, he would coordinate all Ottoman forces with those of Russia. From Saint Petersburg, Foreign Minister Sergey Sazonov brushed aside any such plans. The Ottoman army posed no military threat to Russia, he told Giers. Sazonov instructed his ambassador to stall negotiations and answered Enver's proposal with a threat: if the Ottoman army made any move deemed hostile to Russian interests, the Ottomans would face the partition of their empire.[101] That was August 10. It was only now, after a week of negotiation with the Entente, that Enver finally issued permission for the *Goeben* and the *Breslau* to enter the Straits and to proceed to Istanbul.[102] In the days prior, the German ambassador, Baron Hans von Wangenheim, had been fuming over the wait and threatened that Germany would go together with Russia and partition the Ottoman Empire if Enver denied the ships' entry any longer.[103]

The arrival of the two German ships in the Straits appeared to have punctured Ottoman neutrality and made official the empire's joining Germany. Interior Minister Talat and President of the Assembly Halil arrived at the grand vizier's house. Together they convinced Ambassador Wangenheim to pass on a request to Berlin: the Ottomans would declare the two ships to have been purchased by the Ottoman navy. Wangenheim could not believe his ears. The meeting ended after an acrimonious night at three o'clock in the morning. Before Berlin could send back a reply, the Ottoman government ceremoniously proclaimed in the morning papers that it had bought the ships.[104] The *Goeben* was renamed the *Yavuz*, after the sultan who had conquered Egypt back in the sixteenth century; the name signaled that Egypt, occupied by Britain in 1882, remained Ottoman. The *Breslau* was renamed *Midilli* (Mytilene) after the Aegean island on which Cemal, the navy minister, had been born; it was also one of the key islands Greece had captured in the First Balkan War in 1912. The names of the famous new ships were meant to serve as reminders of these wounds and symbols of the empire's life-and-death struggle.

Much like the Russian foreign minister, Churchill sought to press the Ottomans into neutrality. The Entente was focused on Germany, and the Ottoman theater was to stay quiet. Writing personally to Enver on August 15, Churchill conveyed something between a warning and an ultimatum:

> But siding with Germany openly or covertly now would mean the greatest disaster to you, your comrades & your country. The overwhelming superiority at sea presented by the navies of England, France, Russia + Japan over those of Austria & Germany renders it easy for the four allies to transport troops in almost unlimited numbers from any quar-

> ter of the globe and if they were forced into a quarrel by Turkey their blow could be decisive at the heart.[105]

Churchill and Sazonov were strongly advising the Ottoman government to sit still and await events. This was a tall order for a group of battle-worn revolutionaries intent on saving an empire, whose worldview was shaped by (if simplistic) Darwinian ideals of survival of the fittest, new technologies, modernity, movement, and action and who abhorred passivity.[106]

There seems to have been little consideration in London of the effect that delivering, rather than confiscating, the Ottoman ships would have had. Sending the ships to Istanbul, it seems, would have given the British navy a great deal of control over what would become a key strategic choke point in the First World War, not to mention its incredible symbolic importance. Ottoman crews were far from mastering navigation of the two new dreadnoughts in August 1914, so the vessels would have remained in British hands for the foreseeable future. Moreover, at this point there was still a high-profile British naval mission under the command of a senior officer, Admiral Arthur Limpus, in the Ottoman capital. Given the vital role of the Straits for supplying Russia and the great cost of the failed Entente offensive and the ensuing bloodbath at Gallipoli in 1915, one wonders how the war's history would have differed had the British government not withheld the two ships but instead had moved them to Istanbul in August 1914.

Be that as it may, the Entente powers refused to make any assurances as to the Ottomans' future. The Entente's perfunctory nods and verbal half-pledges did not inspire much confidence in Istanbul. Even the moderate Cavid, the finance minister—a dove by most accounts in August 1914—"of course did not find such a *note verbale* sufficient," as he noted in his diary. To the contrary, Cavid was fuming; he found the Entente's vague statements and evasiveness insulting and insisted on concrete objectives.[107] Given that in a world war neither Germany nor Austria-Hungary would pose a military threat to the Ottomans, the Unionists searched for an Entente promise not to use the conflict as an opportunity to grab further Ottoman territory. More specifically, the Unionists pursued a British pledge to restrain Russia from moving on the Straits or Eastern Anatolia. As the evidence shows, such a British policy was far from Grey's mind. In fact, it ran contrary to visions being articulated and concrete plans being laid for the future of the Ottoman Empire in the capitals of the Entente.

In early 1914, simultaneous with the negotiation of the Armenian Reform Proposal, Sazonov had been eager to move ahead with Ottoman partition. The Straits had become an economic necessity to Russia's empire: "The ultimate aim of Russian policy," he noted after the war, "was to obtain free access to the Mediterranean." Control of the Straits had become of vital importance for Russian trade and thus "for her economic development and for her safety of the more vulnerable part of her territory."[108] Second, he believed that Ottoman rule in the Balkans had been "a monstrous anachronism."[109] It had been "Russia's historical mission," he continued, to provide for "the emancipation of the Christian peoples of the Balkan Peninsula from the Turkish yoke."[110] Hence, following the Balkan Wars, he commented quite triumphantly on the defeat of the Ottomans, whom he declared to be "the enslavers of the Christian peoples of the Balkan Peninsula."[111]

The choice before the Unionists in August 1914 was not whether to side with the Central Powers or the Entente. Instead, the choice was between siding with the Central Powers and risking active participation in a world war, on the one hand, and remaining neutral and placing full trust in the pronouncements of the Entente, on the other. Even the basic Unionist request—a written commitment to respect Ottoman borders and territory—met with Entente equivocation, however. Cavid, for example, asked for any Entente guarantee to be effective for a duration of fifteen to twenty years, plus an end to the Capitulations.[112] When the Unionists' offered their neutrality in exchange for the Ottoman seizure of German businesses and concessions inside the empire, French officials rejected the proposal. The Entente's joint declaration on August 18, supporting Ottoman neutrality but leaving out all other requests, therefore, did little to reassure Ottoman leaders.[113]

In the weeks after the signing of the alliance with Germany, Grand Vizier Said Halim instructed Finance Minister Cavid to continue pressing for a wartime agreement with the Entente. The grand vizier asked for a guarantee of Ottoman territoriality—that is, in effect, a promise that none of the Entente powers would help themselves to Ottoman territory during the war—and termination of the Capitulations. Cemal Pasha supported this renewed effort. Navy minister for much of the war (at least nominally), Cemal, beginning in November 1914, was also appointed commander of the Fourth Army, ruling the Syrian Mediterranean coast from Aleppo to the Sinai Peninsula. Cemal thought the two warships the Navy had ordered from British companies, and which London had confiscated by the end of July, should be delivered as part of an Entente-Ottoman agreement. The central demands, however, remained the termination of the Capitulations and a pledge that the Entente keep their hands off Ottoman lands. The meeting on August 19 between Cavid and the British ambassador, Mallet, can be considered a pivotal moment. The meeting made clear that the Entente never seriously entertained presenting the Unionists with a substantive offer. Instead, Mallet repeated Churchill's threat: the Ottomans must stay neutral. If instead they joined Germany and Austria-Hungary, then the Ottoman Empire's coastline would fall under the control of whoever controlled the seas, that is, the British navy. Mallet was signaling the impending Anglo-French naval blockade that was, as it turns out, already in preparation and that would bring famine and devastation to the people of Syria in 1915. At this point, on August 19, even Cavid, who was highly skeptical of the German alliance, felt bitterly disappointed about the Entente, and the British in particular.[114]

Grand Vizier Said Halim and Navy Minister Cemal also pressed for a written statement addressing the two principal Ottoman demands: to leave Ottoman territory intact and to end the Capitulations.[115] They, too, were turned away. Given British deflection and evasiveness throughout the summer, Cavid grew convinced that Mallet had no instructions for serious talks to reach a formal agreement with the Ottomans.[116] And Cavid was right: we know because Mallet, too, put his thoughts down on paper. Summarizing the meeting for Grey on August 20, Mallet listed the Unionists' requests and added that Cemal had "asked for renunciation of any interference with the internal affairs of Turkey." Mallet commented, "This need not be taken seriously, and is, of course, an absurd proposal." Little wonder that Ottoman leaders found themselves mistrusting the Entente.[117]

This disappointment notwithstanding, Cavid continued negotiations with the Entente. He discussed the termination of the Capitulations with Konstantin Gulkevich, the chargé d'affaires at the Russian embassy, and shortly thereafter with the Russian ambassador, Giers, himself. As finance minister, Cavid was especially attentive to both the real and the perceived injuries the Capitulations inflicted on Ottoman social and economic life. The Great Powers' insistence on maintaining the Capitulations, he believed, was just another reprehensible European double standard, strangling the empire's potential development. Those parts of the Ottoman Empire captured and now part of Bulgaria, Greece, and Serbia in the recent Balkan Wars, for example, had shed immediately their subjugation to the Capitulations, he noted in his diary.[118] Giers, like his British counterpart Mallet, equivocated when meeting with Cavid. The Unionists were getting no traction with the Entente.[119] Nonetheless, Cavid continued to openly oppose the alliance with Germany. On August 22, 1914, he told the Unionists' Central Committee that such an entanglement would "drag the homeland into catastrophe."[120] Meeting with Ambassador Giers on August 22, 1914, Cavid found him evasive and vague.[121] By that time, the Russian army had reinforced its military positions on the Ottoman border in the Caucasus, and the Russian agriculture minister, A. V. Krivoshein, was pressing for military conflict with the Ottomans.[122]

On August 28, 1914, the Entente finally produced some written assurance guaranteeing the empire's territory and agreed to consider a review of the Capitulations.[123] Given the Entente's repeated rejection throughout the month of August, not to mention an Anglo-French naval blockade building along the Syrian coast, the Entente's "guarantee" accomplished little in convincing the Unionists of Entente friendship. Sensing the Unionists' distrust, Mallet had sarcasm on offer: he was "personally somewhat relieved, as to guarantee integrity and independence of Turkey was like guaranteeing the life of a man who was determined to commit suicide." The Unionists were calling out the Entente's repeated equivocation, which Mallet understandably did not appreciate. Meeting with Talat, Mallet now issued a threat: Talat "must not imagine that Great Britain was afraid of

Turkey, or that we [Great Britain] feared to face alternative if forced." Talat steered clear of Mallet's provocation and offered another proposal. The "Turkish Government now wished to sell" Britain "two Turkish ships outright." Talat did not specify which ships, but it is difficult to imagine that he was referring to anything but the *Goeben* and the *Breslau*. This Ottoman attempt to engage the Entente, like those made previously, also met with rejection. Apparently surprised, the British ambassador responded evasively, noting that he "did not know His Majesty's views." He would inquire but told Talat that "personally, I should be reluctant to inflict so mortal a stab on the wounded heart of the Turkish people, who were already suffering so much by temporary detention of their ships." In his report to Grey, Mallet noted that the Ottoman government needed "money badly, as the economic situation was desperate." But Mallet already knew Grey's views on the question of loans to Istanbul.[124] What these exchanges show is that the British government did nothing to win over the Unionists and that the Ottomans tested this British stance exhaustively before they were convinced that a British alliance was not an option.

Talat's alliance offer to the Russian foreign minister, Sergey Sazonov, in late May 1914, marked another potentially pivotal moment, but one the foreign minister cast aside quickly. Sazonov feared that Austria-Hungary and Germany's response to such an alliance would prove too costly.[125] Instead, Sazonov was holding out for a moment of crisis, such as had appeared after the First Balkan War, when an alliance comprising Bulgaria, Greece, Montenegro, and Serbia took up arms against the Ottomans. Such a crisis could offer the opportunity for seizing the Straits in a fait accompli and not through diplomatic means where Russia would have to make trade-offs and offer compensation to the other Great Powers. With the Black Sea fleet now being modernized and expanded, Sazonov was waiting for the right moment (as Giers noted explicitly in early August 1914). In 1908 and again in 1911 the Russian government attempted to redefine the status of the Straits through diplomatic means, and it tried to do so again militarily during the Second Balkan War in 1913. During this time Sazonov also threatened at least twice to invade and occupy eastern Anatolia.[126]

The outbreak of war in late July 1914 altered the fundamental dynamic between the Entente and the Ottoman Empire: if before the war the Entente powers had to consider the interests and desires of Germany and Austria-Hungary and face the risk of a European conflagration in case such interests were violated, this factor now had become a moot point.

In November 1914, as Keith Wilson has observed, the "declaration of war by the Ottoman Empire on Russia and Britain in that month had solved for Grey a problem insoluble otherwise." Grey now could present to Sazonov the Ottoman Straits and Istanbul as "the greatest prize of the whole war."[127] Grey was holding the Straits as a card he could offer Sazonov for a hefty price at the right moment, with the greatest maximum gain for Grey and England. In Wilson's words, in "the final analysis" Grey and the Foreign Office were prepared and willing, when necessary, to trade the Straits in exchange for the safety of India on its northern frontier. Grey had made his point already in early 1906, and it was "strictly adhered to subsequently by the Foreign Secretary himself." In July 1914 both Sazonov and Paul Cambon, the French ambassador to London, made unmistakably clear to Grey that India would be at risk if Grey did not fully support his allies. In Wilson's words, Grey's foremost concern rested with the security of India, but it also meant that his policy "encouraged Britain to encourage Russia in particular to dismantle the Ottoman Empire."[128]

The Entente's posture toward the Ottoman Empire in July and August 1914 grew out of the three powers' well-established stance of the prewar years. In theory, the new situation created by the outbreak of war in July 1914 could have brought about a rethinking on the part of the Entente. The evidence suggests, however, that the Entente not only continued their pursuit of objectives in the Ottoman Mediterranean but in fact now saw opportunities for doubling down on these goals.

Despite the British government's consistently dismissive stance, the Ottomans kept testing the possibility of a British alliance until they were entirely convinced that such an alliance was not in the cards. By September 1914, France and Russia were prepared to move actively against the Ottoman Empire but decided instead to let the Ottomans take the first shot, which they did.[129] Théophile Delcassé, the newly appointed French foreign minister and a former minister of colonies, told the Ottoman ambassador at Paris that the Ottoman Empire's "territoriality no longer was a vital matter to France."[130] When Cavid heard this, he warned Maurice Bompard, the French ambassador in Istanbul, that such statements only served to push the Ottomans into German arms. That same day, the Ottoman cabinet approved and voted on the unilateral termination of the Capitulations.[131]

Rumors of the impending end to the Capitulations had been circulating for weeks. On August 21, 1914, a solar eclipse covered the sun and darkened the sky, "as if pointing toward the General War [*harb-i umûmî*] that had broken out." Mediha, the twelve-year-old in Trabzon, recorded in her diary the mix of excitement and trepidation she felt. She ran to the window, "gazing out at the stars and the moon."[132] She was excited about the news swirling around her neighborhood: the government was finally ending all the legal advantages and commercial privileges that foreign citizens and businesses enjoyed in the empire. Young Mediha believed that these immunities granted to anyone with foreign papers were strangling the empire's economy and stealing the livelihood of ordinary Ottomans. The Capitulations were one of several powerful symbols of foreign domination and the daily injustices European powers inflicted on the empire's people. Mediha described the fireworks, drum performances, and rifle fire that celebrated the Capitulations' demise. There was "so much excitement" and "the streets were full of joy and happiness," while "parents were crying tears of joy at home." Flags flew "everywhere" and "an army parade" caused Mediha's heart to flutter.[133] Amid the crisis engulfing European powers in the summer of 1914, the Ottoman government sought to advance its political goals by removing a crucial mechanism of foreign control.

Between June 28 and October 29, 1914, the Unionists sought to exploit the realities of war in Europe. They unilaterally declared the Capitulations null and void in September 1914, an enormously popular step greeted with celebration in streets across the empire. Next, the government raised import tariffs to 50 percent and declared foreign companies subject to taxes on profits earned inside the empire.[134] The Unionists had claimed their first successes and could make the case that only they could defend the empire and reclaim its sovereignty and unfettered independence.

By September 25, Entente cabinets were calling explicitly, though not publicly, for war with the Ottoman Empire. The British ambassador at Saint Petersburg, George Buchanan, reported to Grey in London that "opinion seems to be gaining ground that it can only be at the expense of Turkey that Russia can obtain any material advantage as the result of the war."[135] Agriculture Minister Krivoshein "remarked to me yesterday that he personally would be glad if the Turks declared war on Russia, as then the Turkish question would be finally settled."[136] From Istanbul, Mallet was reporting that the French government was ready to sever relations with the Ottomans. He told Grey on September 26, 1914, "I gather from the telegrams from the French Minister for Foreign Affairs that he thinks that we should take a stronger line with the Turks. Nothing would give me and my Russian colleague greater pleasure if our Governments are ready to accept the consequences which both of us think would be of the most serious character."[137] The Entente ambassadors were ready to cut off relations.

The Unionists Take Matters into Their Own Hands

For over a century, the Ottoman war minister, Enver Pasha, has been remembered as the man who dragged the empire single-handedly into the First World War and brought about its ruin. But such an interpretation has served primarily the interests of the Entente. The German admiral Wilhelm Souchon, who led the naval attack on Russia, believed that between late August and early September 1914, all the leading Ottoman statesmen favored holding on to neutrality, "including the war minister [Enver Pasha]."[138] As the Unionists' in their negotiations with the Entente repeatedly ran into a brick wall, and Germany lost patience for any further Ottoman delays, the Unionists were forced to act. Souchon concluded that when the Unionists finally decided to enter the war, they did so "in order to fight for the achievement of the Ottoman Empire's national hopes and for its future."[139]

For contemporaries in 1914, it was not hard to see what the Ottomans hoped to get out of the war: sovereignty and freedom from foreign financial control. Sovereignty was what the Entente denied and what Berlin held out as a promise. Admiral Souchon knew how to operate this lever; he told the Unionists that not joining Germany—and providing the Central Powers with much-needed relief in a September of military setbacks for them—would cost the empire dearly. Failure to enter the battlefield would result in the Ottomans' "strong political humiliation" at the hands of all the Great Powers. By not jumping into the war on the side of Germany, Souchon later wrote, the Unionists would relinquish "their right to self-determination [*Selbstbestimmungsrecht*] and the fulfillment of national goals."[140] Already in August 1914, the Anglo-French fleet in the Eastern Mediterranean began assembling the blockade of the Syrian coast. It was becoming increasingly clear to the Unionists that rupturing the alliance with Germany meant entrusting the empire to the interests of the Entente. They were running out of time.

In late October, the Unionists opted for war on the side of Germany. On October 25, Navy Minister Cemal provided Souchon with sixteen identical orders, in sealed envelopes, one for each ship that would participate in the raid on the Russian Black Sea coast. The letters were signed by Enver and instructed all Ottoman crew to follow orders from the most senior German officer on board for the duration of the raid.[141] "Battle-ready," a small fleet of Ottoman vessels—including *Berk-i Satvet*, *Gayret-i Vataniye*, *Hamidiye*, and *Muavenet-i Milliye*—lifted anchor off Haydarpasha in the Bosphorus around five o'clock in the afternoon on October 27. They sailed sixty-six degrees northeast at twelve knots for the Russian port city of Novorossiysk. At 10:50 in the morning on October 29, according to the ship's logbook, they opened fire.[142] At 10:37 p.m. on October 29, 1914, Souchon reported that the *Goeben* had sunk the Russian steamer *Pruth*. The Ottoman *Berk-i Satvet* had destroyed communication facilities in Novorossiysk, while the *Breslau* had set petroleum and grain reservoirs on fire. The *Goeben* had also fished three Russian officers and seventy-two crew out of the water. According to the captured Russian crew, *Pruth* had been loaded with explosives, including seven hundred sea mines, and was headed for Istanbul. The prisoners were due to arrive in the Ottoman capital on October 30.[143] Simultaneously, Ottoman torpedo boats attacked Odessa, a major outlet for wheat exports. *Gayret-i Vataniye* sank a Russian gunboat. *Muavenet-i Milliye* hit another. They destroyed five petroleum tanks on the coast.[144] The Ottoman side did not suffer any casualties, though the *Goeben* had taken two hits and heavy damage. The fleet then gathered near the Bosphorus, on October 31, 1914. Souchon's report to Ottoman headquarters claimed, falsely, that "the Russian fleet on October 27 and 28 monitored all maneuvers of the Ottoman fleet, systematically disrupted exercise, and opened hostilities on October 29, 1914." Throughout the war, the Unionists claimed that Russia had opened fire first.

Speaking to a reporter from Chicago in February 1915, Grand Vizier Said Halim Pasha justified the Ottoman decision for war: the Entente states had offered "so many guarantees" that they could no longer be trusted. Not without a touch of melodrama, he claimed that "when it comes to guarantees we Turks could tell a tale of woe that would bring tears to the eyes of a stone image." "We have had our fill of guarantees," he fumed. "We really want no more of them." He had "no faith in guarantees."[145] He asked, "What does a guarantee mean?" and answered his own question: "It means that you admit that somebody has the right to—well, protect you. And this, in turn, means that you surrender your sovereignty, lock, stock, and barrel. It means that thereafter you ask permission of some other government if you want to do anything—perhaps the very thing that ought to be done." Like Talat, Said Halim understood the Ottoman road to independence to lead through war:

> We have asked other governments long enough, and the Entente governments have been among them. We know what bargains to make. A protected Turkey means a dependent Turkey. We believe that we ought to be independent—more independent than we have been in the past. Others do not think so, of course. But we do. That is a matter of opinion which this war may settle forever. We are all entitled to our opinions. You are, I am, we are.[146]

That the alliance with Germany was not that different from a bid for protection did not seem to have bothered Talat or Said Halim. They believed that an alliance with Germany could be managed without compromising Ottoman sovereignty.

Grand Vizier Said Halim cited ending the Capitulations as a crucial factor in the decision for war. He told the Chicago reporter that "we have abolished the capitulations. Hereafter the foreigner who thinks Turkey good enough to live in must think our laws and courts good enough to conform to. We also propose to show more interest in the future in the foreign schools and missions in the empire. Some of these establishments have turned out young men who are not satisfied with our government. That will have to stop."[147]

On February 22, 1915, Said Halim told the *New York Times* that his government was "tired of the hypocrisy" so palpable in the Triple Entente's "dealing with Turkey." He and his colleagues had seen enough. History had taught them that "to enter into relations with Great Britain, France, and Russia would have been a harmful factor in respect to the country's interest." The Ottoman "people want a chance to work out their destiny."[148] What was the war for? The Grand Vizier averred that for the Ottomans the war was about making "a modern state." The empire needed time to reform—to rebuild its army and develop its industry and infrastructure. "To get that time is the thing we are fighting for," he claimed.[149]

During the war, members of the government appeared frequently before both chambers of parliament, the Assembly of Deputies and the Senate, to address questions concerning proposed laws and budgets. Cabinet members were frequently criticized for the miserable conditions the war had brought on the people. By February 1916, after some fifteen months of war, Talat defended his government's actions before the Senate, claiming the empire had "today an incredible opportunity to rebuild its entire structure." He laid out a great future for the empire, telling the Senate that "just as Fredrick the Great took advantage of extraordinary circumstances and got Germany to climb to the pinnacle of progress, we, too, must work to move the Ottoman state to the pinnacle of progress."[150] As the next chapters demonstrate, no such pinnacle came into view at any stage of the war.

2

An Empire's Domestic Revolution

THE FIRST World War in the Ottoman Empire mobilized the state against the people and the people against the state. In the years leading up to 1914, the Unionist government had begun losing political support at home, not least because they objected to any decentralized, or federated, system of government, such as the kind proposed by Prince Sabahaddin Bey, the main opposition figure and the leader of the Freedom and Entente Party (Hürriyet ve İtilâf Fırkası). Facing formidable opposition, the Unionists resorted to repression and criminalized dissent. Opposition groups sought refuge underground. The outbreak of war in 1914 provided the Unionists with further tools of control. But the war in Europe also touched off a wave of mobilization among parties, organizations, secret societies, activists, intellectuals, political leaders, and local figures aiming to pry open the strong fist of the Unionists. Groups mobilized both inside the empire's borders and beyond it, among exiles in Europe and migrant communities in the Americas. Their opposition to the Unionist government stemmed from a range of grievances and demands that predated the war. Global war turned political contestation into military conflict.

To be clear, opposition groups' mobilizing in summer 1914 was not the result of nationalist movements. Rather, it arose out of the strong opposition to the Unionists' heavy centralism of the prewar years. Groups that mobilized in 1914 comprised small segments of the population. Prominent among them were the Ottoman Armenian volunteers—numbering some four thousand—who joined the Russian army as early as August 1914. These volunteers, a small proportion of all Ottoman Armenians, saw the war as an opportunity to end Istanbul's rule over eastern Anatolia. Zionist leaders sought ways to claim Palestine, and young American and European Jewish men formed the Jewish Corps and eventually joined with British forces in the occupation of Jerusalem in December 1917. Lebanese communities in Egypt as early as September 1914, prior to the Ottoman entry into the war, notified French authorities of their support for an Entente invasion of Lebanon; in November they submitted lists of men ready to take up arms and join such a campaign.[1] Once the empire was at war, Bishara al-Buwari, the mayor of the predominantly Maronite Catholic town of Jounieh, situated just north of Beirut, expressed delight on hearing that the Unionists had jumped in on Germany's side. He thought this decision would bring about Ottoman defeat and subsequently "liberation from Turkish control," although he did not specify liberation for whom exactly, whether for all the communities then inhabiting Lebanon and Syria, all Ottoman Arabs, or all Ottomans in whatever part of the empire they may be. Mayor al-Buwari personally gathered pieces of intelligence and passed them on to French contacts. After the armistice, having witnessed the suffering of the people of Beirut and its environs, al-Buwari remarked bitterly that if he had known the "extent of the sacrifice," which he was "far from being able to imagine" in 1914, he would never have found this "liberation" to be "worth such a high price."[2] Edward Said, whose 1978 book *Orientalism* transformed the study of the Middle East, relates his father's story in his memoir. On hearing news of the Ottomans' entry into the First World War on the side of the Central Powers, Wadie Said, a young Palestinian Christian who—like hundreds of thousands of Ottomans since the 1890s—was looking for work in North America at the time, immediately sought to join the war against the Ottoman Empire. He first tried enlisting in the Canadian army, then in the American Expeditionary Force. Private Said made it as far as France.[3]

Thus, even as the Unionists were exerting great efforts to exploit the global war and cement their rule, numerous opposition movements also recognized opportunity in the war. For groups that formed their own alliances with the Entente powers and had access to arms, the conflict opened new possibilities for fighting the Unionist regime. At the same time, such mobilization exposed entire communities to accusations of supporting the enemy and playing the role of a "fifth column."[4]

The interests of the Entente and certain groups within the empire aligned in new and powerful ways: if the outbreak of war made it possible for the Unionists to sign an alliance with a Great Power, Germany, it also made it possible for their opponents to forge ties with the Entente. Contemporaries recognized this dynamic and, in addition to opportunity, could see the danger that resided in such alliances. This chapter explores the extent to which the Unionist government from July 1914 onward employed the crisis of the First World War as a way of clamping down on the political demands voiced by various segments of the population, especially in the aftermath of the Balkan Wars and the new dynamics they generated. At the same time, as the Unionists used the First World War to impose "union and progress" by force rather than incentivizing, let alone inspiring it, groups mobilized against the Unionists and seized the opportunities engendered by global war.

Parliament Is Closed and the Servant of Humanity Jean Jaurès Remembered

When the Unionists launched their revolution demanding a constitution in July 1908, they called for empire-wide elections and oversaw the opening of parliament that same year.[5] Once the parliament opened its doors, the Unionists worked to shift power away from the sultan and his court and toward the new parliament. They did so primarily by amending, rewriting, adding, and removing articles of the constitution, a document they inherited from the first Ottoman parliament of 1876–1878.[6] The revised constitution replaced the centrality of the sultan with the new centrality of parliament. In the heady days that followed the revolution, the Ottoman Committee of Union and Progress held itself out as the principal defender of the new constitutional order. But once the Unionists fared poorly in electoral politics and risked losing their dominance and control over the legislature, they reversed the liberal changes they themselves had implemented. After empowering parliament, the Unionists undermined and restricted it; they prized controlling the institutions of power over democratizing them. For all those who were not supporters of the Unionists, the revolution turned repressive. This process was still unfolding in 1914, and it took on new forms after the June 28 assassination of Archduke Franz Ferdinand, indelibly shaping the course of the war.

The years 1911–1913, as we have seen, threw the country into crisis. In late September 1911, Italian forces invaded Ottoman Tripolitania in North Africa and imposed a ruthless, decades-long occupation on its population.[7] Then, on November 21, opposition groups merged under the leadership of Sabahaddin Bey to form a massive alternative to the Unionists, the Freedom and Entente Party.[8] Alarmed and seeing no other path to electoral victory, the Unionists resorted to rigging the general election, held in April 1912. The move incensed a group of military officers, who styled themselves the Savior Officers (Halâskâran) and forced the Unionist government to resign. The Savior Officers dissolved the parliament and called for new elections. The Unionists scrammed, with many going into hiding abroad.

The First Balkan War, in some ways, handed the Unionists an unexpected gift. In October 1912, following the Unionists' dispersal by the Savior Officers, a coalition of four Balkan states—Bulgaria, Greece, Montenegro, Romania—declared war on the empire. The new government that succeeded the Unionists was barely in place when it presided over the loss of much of the empire's European provinces and the arrival of hundreds of thousands of refugees. In January 1913, the Great Powers dictated that Istanbul relinquish the city of Edirne to Bulgarian forces. Spreading the news that the caretaker government was giving away Edirne, the Unionists exploited the crisis and staged a coup. In what became known as the Raid on the Sublime Porte (*Bab-ı Âli Baskını*), on January 23, 1913, an armed group led by Enver stormed the offices of the grand vizierate, killing the war minister and forcing the grand vizier to resign. With pistols drawn and pointed at him, Grand Vizier Kâmil wrote out his resignation letter, his hand, the penmanship suggests, shaking: "I have been obliged by the army to submit my humble resignation to your royal highness and omniscient wisdom." Kâmil was then ordered by the revolutionaries to insert the words "by the people and" so that the letter would read, "I have

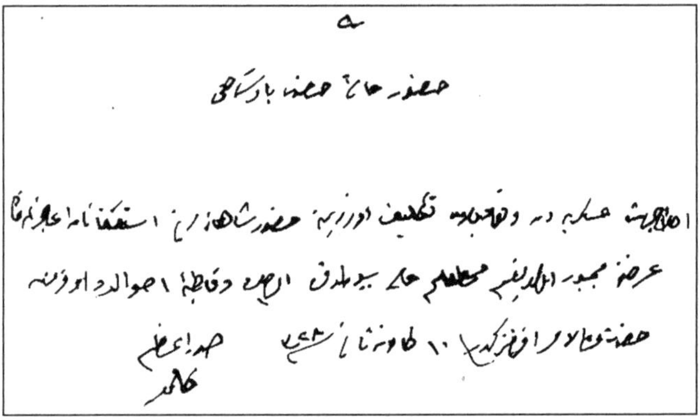

FIGURE 3. The resignation letter of Grand Vizier Kâmil Pasha, written at gunpoint on January 23, 1913. Note the insertion of "the people and" (italicized below), at the beginning of line 1. Grand Vizier Kâmil was ordered to add the phrase to give the coup a populist veneer. The event became known as "The Raid on the Sublime Porte (*Bâb-ı Âli Baskını*)." *Source*: BOA, BEO, A.AMD 1345/41, Ottoman Archives, Istanbul

Huzûr-i Âli-i Hazret-i Pâdişâhî[ye]

Ahali ve cihet-i askeriyyeden vuku' bulan teklif üzerine huzûr-u şâhânelerine istifanâme-i âcizânemin arzına mecbur olduğum muhat-ı ilm-i âli buyruldukda ol babda ve katıbe-i ahvalde emr ü ferman hazret-i veliyy'ül-emr efendimizindir.

Fi 10 Kânun-ı Sâni 328

Sadr-ı Âzam

Kâmil

[To] the Esteemed Presence of His Imperial Highness

I have been obliged by *the people and* the army to submit my humble resignation to your royal highness and omniscient wisdom. In this and every matter command belongs unto him our protector to whom all commanding belongs.

23 January 1913

Grand Vizier

Kâmil

been obliged *by the people and* the army to submit my humble resignation to your royal highness and omniscient wisdom."[9] With their political appeal melting, the Unionists craved popular support.

Days before the coup,.the cabinet had discussed plans for arresting Unionist members and closing all offices of the Unionist organization in the capital.[10] In the coup's aftermath, the Unionists clamped down on any calls for expanding local political authority in the provinces. Such calls had come primarily from the Decentralization movement (Arabic: *la markaziyya*; Ottoman Turkish: *adem-i merkeziyet*; literally, no centralization), whose most prominent advocate was Prince Sabahaddin and which had adherents all across the empire.[11]

Ironically, it was under the Unionists that the government ceded Edirne (Adrianople) to Bulgaria. In May 1913 in the Treaty of London, they did exactly that for which they had excoriated Kâmil Pasha before then. A few weeks later, on June 11, 1913, the new grand vizier, Mahmud Şevket Pasha, riding in one of the country's few automobiles, was shot dead. That same month, Bulgaria, dissatisfied with the division of the spoils in the First Balkan War, attacked Greece and Serbia in a Second Balkan War. Capitalizing on the situation, Enver marched back into Edirne and occupied the city without firing a single shot. Enver, donning the mantle of the hero, was the first to ride into the city, a former capital of the empire. As the Balkan Wars posed an existential threat to the empire, the Unionists managed to turn military losses into political victory at home.

The assassination of Mahmud Şevket Pasha in June 1913 served the Unionists as a pretext for deporting hundreds of opposition members from the capital. A prominent journalist observed, "The opposing sides no longer constituted regular political parties seeking to further their special aims by means of discussion and persuasion."[12] It was no longer about politics or governance but about controlling the levers of power. "They had become fighting groups, resolved to keep, or obtain, public power at any cost."[13] The Unionists claimed for themselves "exclusive proprietorship of the public powers." Having overthrown Sultan Abdülhamid II, they now undermined the powers of the parliament. And "under the pretense of safeguarding liberty, liberty was sadly crushed."[14] The Unionists' "chief concern," the journalist went on, "became the maintenance of their political power as a group." Their goal was to achieve "a strict submission to the authority of the central Government" of all groups and organizations across the empire.[15]

Hüseyin Cahid, the owner and editor of the major daily newspaper closest to the Unionists, *Tanin*, commented at length on the politics of this period in his memoirs. He thought a century of upheaval had left its stamp on the various regions of the empire. Looking back, he surmised that "it would have been foolish to believe that because there was now a constitution in Istanbul, all the turmoil across the empire would simply cease to exist." The state had little legal or political authority in "those faraway, embroiled places." There—without specifying where exactly—"the word of the government could be made audible only with the help of the government's fist." It was simply unrealistic to expect that because of the constitution "all parts of the empire would now bow their heads to the government and its laws." Hüseyin Cahid explained that "the government wanted to collect taxes from every jurisdiction of the empire, and naturally it was met with opposition, resistance, and rebellion. The Albanians, refusing to pay taxes, gathered in Firzovk and organized protests."[16] And yet, Hüseyin Cahid, and all the Unionists, were aware of alternatives to their highly centralized rule. Shortly after the founding of the main opposition party, Freedom and Entente, Hüseyin Cahid wrote in *Tanin* in November 1911 that a coalition of liberal parties in opposition to the Unionists had formed in order to "strengthen the foundations of the constitution" and "to bring about a genuine understanding and agreement [*gerçek bir anlaşma ve uyuşma sağlamak*]."[17] Sabahaddin Bey's Freedom and Entente Party argued for empowering regional parties while maintaining imperial unity intact.

The alliance with Germany in August 1914 and the Ottoman entry into war at the end of October, therefore, came at a time when the Unionists faced a crisis of legitimacy at home. Hours after signing the German alliance, still on August 2, Unionist leaders shut down the Assembly of Deputies. With imperial decrees tucked into their pockets and carrying the sultan's signature, Interior Minister Talat and Finance Minister Cavid made their way to Nazime Palace, the mansion on the shores of the Bosphorus where the Assembly and Senate held their sessions.[18] Halil, president of the lower house, opened the session at 4:20 in the afternoon.[19] Before Talat could take the podium, the deputy from Karesi rose to speak: "I would like to propose that we as a body convey our condolences to the family of Monsieur Jaurès. He was deeply committed to serving humanity and had so much respect and affection for the Ottoman world [*osmanlılığa*]." Jean Jaurès, the popular French socialist politician, who had advocated so staunchly for peace in the days following the Sarajevo assassination, had been shot and killed in an attack on July 31. The deputies adopted the proposal unanimously. If the gesture was intended as a call for the preservation of peace, it went unheeded. Then Talat read the same imperial decree Cavid had already delivered in the upper house, the Meclis-i Ayan.[20] "Because the war between Austria-Hungary and Serbia has now acquired the form of a general war," Interior Minister Talat intoned, "I declare this session of the Assembly adjourned."[21] The meeting lasted ten short minutes and closed without debate or apparent objection. The Ottoman Committee of Union and Progress—the organization that had overthrown Sultan Abdülhamid II for suspending parliamentary rule—now shuttered the very institution for whose reinstatement it had struggled from Salonika to Istanbul and from Cairo to Paris.[22]

Parliament emptied and silenced, the next day the War Ministry issued an official declaration of the empire's neutrality in the current war. It then announced the mobilization of the army, as a precaution in the event of an attack. Although they had signed a secret alliance with Germany, the Unionists at this stage, as we have seen, were still hoping for an understanding with the Entente.

The parliament reopened four months later, in December 1914, and continued to meet throughout the war. Often deemed a toothless hall of yes-men, more form than substance, in reality the parliament became an extraordinary forum in which rare voices of opposition could make themselves heard. The number of those openly questioning government policy was small, but their criticism was relentless and searing. Deputies and notables in both houses castigated the actions of the government, in many cases fully aware that their pleas would be dismissed by the majority and that speaking up would place them in the crosshairs of the Unionist regime. At times they expressed opposition with the sole purpose of having their words recorded in the official parliamentary gazette, an invaluable source for historians today. The floors of the Assembly and Senate offered a way around the heavy hand of state censorship that muzzled the press and other public fora during the war.

The parliament was more than just a thorn in the government's side. The Unionists attempted to amend the constitution and curb the legislature's powers, and they repeatedly tried to close it down altogether. They also ordered the covert assassination of several parliamentarians and the public execution of several others.[23] By 1915 Grand Vizier Said Halim saw no reason to hide his dislike for the parliament. He opined publicly that improving the empire's economic development while also adopting electoral politics all at the same time, had failed: "We thought at first we could apply here some form of government that had been used with success in the Occident." However, he continued, "we tried that, but found it to be a mistake." The empire required deep reforms first, the grand vizier claimed. "Before a Western form of government can be established," he went on, "the attitude of the population toward government must be changed." Hence, "we are somewhat in the position of the Latin American countries whose constitutions prescribe a democratic form of government, but whose heads are dictators at best."[24] This was Said Halim acknowledging that his government had abandoned the experiment of representative government and the idea of allowing legitimate opposition.

Thus, shedding European financial control and colonial dominance were not the only issues unresolved by 1914. The place of the empire's ethnic and religious communities within the swiftly shrinking Ottoman space, too, remained a source of deep tension in government circles and across society.

"In Their Hearts and Minds the Maronites and Orthodox Support France and Russia"

In August 1914, the district governor of Jerusalem anxiously followed the gradual build-up of an Anglo-French naval blockade. Five days after Churchill's threat, on August 20, 1914, Jerusalem's governor respectfully but pointedly notified the Interior Ministry of the dangerous effects the declaration of mobilization was having on the region. After some polite praise for the government's decision to mobilize as "entirely prudent and laudable," he quickly changed tack, pointing out to his bosses in Istanbul that "this wide-ranging and rapid preparation" had prompted "speculations that we are planning an attack on Russia or our return to Egypt." He added that these rumors were "spreading among the public" and that the "concealment of the pro-German stand" had become pretty much impossible. The Ottomans' German allies were no help in this respect: "The Germans who wish to create problems for their adversaries in the East are spreading these rumors and thus fueling the anxieties of the Entente governments." The Jerusalem governor believed Berlin was exploiting the Ottomans for German strategic interests at the Ottomans' expense. More specifically, the governor's intelligence agents had learned that because of the ongoing mobilization, the Entente now planned a naval demonstration (*nümayiş-i bahrî*) along the Syrian coast, in which it would deploy over one hundred British, French, and Italian vessels.[25]

In the first weeks of the war in August 1914, while the Ottoman Empire was still neutral, the governor of Bekaa district voiced his distrust of the "malicious population of Mount Lebanon and especially the city of Zahle." Bekaa, a fertile valley just east of Mount Lebanon, was home to sizable Christian communities of various denominations—Maronite Catholic, Greek Catholic, and Greek Orthodox. Zahle's newspapers, the district governor of Bekaa claimed, displayed "an excessive support for France" that was "wounding the hearts of the Muslim ummah." What's more, he warned, this had been going on "since the Balkan Wars." Now, in the first days of the First World War, the people of Zahle's "affection for France" had risen to the "level of worship," which was unacceptable. He recommended the immediate dismissal of Zahle's top official, Ibrahim Abu Khatir, who was turning a blind eye to this "open" hostility to the Ottoman state. The offices of the local newspaper, *Zahle al-Fatat* (Young Zahle), furthermore, should be shuttered immediately and indefinitely.[26]

A few days later, Ibrahim Abu Khatir met with Philippe Zalzal, a Maronite Christian and a translator at the French consulate in Beirut. Their meeting further intensified the governor's red-hot suspicion of Maronite-French collusion. The governor now demanded the posting of "a superintendent of police," someone "very diligent and experienced," to monitor the situation, especially at Zahle's train station. It was "probable that with the influence of the [French] consul in Beirut and the connivance of the railway company, weapons will be smuggled into Mount Lebanon." He urged that "each and every train departing Beirut"

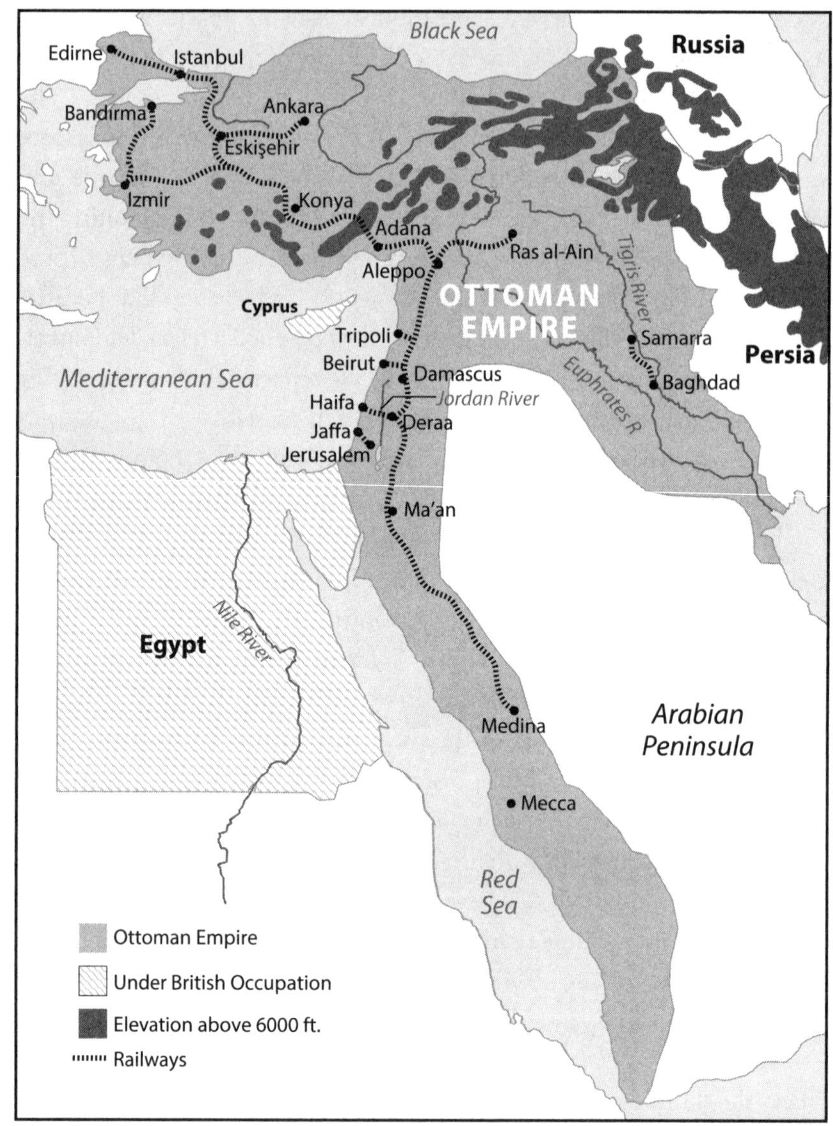

MAP 3. The Ottoman Empire, 1914.

for Zahle "be placed under continuous and secret surveillance."[27] The fighting that had broken out in Europe had prompted Ottoman authorities to clamp down on the suspected fifth column activities of Mount Lebanon's Christian population and, as we shall see, Christian populations across the empire.

The governor of Syria province, Hulusi, immediately approved the recommended measures. He also fired Zahle's district governor, who had stood by and watched "the already poisoned public opinion of the local population be incited to yet an even greater degree" after the war broke out.[28] Then Hulusi notified the military authorities that the lax district governor had been dismissed and wrote to the Directorate of Police requesting that a special officer be posted to Zahle's train station for the necessary surveillance work.[29]

The governor of neighboring Beirut province, Bekir Sami, also grew alarmed. He, too, was beset with anxieties about how best to control the population of Mount Lebanon. Not bothering to distinguish between political groups and the general population, he categorically described the people of Mount Lebanon as hostile: "In their hearts and minds [*kalben ve ruhen*] the Maronites and Orthodox support France and Russia."[30] Bekir Sami, like Talat, came from a family of refugees. While Talat's had been driven out from what became Bulgaria, Bekir Sami's family originated in the Northern Caucasus. The loss and anguish Muslim populations had suffered at the hands of, as he saw it, Christian states, was deeply personal and real to him.[31] Both Bekir Sami and Hulusi were prominent figures in Unionist circles. Hulusi, an accomplished engineer, had been the first president of both the Society of National Defense (Müdafaa-i Milliye Cemiyeti) and the Turkish Strength Association (Türk Gücü Derneği), the paramilitary youth movement established to train Ottoman youth. In late August and early September 1914, correspondence between Bekir Sami, Hulusi, and the district governor of Bekaa focused on the potential threats emanating from the local population.

During the war, hundreds of thousands of Ottoman citizens in Mount Lebanon would perish of hunger. The Governorate (Arabic: *mutasarrifiyya*; Ottoman: *mutasarrıflık*) of Mount Lebanon, with a Christian population of nearly 80 percent, had been under autonomous rule since 1861, a status granted by an international agreement between the Great Powers and the Ottoman government. On the eve of the First World War, relations between Mount Lebanon and the central government were tense. Over the past several years, with French support, the local council had sought to expand its fiscal and administrative powers.[32] In the aftermath of the 1908 Ottoman Revolution, the district had opted not to send deputies to the parliament, hoping thereby to retain its special self-governing status.[33] Under the strains of war, relations snapped. The recent international imposition of the Armenian Reform Agreement over eastern Anatolia, moreover, had suffused the Mount Lebanon *réglement*—an arrangement that enabled outside interference—with a new layer of opprobrium from many Ottoman observers, and especially the Unionists. In July 1915, amid horrifying wartime conditions of hunger and starvation, the Unionists terminated Mount Lebanon's autonomous status. The government's policies toward Syria, and Mount Lebanon in particular, proved disastrous. The hunger and disease that claimed the lives of half a million people—or 12.5 percent of Greater Syria's entire population—had its epicenter in Mount Lebanon and Beirut. The Governorate of Mount Lebanon lost between one-third and two-thirds of its population. The city of Beirut, wedged between the governorate and the Mediterranean Sea, lost over half of its population between 1914 and 1916, largely due to famine and hunger-borne disease.[34]

About 11.4 percent of Mount Lebanon's population was Druze, a religious community whose origins dated back to the eleventh century. In early September 1914, Governor Bekir Sami warned the government that the British consul "is working day and night to win over the Druze" to the British side. He surmised that the Druze population, "because they are more or less related to Islam, in their hearts they are leaning towards the Exalted Government" of the sultan. But Bekir Sami counseled caution. The British consul, he noted, was aided by two Druze leaders, Mustafa Imad, head of the local court of appeals, and Nasib Janbulat, a notable. "Strict orders" for the dismissal of Mustafa Imad and his staff should be issued immediately.[35]

At this point, neither Bekir Sami nor Hulusi knew that thousands of miles away officials in the French government were discussing the possibility of an Arab revolt and whether they would back it.[36] On September 5, 1914, François Georges-Picot—of Sykes-Picot fame and former French consul-general at Beirut—was lending his support for a Lebanese fighting force that would join French troops in any offensive on the Ottoman front.[37] At the beginning of the war, Picot had decamped to Cairo, where he was in contact with leaders of Lebanese groups. By September 9, these contacts had pledged their services to Picot, and by December 1914 they had submitted lists of names of volunteers ready to enlist in a Lebanese legion.[38]

In this cauldron of a growing war, a small incident caused the governor of Beirut province, Bekir Sami, to blow his top; it is unlikely that in peacetime the incident would have attracted much attention. I include the episode here because it became emblematic of the Ottoman state's posture toward large swaths of its citizens. On September 11, 1914, a man named Najib Shufati turned a personal dispute into a public spectacle in the village of Suq al-Gharb by taking down "an Ottoman flag flying over one of the shops and trampling it under his feet." A police officer instructed the man to return the flag and left the matter there. When Bekir Sami heard about the incident, he penned an angry report to the capital. The man's action, he wrote, represented much more than a brief instance of local disrespect; rather, it "proved the overt and blatant hatred the people of Mount Lebanon harbor against the government." Unless strict measures were taken now, he warned, more "incidents such as this one" would follow. "I believe the moment has come to take necessary measures against the Mountain [*Cebel'e karşı tedabir-i lazıma ittihazı zamanı geldiğine*]."[39] A seemingly insignificant incident resulted in the call for a fundamental change in Mount Lebanon's place in the empire.

A small dispute had turned into a call for big change: the governor demanded that Mount Lebanon's autonomous status be abolished, ending a decades-old international agreement. He argued that ruling Mount Lebanon directly would let the state tighten its grip on the population and region. The key to terminating home rule in Mount Lebanon without fanning the flames of opposition too much, he suggested, would be to preserve, for now, its male inhabitants' exemption from military service and any special war taxes that were being collected in the surrounding areas.[40] All other previous political and administrative privileges should be abolished, however.

In Mount Lebanon, and all around the empire, the Unionist government exploited wartime conditions to clamp down on opposition groups. The dangerous situation in which the people of Mount Lebanon and Beirut found themselves in this conflict was no secret. The representative of the Maronite Patriarch at Paris, Emmanuel Pharès, called on the French government for quick action. It was only a matter of time, he told French officials, before Ottoman authorities began deporting the Maronite population to Damascus, where, he claimed, it would be massacred. To prevent this from happening, French arms should be shipped immediately from Egypt to Beirut.[41] Talk of deportations and massacres were part of the war from the very beginning. The French government held off on any explicit cooperation, fearing that any open partnership would expose the people of Mount Lebanon and Beirut to the punitive measures of the Ottoman state.[42]

Perhaps Father Emmanuel was privy to knowledge of a key event that took place in the early days of November. At the start of the war, the French consul, General Picot, was forced to leave Beirut. He entrusted Philippe Zalzal, the chief translator at the consulate, with secret information: Picot told Zalzal of the existence of a hidden vault behind one of the walls inside the consulate. It contained a batch of sensitive documents that incriminated some of Beirut's citizens, both Christian and Muslim, in pro-French, anti-government revolutionary activities. When Ottoman authorities arrested Zalzal, he offered the vault in exchange for his freedom. Upon Cemal's arrival in the region as the Fourth Army Commander in November, Governor Hulusi handed Cemal the documents, saying he had waited for Cemal before taking any action. Cemal decided to sit on the documents and keep a close watch. He would bring them out in spring 1915.[43]

In Egypt, the British military governor, General John Maxwell, was not worried about the Ottoman army. Ottoman troops could not do "much harm or force the passage of the [Suez] Canal," he reported to London. Rather than worry about an Ottoman attack, Maxwell recommended his government take steps to win over, as he called it, the "Arab movement." He advised Kitchener, the war secretary, how to go about this: "I hope you favourably considered the suggestion of supporting the idea of the Christians of the Lebanon arming themselves from Greece." Once armed and on Ottoman soil, "the Turks would have practically impossible difficulties in getting at them, whilst they would be always a menace in their rear, if they came on!"[44] Even though the Ottoman Empire was not yet at war, and officially neutral, a war behind the war had already commenced.

"The Caucasus Armenians Are Entirely Against Us"

In the empire's eastern provinces, along the Russian border, within days of the Sarajevo assassination, a group of Ottoman Armenians in eastern Anatolia pledged to the local Russian consul that the Armenian population there would fight for Russia if supplied with equipment and guns.[45] At the same time, Catholikos Kevork V of All Armenians, proposed to the Russian government that it bring "Turkish Armenia" under Russian control and make it autonomous. Intent on keeping the Ottoman front quiet for now, in August the Russian government replied that after the war "the Armenian question will be resolved in accordance with Armenian expectations."[46] Sazonov took note but counseled delay since the Ottoman Empire was not yet in the war and had declared neutrality. Some ten days later, however, Sazonov changed his position. He ordered the preparation of weapons and equipment for the proposed Armenian volunteer force.[47] Ottoman authorities obtained some of this correspondence.[48] By September 6, additional Armenian, Assyrian, and Kurdish groups had approached Russian officials. The viceroy for the Caucasus region, Prince I. I. Vorontsov-Dashkov, now formally requested arms to be distributed to such volunteer formations.[49] On September 18 Sazonov approved the distribution of arms to groups along the Iranian frontier, and, two days later, to groups inside Ottoman borders.[50]

The start of the war triggered both new wartime politics and touched off dangerous rumors, as waves of suspicion and anxiety spread among both civilian populations and government authorities. From Erzurum, on August 16, 1914, intelligence agents reported that "the Caucasus Armenians are entirely against us." According to the report, "Armenian revolutionaries" were sending their families across the border into Russia. It also maintained that "Armenians in the Caucasus generally" were "threatening the Muslims there and saying they were going to exact revenge for the events of 1895," referring to the outburst of ethnic violence in which Ottoman Armenians were massacred in great numbers.[51]

Some high-ranking military officers and civilian officials responded with skepticism to such reports. And they sought to cut off such talks and ease tensions—at least during the first months of the war. The governor of Van province, Tahsin, reported on August 25 that there was no "thought of rebellion" (*fikr-i ihtilal*) among the Armenian population in Van. The government need not worry, he insisted. In fact, "to the contrary," members of the Armenian Dashnak party were "aiding and supporting the government" in its "mobilization" efforts and in the collection of "war taxes." He noted that on the Russian side of the border, Armenians of the Hunchak party were greatly engaged in aiding Russia "as a result of the current war." But inside Ottoman borders, "in Van province the Hnchak committee [*komitesi*] are more or less nonexistent and therefore cannot do anything [*hiç bir şey yapamazlar*]." He conceded that a few young Armenian intellectuals hoped for a German defeat and Russian victory, because they considered Russia to be the staunchest backer of the Armenian Reform Agreement. But beyond that, he concluded, "there is not a single movement or activity coming from the Armenians."[52] In Van province, therefore, the governor tried to send a message loud and clear that Armenian Ottomans posed no risk. It is important to note that the governor's language, intended to calm anxieties about Armenian action, talked about Armenians as a national, unitary collective rather than as Ottoman citizens of the empire and regarded them as having the potential to threaten the state. In other words, Armenians in this correspondence were considered primarily in the context of posing a potential threat to the empire's security.

Then in October 1914, Governor Cemal Azmi informed his government about news he was getting from Erzurum. He had received information that İzzet Paşa, the army commander there, was telling troops that Armenian revolutionaries were inciting the Armenian population of the Ottoman Empire [*Memâlik-i Osmâniye'deki Ermeniler*] to "rise up [*kıyâm*]" and commit atrocities against Muslims. This warning had been shared with conscription offices and was now circulating among the population at large. The governor strongly urged the government to curb such talk immediately, pointing to the grave danger it posed to the empire. He asked that this request be presented to the War Ministry as well.[53]

Thus it was not the degradation of the empire's communal relations that ushered in its demise but rather the Unionists' policies, in the context of global war, toward the Entente and toward groups and, eventually, entire communities inside the empire associated with the Entente.

"The Dear Empire" in Jerusalem

In 1914 Yitzhak Ben-Zvi and David Ben-Gurion, the president and prime minister of Israel after 1948 respectively, were in the Ottoman capital studying law at Istanbul University (the Darülfünûn). They had studied Ottoman Turkish and embarked on their legal studies in the hope of one day serving in the Assembly of Deputies as elected representatives from Jerusalem. With war on the horizon, they made their way back to Palestine, where they volunteered for military service in the Ottoman army. They also proposed the formation of a Jewish legion to fight under the Ottoman banner, but their initiative fell on deaf ears. Instead, upon their arrival in Palestine in December 1914, the two, both carrying Russian papers, were arrested for not holding Ottoman citizenship. Ben-Zvi had immigrated to Jaffa in 1904, Ben-Gurion to Jerusalem in 1906. After some time in prison in early 1915, the two were deported to Egypt, from where they left for the United States. They spent the next two years recruiting and organizing a force that eventually fought in the First World War as part of the British army to "liberate" Palestine from Ottoman rule.[54] We have no way of knowing how things might have turned out had Ben-Zvi and Ben-Gurion been allowed to suit up in Ottoman uniform.

Ben-Zvi and Ben-Gurion were not the only Jews in Palestine rallying to the Ottoman colors in August 1914. *Ha-Herut*, the Hebrew language daily of Jerusalem, printed the patriotic words of a Jewish conscript, Yitzhak Shirizli, who urged his readers to take up arms and defend "the dear Empire" in any way possible.[55] This kind of public embrace of the Ottoman state echoed previous pledges of patriotism by the empire's Jewish communities, notably during the Italian war of 1911 and the Balkan War of 1912. Moshe Sharett, another future prime minister of Israel and said to have been fluent in both Arabic and Turkish, served in the Ottoman army during the Balkan Wars and all through the First World War, even beyond the announcement of the Balfour Declaration and the British occupation of Jerusalem in December 1917.[56] For many, being a Jewish patriot of Palestine in no way precluded loyalty to the Ottoman Empire.[57]

Most accounts describing the experience of Jewish soldiers in the Ottoman army, not unlike those of their non-Jewish peers, speak primarily

FIGURE 4. David Ben-Gurion and Yitzhak Ben-Zvi as law students in Istanbul, October 1, 1912. They planned to run for office and represent Palestine in the Ottoman Assembly of Deputies, the Meclis-i Mebusan. *Source*: D683–118, The National Photo Collection, Jerusalem.

of anguish in the face of battle, personal hardship, and homesickness rather than of political purpose or objectives.[58] Authors like Yehuda Burla and Ya'akov Hurgin left behind largely forgotten portrayals of their lives and camaraderie in the ranks alongside Christians and Muslims. In 1915 Burla participated in the First Suez Canal campaign as a translator and penned short stories describing what he saw and how he felt. His fictional Jewish soldier, Shimon/Simon, shared the heart-stopping fear of battle with his fellow Arab, Armenian, and Kurdish soldiers.[59] After the war, such accounts no longer fit the postwar world and were quickly discarded, both by Jews in the new British mandate and by Turks in the new Turkish Republic.

The war opened new opportunities and paths; weeks into the war, in September 1914, Pinhas Rutenberg, a Russian businessman, traveled from Italy to Manchester to meet with the chemist Chaim Weizmann, considered by many as the key force behind the Balfour Declaration of November 1917.[60] Weizmann would become the first president of the state of

Israel in 1949. Rutenberg and Weizmann met to discuss the possibility of creating a Jewish fighting force to join the Entente in Palestine.[61] Their paths would cross with that of Ze'ev Jabotinsky, who was pursuing similar goals in Paris in talks with French officials. Like Ben-Gurion and Ben-Zvi, Jabotinsky had been in Istanbul before the war, but unlike them, he believed the empire needed to be broken up if Jews were to achieve a homeland in Palestine; to Jabotinsky, rights through Ottoman citizenship would not be enough. This had been a minority view in 1914, but the global crisis of a world war had brought such a scenario into reach. In March 1915 Jabotinsky and Yosef Trumpeldor, a seasoned military officer who had served in the Russian army, made contact with General Sir John Maxwell, the British military commander in Cairo. These efforts resulted in the creation of the Zion Mule Corps, established in April and consisting of some 375 Russian Jews, most of whom Cemal had deported from Palestine. The Zion Mule Corps was attached to the British Mediterranean Expeditionary Force and taken to Mudros, on the island of Lemnos, which had become a staging ground for the Entente's Dardanelles campaign, just a few weeks old at that time.[62]

Syria, which included Jerusalem, Palestine, and Lebanon, had been under Egyptian rule from 1831 to 1840. The Ottoman state had been slow to come back and reassert control after that interregnum. From the late 1860s on, centralizing measures began to transform the urban landscape and by the turn of the twentieth century, Jerusalem, alongside Aleppo, Beirut, and Damascus, had emerged as one of the empire's principal economic and political urban hubs.[63] In 1914, after several waves of Jewish immigration, the Jewish population of Palestine stood at around 10 percent. Most Jewish organizations and newspapers urged recent immigrants from Europe and Russia to take up Ottoman citizenship, serve in the Ottoman military, work and do business with their Muslim and Christian neighbors, and thereby build a Jewish community within the House of Osman, the Ottoman dynasty.[64]

The Ottoman state had endeavored to restrict Zionist immigration to Palestine before 1914 by repeatedly issuing regulations aimed at preventing foreign nationals from acquiring land and settling in Palestine. But Jews hoping for an escape from rising tides of antisemitism in Europe found ways to circumvent legal barriers, often with the backing of European consuls, who, under the Capitulations, could invoke special provisions for entry to those who declared themselves visitors to holy sites, for example. Bribes also did the trick. Large real estate and agricultural companies, the most extensive of which were run by the Sursock family and its subsidiaries, sold huge swaths of agricultural lands to European companies for settlement. Such sales pushed Palestinian peasants off their land, as Zionist purchasers replaced Arab workers with a Jewish labor force. Arab papers from Aleppo to Cairo were filled with stories of Palestinian peasant plight caused by concerted Zionist land purchases.[65]

Unable to address these problems effectively, the Unionist government's legitimacy waned in the eyes of its citizens in Syria and Palestine. The Unionists' inability to resolve legal disputes and crimes, including, for example, the alleged murder of a Muslim man by Jewish settlers for trespassing on land in 1914, undermined the promises of the 1908 Revolution.[66] Such incidents exposed the incongruity between the Unionists' centralist vision, on the one hand, and the state's actual capacity in many locales around the empire, on the other. Insisting on governing the various regions of the empire directly from Istanbul, the Unionists refused to grant greater authority to local administrations, as proposed and articulated, most clearly, in Sabahaddin Bey's decentralization program.[67]

In 1914, even Zionist leaders who later would be considered canonical envisioned a multiethnic, multireligious future for Ottoman Palestine. Leon Pinsker, one of Zionism's founders, imagined a Jewish "autoemancipation" in a Palestine ruled by the Ottoman state "as one of its *pashaliks* [principalities]."[68] Another leading Zionist figure, Ahad Ha'am, differentiated citizenship from nationality and posited that Jews should live their lives as both "sons of the *Jewish people* and the *Ottoman state*."[69] Writing four years after the Balfour Declaration—and three years after the Armistice—he wrote about the Jewish people's ancient links to the lands of Palestine but added that

> this historic right does not cancel out the right of the rest of the land's residents, who press their claims by virtue of the concrete right that comes from working and residing in the land for generations. This land

> is presently their national home as well, and they also have a right to develop their national resources to the best of their abilities. This situation makes Palestine a joint home of different nations, each of which is trying to build its own national home.[70]

A "national home," to Ahad Ha'am, was not the same as the surgical, territorial separation of ethnoreligious groups.

Even Theodor Herzl, six years after his programmatic, blueprint-like *The Jewish State* (*Der Judenstaat*) and two years before his death in 1904, published a novel, *Altneuland* (*Oldnewland*), that imagined future Palestine as part of the Ottoman Empire. As its protagonist, the novel featured Reshid Bey, the modern, elected, and Muslim parliamentarian representing Palestine in the Assembly of Deputies.[71]

Ze'ev Jabotinsky, who in the 1920s and 1930s embraced fascist and racist views, imagined a different kind of Jewish life in Palestine prior to the violent upheaval of the First World War. He distinguished between nation and state and advocated for a federation of nations within multinational states. Writing in 1906, he argued that "simple logic teaches us that no people would think of quitting a strong union as long as this union, which protects that people from various kinds of external aggression, does not forcefully stymy that people's free internal development. Only oppression by that union can force such a people to prefer breaking off, because insecurity is certainly preferable to slavery. But the liberty of nations within a state is the best guarantee of the strength of the state's unity."[72] These prewar views of even the most prominent and staunchest advocates of Zionism were transformed—in some cases, beyond recognition—by the Unionists' wartime policies and the events of the war.

Following the Balkan Wars and the loss of Salonika, divisions deepened between Zionists and the Muslim and Christian Arab population in Palestine. Arab intellectuals, and at times the Ottoman state—were highly critical of the antisemitism they observed in Europe. They closely followed the Dreyfus Affair and were shocked by the racist anti-Jewish chants ringing through the streets of Paris.[73] But they also increasingly decried the tensions resulting from the arrival of tens of thousands of Jewish immigrants in Palestine. Ottoman Jews, too, grew critical of Zionism. The editor of the Jewish Ladino newspaper *El Tiempo*, David Fresco, was perhaps the most prominent such voice. Already in 1909 he had written that

> I think the central leadership of Zionism is committing a huge crime in its desire to drag the Ottoman Jews after their crazy movement.... The Zionist shelter must be in Turkey [*sic*] itself, and because of that Ottoman Jews cannot participate in this movement without being traitors in the eyes of their friends who belong to the other peoples. The heads of Zionism should think a little about the existence of half a million Jews who live quiet and peaceful lives without any pressures, faithful to their homeland.[74]

Fresco was, of course, excoriated by Zionists for expressing such views. Some Zionist groups were building institutions and forging an economy that primarily served Palestine's Jewish population and operated increasingly in Hebrew. Without the First World War and the occupation that followed, however, it is difficult to see how even the most devoted Zionist movement could have gotten far in the establishment of an independent state. In 1914, even Ben-Gurion and Ben-Zvi, as we have seen, were imagining their future as Jewish Ottomans. But the outbreak of war and Ottoman participation in it fully transformed this outlook. In August 1914, the Unionists closed the borders to Jewish immigration and deported Jews who did not hold Ottoman citizenship from Palestine.[75]

Without foreign control over Palestine, Zionists had few alternatives to continuing their coexistence with their much more numerous Christian and Muslim Arab neighbors. This circumstance, perhaps, explains why the Ottoman parliament remained largely unmoved by the alarm bells Arab deputies were ringing in 1911—Jews comprised a small percentage of Palestine's total population, such that Arab fears of displacement before 1914 appeared exaggerated to many deputies in the Assembly.

Sharif Husayn and the Arabian Peninsula

Husayn ibn Ali was appointed Grand Sharif of Mecca in November 1908. This made him the custodian of the holy cities of Mecca and Medina. While his office was defined by spiritual leadership, his day-to-day rule was shaped by political and economic imperatives. In 1908 a principal goal was the military defeat of rival figures in the neighboring territories of Asir and Najd. As the Unionists' regional agent, Sharif Husayn was charged with controlling these local strongmen. Husayn, in turn, sought to leverage the central government's backing and resources into predominance in the western and northwestern parts of the Arabian Peninsula. This balance no longer held under the conditions of the war, however, and it broke down openly in June 1916 in what became known as the "Arab Revolt."

At the time of Husayn's 1908 appointment, local leaders in the Hijaz had risen in armed resistance against the central government. The opening that year of the Hijaz Railway connecting Damascus to Medina undermined the political and economic position of local leaders who made a living by providing transportation and the security of goods and travelers, especially during the annual pilgrimage season to Mecca.[76] Wedged between the Hijaz and Yemen, the ambitious leader of Asir, Muhammad ibn Ali al-Idrisi, called for jihad against the Ottoman government and proclaimed himself "messiah" (*mahdi*). The sharif dispatched his local forces to fight alongside Ottoman regulars to put down the defiant leader. Husayn blamed the unrest on the lack of government resources, officials, and manpower at his disposal. He grew furious when the government in Istanbul not only dismissed his request for additional support but struck a conciliatory tone with Idrisi, whom Husayn considered an outlaw. In 1912, during the Ottoman-Italian war, Idrisi secured Italian support against the Ottoman central government. While Husayn insisted on greater military resources to confront both Idrisi and a second rival, Abd al-Aziz Ibn Saud, Istanbul issued an amnesty to Idrisi, preferring to let the three leaders exist alongside each other rather than allowing the sharif to eliminate his rivals.[77] For the Unionists, it was expedient to maintain a balance among several centers of political power rather than let Husayn consolidate his rule over a massive territory. In 1910 the Unionist government detached Medina and its environs from Hijaz province, linking it administratively to the central government in Istanbul. This move reduced the sharif's jurisdiction and pointed to the central government's desire to play a new and expanded role in the peninsula.[78] Nor were the Unionists eager to fan the flames of internal military conflict that tore at the Ottoman fabric and could pull in the Great Powers. This policy rendered Husayn one among several regional notables and power brokers: Ibn Saud and Ibn Rashid in Najd to the east, al-Idrisi of Asir to the south, and, even further south, Imam Yahya of Yemen. The Unionist government was relying on "Sharif Husayn, the most influential notable of the Hijaz, if not of the whole Peninsula, as a proxy."[79]

As a result, tensions between the Unionist governor of Hijaz province, Vehib, and Sharif Husayn, were high even prior to the outbreak of war. In early May 1914 Vehib received intelligence reports warning that Sharif Husayn would send Bedouin tribes to attack Medina and its environs as well as railways.[80] Already on June 21, 1914, before the assassination of Franz Ferdinand, Governor Vehib reported to the Interior Ministry that Sharif Husayn's son, Abdullah, an elected member of the Assembly of Deputies in Istanbul, was "busy with intrigue and sedition [*ika'-yı fesadla meşguldur*]."[81] Just as war broke out in Europe, in July and August 1914, Vehib called for Husayn's immediate dismissal, "for the sake of Ottomanism."[82] He claimed that if the war continued and spread, the sharif would undoubtedly join a foreign power. Once the war in Europe had started, Vehib wrote that he had learned "from multiple sources" that Husayn "especially right now" has been in "frequent and serious communication with the English government in Egypt." He added, "His sons who are also deputies will be returning here from Egypt. The roughly ten-day period they have spent there [in Cairo] confirms suspicions."[83] In the Hijaz, as in eastern Anatolia, Mount Lebanon, and Palestine, another imperial fissure threatened to burst under the weight of global and total war.[84]

The 1908 Ottoman Revolution promised to usher in a new era of justice. But unseating the old, three-decades-long authoritarian regime of Sultan Abdülhamid II was not a task that could be accomplished overnight. Righting the wrongs of his reign would take even longer. On the floor of the new parliament, deputies advocated the interests of their constituents and aired their grievances. Faced with wars in Tripolitania and the Balkans and growing political opposition at home, the Unionists struggled to maintain control. As internal and external conflict fused, they used the world war to silence political opposition and consolidate their power.

3

An Empire's Bloody War

SARIKAMIŞ, SUEZ, GALLIPOLI

SPURNED BY the Entente, the Unionists secured an alliance with Germany and began cementing their control at home. At this point, they could have adopted a wait-and-see, mostly defensive posture. The military failures of the armies of Germany and Austria-Hungary rendered such a course impossible, however. In the opening months of the war, the German attempt to sweep swiftly through Belgium and into France bogged down in a sea of blood, while Austro-Hungarian forces failed to steamroll over the Serbian army as promised. Facing unexpected setbacks, Erich von Falkenhayn and Franz Conrad von Hötzendorf—the German and Habsburg chiefs of the general staff, respectively—looked to Ottoman forces for crucial relief. Planners in Berlin and Vienna called for Ottoman action in the Russian Caucasus to ease pressure on their armies along the Eastern Front. They believed the Ottoman army could threaten British positions in Egypt and India by concluding an alliance with Afghanistan and threaten British and Russian interests in Iran. Strategists in Berlin wagered that if the Ottoman sultan-caliph made a public proclamation of jihad—the Islamic principle of personal struggle and defensive war—against the Entente, millions of Muslim subjects in the colonial empires of the Entente would rise in a global Muslim revolution and bring disruption to Berlin and Vienna's enemies. In November 1914, War Minister Enver Pasha and those around him saw an opportunity to save not only the Ottoman Empire and the Unionist government but also their German and Austro-Hungarian allies. They also saw a way to anoint themselves as the liberators of the world's Muslims under Entente colonial rule.

The Unionists embraced the idea of two brazen military campaigns. The first aimed to strike the Russian army in the Caucasus; the second targeted the Suez Canal by invading Egypt. Both campaigns would be launched into territories that until recently had been under Ottoman rule. Russia had annexed three Ottoman provinces in eastern Anatolia, Ardahan, Batum, and Kars, in the war of 1877–1878: this area would be the destination of the Ottoman Third Army. Britain had occupied Cyprus in 1878, and some four years later, in 1882, Egypt. Militarily, the two Ottoman campaigns faced tremendous challenges. Politically, they abounded with promise. They aimed at lands with Muslim populations—in the case of the Caucasus, the grandchildren of former Ottoman citizens, and in the case of Egypt, Ottoman citizens until December 1914—whose sense of belonging the Unionists hoped to rekindle and mobilize. With the empire's "Christian" lands lost in the Balkans, this was an opportunity to recover "Muslim" territories.

To prepare these campaigns ideologically and win over Muslims in the Caucasus and Egypt, the state invoked jihad in November 1914. Like the other belligerents in the First World War, the Ottoman state instrumentalized religion to rally its citizens behind the flag and motivate its army; it also sought to inspire Muslim populations in the Entente empires. This was not Istanbul's pan-Islamist dream but part of a strategy for defeating the Entente and winning the war. But getting Muslim populations to rise required more than pledges; it required guns, money, and political promises—not to mention channels of communication and distribution, all of which were in short supply. More crucially, populations mobilized around their own self-interests rather than directions from foreign powers. When Muslims in Central Asia revolted in 1916 against Russian rule, they did so not because they were heeding the Ottoman caliph's call to jihad or supporting the Ottoman war effort, but because they were protesting conscription into the Russian army and wartime deprivation.

Both campaigns failed. Cemal Pasha, as commander of the Fourth Army, led troops to the Suez Canal, intending to rattle if not dislodge the

British from Egypt. Ending in fiasco, the Suez campaign compounded the disastrous defeat in the Caucasus. In the aftermath, Istanbul turned on its Armenian and Arab populations. Just as the Ottomans perceived some populations beyond their borders as potential allies, they saw certain populations within their borders—Christians, especially, but also Muslim Arabs and Kurds—as potential enemies. This was not an entirely new calculus, but in wartime it turned deadly.

The two campaigns aimed to suck in Entente troops, matériel, and money and offer relief to Ottoman allies in European theaters of war. Enver was determined to render the Unionist contribution to the war effort highly visible so as to secure the empire's seat at the table when it came time to negotiate peace and rewrite the postwar order. If the German side won, Istanbul would demand some of the spoils; if the war ended in stalemate, then the empire's interests would be represented in whatever settlement was reached. But these calculations proved to be catastrophically erroneous. Even though by war's end the Ottomans reclaimed the provinces of Ardahan and Kars, that success was made possible only by the Russian Revolution of 1917 that removed the tsar's empire from the war. Two years prior, the Ottomans had lost tens of thousands of soldiers to cold and disease over a few short days near the town of Sarıkamış. That defeat was blamed on the region's Armenian population and Ottoman Armenian fighters who had joined the Russian army as volunteers. Once the battle was lost, Istanbul punished its Armenian population, culminating in the notorious deportation order of May 27, 1915.

Both Enver and Cemal failed in their first major military campaigns of the war. Both felt greatly embarrassed, if not humiliated, and accused each other of incompetence. The call for jihad also did little to rally the people behind the leaders: not only did Muslim populations in the Russian Caucasus and British-controlled Egypt not respond as hoped, but the people within their own borders did not support the effort as Enver and Cemal had envisioned. Little could be done about the absence of revolution across the border, but local populations inside Ottoman borders could be punished for their lack of support. The bitter defeats at Sarıkamış and Suez, with a third possible defeat brewing at Gallipoli, heightened the perceived threat to the empire and explain, in part, the violent and bloody fashion in which the Unionists meted out collective punishment to populations whose loyalty they questioned.

Jihad as Anti-Colonial Struggle

Throughout the nineteenth and twentieth centuries, the principle of jihad served as a vehicle for anti-colonial struggles, both armed and unarmed, from Indonesia to West Africa.[1] In Arabic, *jihād* means "striving." The concept appears in the Quran without a definitive explanation and over the centuries was interpreted by scholars as the internal, entirely peaceful struggle carried on by the individual believer "striving" to honor divine expectations. It also has been understood as legitimate, defensive warfare waged against other Muslims and non-Muslims.[2] The internal, personal, daily form was more often referred to as "greater jihad," with the external, armed form considered "lesser jihad."[3]

In the case of the Unionists' declaration of jihad in November 1914, it is conventionally claimed that the jihad proclamation was the product of a German scheme to get Muslim subjects of the British, French, and Russian empires to revolt. But German interests in the venture in 1914 have obscured the Ottomans' own motivation for instrumentalizing Islam in general and jihad in particular in the context of the First World War.[4]

The Unionists' proclamation of jihad on November 14, 1914, was intended to rally soldiers at the front and civilians at home. It was also intended to prepare the ground for military offensives into the Caucasus and across the Suez Canal, and, at a later point, against Russian forces in northern Iran. Enver, in particular, tried to exploit the symbolism of the caliphate to project Ottoman power into these theaters. The jihad declaration cast Ottoman armies—and Enver himself—as the defender of oppressed Muslims worldwide.

Ottoman military officers and leaders of 1914 had cut their teeth in brutal conflicts in the years leading up to the First World War—in the guerrilla warfare in Macedonia, in the war against Italy's invasion of Tripolitania in 1911, and in the Balkan inferno following hard on its heels. These "Christian" aggressions were the crucible that imbued the Ottoman military and political leadership with a deep sense of violation and victimhood.[5]

Casting war as a sacred endeavor was hardly unique to the Ottomans (or to the First World War).[6] When Italy occupied Libya/Tripolitania, the pope issued a statement declaring that he hoped the Cross would soon replace the Crescent there.[7] The Balkan states, too, employed religious rhetoric in 1912, when they fought Ottoman forces, and it also played an important role on the Western and Eastern fronts during the First World War.[8] The Ottoman state mainly refrained from the use of jihad during the conflicts in Tripolitania and the Balkans, at least officially. During the war in Tripolitania, however, an impromptu play—*The Holy War, or The Ottoman-Italian War in Tripolitania*, was performed in Izmir, and Iranian religious leaders, in an expression of Iranian-Ottoman—and Sunni-Shi'a—solidarity, issued fatwas calling believers to join the defense against the Italian attack.[9] These acts point to the widely held perception at the time that throughout the nineteenth century and into the twentieth the Muslim world itself was under siege.

The forces sent to invade Egypt, moreover, were depicted on postage stamps as "The Islamic Army of Egypt, Savior of Conquered Lands," and those sent into Russian Baku in 1918 marched under the banner of "The Caucasus Army of Islam."[10] When the common soldier (called "Little Mehmet" [*Mehmedcik*], the Ottoman equivalent of G.I. Joe) reported for duty in 1914, he had to pass a basic knowledge exam of some sixty-two questions, starting with "Who created you and all the world?" The correct, prescribed answer was, "God, the Most Exalted, created me and all the world."[11] The next question was "who is your prophet"? Correct answer: "the Prophet Muhammad, the last of the prophets." At this point in the exam manual, there was a note to the officer conducting the lesson: if Little Mehmet was Christian or Jewish, then the correct answer, respectively, was: "My prophet is Jesus, I am Christian," or, "My prophet is Moses, I am Jewish."[12] The exam was oral since nearly all the recruits were illiterate. These questions suggest multiple uses of religion. They show that Unionist military leaders drew heavily on religious ideals and identity to motivate soldiers, a constant across all the armies fighting in the First World War. The questions also reveal a sensitivity to the various religious identities comprising the rank and file, accommodating, at least on paper, men from all backgrounds. The exam asked for the affirmation of loyalty to Sultan Mehmed Reşad V, alongside the more worldly but potentially lifesaving demands of personal hygiene and keeping weapons dry and functional. The questions also suggest that from day one, soldiers were identified by their religious affiliation.[13]

The instrumentalizing of religion was not confined to the frontlines but involved the civilian population at large—youths, women, the elderly, Arabs, and Kurds. With the announcement of mobilization on August 3, 1914, the War Ministry called on villagers above the age of conscription, that is, above the age of forty-five, to designate "senior councils" (*heyet-i ihtiyariye*) to enforce conscription: the senior councils' duties were framed primarily in religious terms. If a village had draft dodgers or deserters, the senior council could be held responsible. The directive read:

> Those of us between the ages of 20 and 45 must be prepared at all times to defend our beloved homeland and sacred religion by joining the ranks of our army whenever it calls us. Whenever there is a call for conscription it is our religious duty and honor to answer that call and rush to the army office immediately. When the army calls it is God's command. In times of war, if the state needs us, then those of us over the age of 45 are also called up. Every able-bodied Muslim is obligated by his religion to fight in the jihad.[14]

Already on August 6, 1914—four days prior to the controversial arrival in Istanbul of the German warships *Goeben* and *Breslau*, and three months before the jihad declaration—Enver wrote to Cavid Pasha in Baghdad, "War with England is now within the realm of possibilities." If that moment came, he told Cavid to contact local leaders, including Ibn Saud, the Sheikh of Kuwait, and other tribal leaders for coordinated action. "Since such a war would be a holy war [*böyle bir harb mukaddes olacağına*] . . . it will definitely be pertinent to rally the Muslim population . . . in Iran." The plan would be to cross into Iran and to get "the Muslim population" there to revolt against British and Russian forces and to "end Christian rule over Muslim peoples."[15]

On August 10, 1914, playing on their shared Muslim brotherhood, Enver wrote to Talib Bey, the powerful notable of Basra. Talib had been a frequent critic of the Unionists, but he also worked with them to stave off ever-growing British influence in the Arab Gulf region. "Should our enemies wish to soil our land with their filthy feet," Enver told Talib, "I am convinced that Islamic and Ottoman honor and strength will destroy them."[16] In the early stages of the war, the predominantly Shi'i provinces of Iraq—Baghdad, Basra, and Mosul—strongly supported the Ottoman war effort. Shi'i clerics buttressed Istanbul's jihad proclamation with statements of their own.[17]

Ottoman officials knew, of course, that jihad propaganda could alienate the empire's Christians and Jews, both of whom had fought in great numbers for the empire as recently as the Balkan Wars. The state's use of Islam and jihad could be divisive and lead to the breakdown of stable relations between Muslim populations and Christians and Jews. Writing in 1916, Major Mehmed Şükrü Bey, a military recruiter from Zonguldak on the Black Sea, an area with a large Christian population, directly addressed the role of non-Muslims, framing jihad as a struggle to defend the empire that applied to all Ottomans, regardless of religion:

> Our Christian and Jewish friends are also the children of this homeland. Together with us they, too, are obligated to fight against the enemy for the defense of our homeland, that is to say, for their mother, and to spill their blood and to kill and be killed on this journey. And so just as Muslims, Christians, and Jews harvest the fields together and make a living, in wartime they must fire cannons and rifles, throw bombs, and wield swords together.[18]

There is something of a running joke in the historiography on the 1914 jihad about how the atheist Young Turks and the Protestant Kaiser Wilhelm II got their jihad wrong by calling it the Greater Jihad (Ottoman: *cihad-ı ekber*; Arabic: *al-jihād al-akbar*). The fact that the Young Turk government referred to the war against Britain, France, Russia, Serbia, and Montenegro as a "greater jihad" seemed at first sight to betray a stunning ignorance of classic understandings of jihad. But rather than a theological error, it is more likely that Ottoman leaders deliberately erased the line between the individual's personal, spiritual striving and efforts aimed at the well-being and future of the state in a time of total war. This would accord with the Unionists' consistent efforts to erase the line between self and state, between the personal and the official, just as the state and the war erased the line between civilians and soldiers, combatants and noncombatants.

By November 1914, the consideration that a proclamation of jihad was a double-edged sword capable of tearing apart the Ottoman body politic apparently no longer mattered to the Unionist brass. Instead, they employed jihad in an attempt to bind the empire's Muslims closer to the state, and especially Muslim populations in the empire's Arab lands.

The Offensive for Sarıkamış

The first major Ottoman military campaign of the First World War was the offensive into the Caucasus. It focused on capturing the small town of Sarıkamış just across the Russian border. Sarıkamış was located in one of the three Ottoman provinces Russia had captured and annexed in 1877–1878, remembered by Ottomans (and later Turks) as The War of '93, a reference to the year 1293 in the Muslim calendar. That war produced over a hundred thousand Muslim refugees.[19] Dominic Lieven, in his book on Russia in the First World War, has observed that there were many Alsace-Lorraines—borderland regions and populations contested by states adjacent to each other—that contributed to the origins of the First World War: the Caucasus and Egypt might be added to Lieven's list.[20]

When Austria-Hungary and Germany demanded Ottoman action, War Minister Enver understood the enormous risks an offensive campaign would entail. Hoping to share those risks, he offered the command of the Third Army in the Ottoman East to Liman von Sanders, the most senior German officer in the country and the head of the German military mission to the Ottoman Empire. Liman refused—ironically, since Berlin had demanded the campaign—and Enver assumed the command himself. Relations between the two men had never been smooth.[21]

The campaign turned into one of the greatest military disasters in Ottoman history. Erroneous intelligence reports, poor planning, bad weather, and difficult terrain undermined the offensive's chances for success. Tens of thousands of soldiers lost their lives. Most died of cold and disease, in a march through the mountains that later appeared stunningly foolish. From the German perspective, the campaign's purpose was to tie down as many Russian troops in the Caucasus as possible and to prevent their deployment in theaters against the Habsburgs. The offensive also pitted Ottoman forces against Armenian volunteer battalions fighting on the Russian side.

The territory on the Ottoman-Russian border, with large Christian and Muslim populations on both sides, became a "bloodlands," as both empires killed and deported border populations they suspected of disloyalty. In January 1915, perhaps as many as forty-five thousand Muslims were killed inside the Russian border, and some ten thousand deported.[22] As staggering as these figures are, they were dwarfed in 1915 and 1916 by Ottoman deportations and mass executions of first Christians, then Arabs and Kurds.

Little attention has been paid to the faulty military intelligence that encouraged the Ottomans to take the offensive. In early August 1914, Ottoman agents tracking Russian units building up alongside the border estimated their strength at about one hundred thousand men. On August 5, 1914, intelligence agents learned that martial law had been declared in the Russian Caucasus and the press put under tight state control. Rumors of an impending German attack on the Eastern Front circulated. The Ottoman consul in Baku reported that Russian mobilization had sparked "riots and disturbances" of resistance.[23] Planners in Istanbul hoped that Russian Muslims just across the border would rush to join up with any invading Ottoman forces. Istanbul wagered that both Afghanistan and Iran would join the war on the empire's side; in fact, in mid-August 1914 Tahsin, the governor of Van, claimed that both Afghanistan and Iran had decided to join forces with the Ottomans in a combined attack on Russia.[24]

Cemal Azmi, the governor of Trabzon province, located on the shores of the Black Sea, summarized what he considered to be highly promising intelligence his men had gathered: Russian Muslims were refusing service in the gendarmerie despite offers of cash payment and the tsar's personal appeals. Ottoman agents counted Russian troops "in Tiflis, Kars, and Sarıkamış at around five hundred thousand men" in early September, and Cemal Azmi argued that these impressive numbers should be taken with a grain of salt: informants reported that the high Russian troop numbers masked the fact that these soldiers were "all untrained." What's more, "hardly any provisions were available in Tiflis." Governor Cemal Azmi then suggested that even though "the Christian Georgians have given Russia a definite promise of loyalty," this was only "a facade." Cemal Azmi had spoken personally with agents who lent further credence to such a view. He surmised that the people of the Caucasus "in general," not just the Muslim Ajars, were "ready to rebel" against Russian rule. He closed by saying that "the Russian civilian and military authorities live in constant worry that the Ottoman army will attack," as the Russian troops were equipped only "with an assortment of weapons and many of them are unarmed."[25] Azmi's report suggested the time might be right for an Ottoman bid in the Caucasus.[26]

Given the growing animosity between Enver and Liman, perhaps it was no surprise that Liman simply said no when Enver asked him to lead the Third Army across the Russian border. On December 6, 1914, the German ambassador in Istanbul, Wangenheim, wired Berlin:

> According to the information here the number of Muslim rebels [willing to join forces with the Ottomans] in the Caucasus region has increased to 50,000. They are more or less well armed. The electricity plants in Batum are destroyed. Enver believes the moment has come for a full strike against Russia. Marshal Liman von Sanders has refused command over the Caucasus Army. As a result, Enver and General Bronsart von Schellendorf have just departed for the Caucasus aboard the *Goeben*. Enver's absence [from the Ottoman capital] is very regrettable as external complications could arise anytime.[27]

Arriving at Third Army headquarters on December 17, 1914, Enver sent a ciphered telegram "to be decoded personally" to Talat. Like the attack across the Black Sea, the operation was "to remain absolutely secret." Only

Talat was to know about it. Russian monitors had been observing his forces closely, Enver said. However, seeing that the Ottomans had not budged, Enver claimed, the Russians were now moving their troops to other locations. "Taking advantage of this," Enver had decided to make a move. His "Third Army in four or five days will attack the enemy." He added, "I will remain here until the outcome of this operation has become clear."[28] The campaign focused on Sarıkamış, a railway hub of strategic importance. Back in Istanbul, Wangenheim worried that Enver's absence might lead to the Ottomans switching sides even at this point in December 1914.

Ten days later, by December 27, 1914, amid the fighting, direct communication with Enver and Hafız Hakkı, Commander of the Tenth Army Corps, had been cut, but the campaign was said to be going well. The army was now somewhere between the towns of Oltu and Sarıkamış, and Governor Tahsin from Erzurum reported that "strong Russian opposition has been broken and one thousand men, one colonel, and six shells and four machine guns have been captured. We have taken [the town of] Oltu. Some units are now advancing to Sarıkamış."[29] Over the next two days, additional reports confirmed the early success. Cemal Azmi, the Trabzon governor, estimated Russian troops for the entire Caucasus region now to stand around two hundred thousand, with about fifty thousand of those at Sarıkamış. But Ottoman reports claimed that the Russians were destitute: "They receive only half rations." The price of bread had risen from three to seven kopeks. Soldiers "are begging in the streets, no rifles." Even better, "the morale of the [Russian] troops has been broken. At the shelling of Batum, the men dropped their rifles and ran." There was news that the tsar had been visiting troops in Tiflis at the time and had to be hurriedly evacuated.[30]

Then a trickle of bad news started that quickly turned into a flood. An intercepted Russian telegram summarized the situation: "On December 30, [1914], we shelled the town of Verkeni, which the Turks had been defending for three days." Soon thereafter, "our volunteer units attacked the farthest part of the village, and two battalions of our Caucasus Regiment launched a bayonet charge. The Turks suffered great losses. One general fell. 20 officers and 1,300 men have been taken prisoner. Fighting continues in Ardahan."[31] It is unclear whether the "volunteer units" mentioned in this Russian document referred to units comprising Ottoman Armenians; regardless, subsequent sources commented that Armenian units contributed significantly to the Ottoman defeat at Sarıkamış.[32] In the Ottoman capital, Talat feverishly followed the downward spiral of events, but there was little he could do. He wrote to Cemal Azmi in Trabzon, "There are no reinforcements to be sent from here [i.e., from Istanbul via the Black Sea], because Admiral [Wilhelm Souchon] cannot guarantee safe passage. You can request men from Ardahan. Try establishing communication [with Ardahan]." Enver was on his own. Perhaps intended to offer encouragement but certain to cause consternation, Talat closed with the words, "There is no reason for panic and useless lamentation . . . fighting against the impossible befits your ingenuity and resourcefulness."[33] Essentially, Talat was counseling him to keep calm and fight on.

By January 6, 1915, it was clear that the initially promising situation had been reversed. Not only had the offensive on Sarıkamış been pushed back, but Enver's Third Army, a force upward of ninety-five thousand men, had been destroyed. On January 7, Governor Tahsin—governor of Erzurum province since November 1914—relayed the latest developments. Russian forces had "attacked Ardahan with superior force." They had pushed the Stange Detachment, commanded by German officer Lieutenant-Colonel Stange and Bahaeddin Şakir, the Unionists' political officer in the eastern theater, and "our irregulars [*çetelerimiz*]" into retreat. Enver's Third Army had suffered "heavy casualties in losses and wounded." Stange and Bahaeddin Şakir were holding their position in Ardanuç, hoping to replace the lost men with new conscripts.

Bahaeddin Şakir's report noted that irregular forces attached to the army had engaged in "pillaging" and were to blame for the atrocities visited on local civilian populations. Tahsin did not include all the information from Bahaeddin Şakir's "detailed telegram," deeming some of it "too upsetting." Unfortunately, the telegram has not surfaced in the archives. According to Tahsin on January 7, the only thing left to do was to push on: Stange thought the Russian troops were subpar, "third class," and that with reinforcements, the Russians could still be turned back.[34]

In reality, things had gone badly since December 22, 1914. An Ottoman Red Crescent report listed thirty officers taken prisoner that day alone. Russian forces captured the commander of the Ninth Army Corps, Major General (*Mirliva*) İhsan Paşa as well as Colonel (*Miralay*) Arif Bey, Lt. Colonel (*Kaymakam*) Şerif Bey, Major (*Binbaşı*) Baki Bey, Medical Major (*Tabib Binbaşı*) Dr. Tevfik Mehmed Bey, along with ten captains and fourteen first and second lieutenants.[35]

In a narrow sense, the empire had met the tactical objective of tying down considerable numbers of Russian troops in the Caucasus, thereby relieving pressure on the German and Habsburg forces on the Eastern Front. But this effort came at great cost, both in terms of the casualties the Third Army suffered and its political consequences.

The First Offensive for Suez

With the bad news pouring in from the Russian border, the Fourth Army headquartered in Damascus under the command of Ahmed Cemal Pasha prepared to cross the Suez Canal. Cemal's telegram, "to be decoded personally" by Interior Minister Talat, explained his immediate military plan. "On Friday," January 8, 1915, "I will go to Jerusalem" and "give the order to attack the Canal." Like Enver, Cemal felt confident—or at least he sought to convey he was. Based on information he had received, he believed "the chance for success is great." His closing lines intimated a somewhat different sensibility, however, and perhaps revealed the unease he was also feeling: "I will press quite rapidly to the Canal myself," he wrote. "You may therefore not hear from me again for some fifteen days. Please take this telegram to my house. I would be grateful if you could see my mother-in-law and give her assurances not to worry. Whatever happens, please do not leave my children without money and support. I kiss the eyes of all our friends, and the hands of the grand vizier. Pray for us. [. . .] May God protect all of you."[36]

Not unlike reports ahead of the Sarıkamış offensive, the intelligence reports in the weeks leading up to the Suez campaign inspired optimism. Agents who had traveled from neutral Greece and Italy to Egypt painted a promising picture. As soon as the Ottoman army crossed the Canal, the Muslim population of Egypt would rise up against the British, they claimed.[37] News arriving from Rome in early February 1915 reported that "over the past week the hostile feelings" of Egyptians against British rule there had risen "with great speed."[38] Another report claimed that the people of Egypt believed steadfastly in the "victorious entry of the [Ottoman] Imperial Army" into Cairo.[39]

Cemal, too, used religion to mobilize soldiers and the civilian population. He sent for "a holy flag" from Mecca, and the Custodian of the Flag presented the glorious artifact to him with great fanfare on December 20, 1914, in Jerusalem. The sixty-five-year-old had personally made the trip from Mecca to Jerusalem. Cemal required soldiers to swear their loyalty on this holy flag while religious leaders gave speeches. The German commander, Kress von Kressenstein, who played an important role in Cemal's Fourth Army in Syria during the war, saw in the gesture Cemal's attempt to compensate for the "lacking patriotic enthusiasm" among his "Arab soldiers" by playing on Muslim brotherhood.[40]

Much like the countdown to the Sarıkamış campaign, there was reason for optimism in the lead-up to the Suez campaign. Before 1914, the Nationalist Party had looked to Istanbul in their struggle against British colonialism. Muhammad Farid, the Nationalist Party's leader, hoped for revolution at home against British rule and the formation of a regional alliance, backed by Germany, against the three Entente powers.[41]

Cemal was also encouraged by some Arab volunteers. Shakib Arslan, a prominent Druze leader, writer, and vocal anti-imperialist, organized volunteers from Mount Lebanon's Druze population. Assuming the command of the Mount Lebanon Volunteer Detachment, he led it to the town of Ma'an in late January 1915. Ma'an was on the famous Hijaz Railway, which had been completed in 1908 under Sultan Abdülhamid II with donations from Ottoman subjects. The railway became a symbol of Ottoman resistance, and it drew the empire closer together. It was intended to fuse the empire's Turkish- Armenian- Greek- Kurdish-speaking northern half of Anatolia with its (predominantly) Arabic-speaking southern half.[42] The Anatolian line would link up with the Hijaz Railway to run from Istanbul through Konya, Adana, Aleppo, Damascus, and Ma'an all the way south to Medina. Ready to join Cemal's army, Shakib Arslan sent an upbeat telegram, as if he were not about to embark on a trek of over two hundred miles through desert territory. "I have arrived in Ma'an with my volunteers. We will continue towards Suez within two days. We will not return," Shakib Arslan promised, "before, with God's help, we have crossed the Canal."[43]

Cemal's army departed Jerusalem on January 17, 1915. The Spanish consul, Ballobar, watched the ceremonious departure. He recorded in his diary, "All in all, they have accumulated a real army now, for the number of those who have passed through the city is no less than 40,000 or 50,000." His next note, however, dripped with sarcasm: "But the organization is admirable: They don't have anything to eat. The officers eat black bread and a thank you very much."[44]

The actual strike on the Canal came on the night of February 2–3, 1915. The plan was to cross the Canal, take up positions on its western banks, and dig in.[45] Instead English forces sat in wait on the other side: they allowed three pontoons with some sixty men to cross the Canal, then unleashed their machine guns, killing most of the men on the water. The British then crossed the Canal themselves, killing or capturing seven officers and two hundred men, according to Kress. Meanwhile, no uprising among Egyptians materialized. Cemal's offensive, not to mention his hopes to conquer Egypt, had been crushed.[46]

Much like Enver's campaign at Sarıkamış, Cemal relied on intelligence suggesting that things would turn out well at the Canal. The news made its way back to Jerusalem, where the district governor of Jerusalem, Midhat, informed Istanbul, falsely, that although he had "not yet received official information," he had heard informally that "some parts of the army" had "crossed the Canal" and that "fighting continued."[47]

In reality, the Ottoman forces were easily repelled, even if Cemal denied it. From Istanbul, he requested British news coverage of "our first attack on the Canal," implying that this was not the end of the story.[48] He warned his colleagues in the capital not to believe "the lies of the British."[49] The news summaries Cemal received were as disparaging as he had suspected, and he may have regretted drawing attention to them. From Cairo, Reuters had reported clashes at Ismailiye, the Canal's halfway point between the Mediterranean and the Red Sea, on February 4, 1915. The "attempt to cross the Suez Canal," it said, had been "met with laughter." According to the piece, "a small English force" had sufficed to drive the Ottomans into retreat, with many Ottoman soldiers fleeing and deserting. A government statement from London said its forces captured 222 Ottoman soldiers and eight officers. It added that both Arab and Turkish soldiers had run over to the British side to be taken prisoner, and only those Ottomans who surrendered reached the western banks of the Canal. British forces, the government noted, had lost two officers and thirteen soldiers in battle, with fifty-eight taken prisoner.[50]

Cemal could not prevent news of the Suez fiasco from spreading. By February 10, 1915, Ballobar, the Spanish consul, recorded in his diary the first rumors: there was talk of the Ottomans having met "tremendous defeat." A few days later, Ballobar wrote, "A day of big, fat lies." He had learned that Ottoman forces, "the Arabs, the only ones who were sent ahead," had been decimated upon reaching the western bank, "all this without seeing the enemy." He also heard about the British counterattack, how "a rain of fire shot by artillery batteries, warships and fifty airplanes, completely destroyed the Turkish army. Nothing like this is remembered in history."[51]

A fighter who was there, Tergeman of Damascus, later relayed his experience to his daughters. He had served in the Balkan Wars as an engineer in the telegraph communication unit and did the same work in the Suez campaign. His food rations were initially more than adequate: "three loaves of bread per man." In addition, there was "butter, lamb and dried dates."[52] Tergeman arrived at the Canal, where his team dug in and kept quiet: "no smoking or talking allowed." On the third night, they put "metal boats" in the water: Ottoman units were crossing the Canal. Tergeman was told to cable Damascus claiming the crossing was proceeding successfully, which gave rise to the early sense of success. In Damascus, the update was greeted with euphoria. However, "just as our sixth boat was crossing the canal, we were overwhelmed by a burst of gunfire—more than a thousand machine guns, it seemed. The bullets were all over, hitting and exploding in the water and making the water of the canal churn like a kettle of boiling water."[53]

The Ottomans had no choice but to abort the crossing and fall back. They set up a field camp under Kress's command along the Canal's eastern bank. Conditions were poor: the sick and wounded were "lying in miserable, bad tents, on rocky floors, without mattresses." The lack of hygiene "defied description" and doctors could not do much given the "great shortage of medication and suitable food."[54] On March 21, 1915, the Ottomans returned to the Canal, with some eight hundred men, a machine gun company, and two artillery batteries. They took up a position just north of Suez city.[55] There was no way to cross the Canal, however, and Ottoman supply lines remained too stretched to sustain any prolonged presence along the Canal.[56]

Gallipoli and a Possible Truce in March 1915

The 1915 Battle of Gallipoli is one of the most famous battles of the First World War. It took on epic proportions as the Entente assembled British and French dreadnoughts and troops from across the British Empire from Canada to New Zealand. Its story has been retold in a blockbuster movie and in countless documentaries and monographs and popular histories featuring Atatürk and Churchill as protagonists and tragic heroes.

In March 1915 an Allied fleet of some twenty-one warships—sixteen British, four French, one Russian—took up position along the southern mouth of the Dardanelles, just off the Gallipoli Peninsula. They began bombarding from a distance, aiming at the Gallipoli Peninsula's outer fortifications while remaining beyond the range of Ottoman guns. At times the Allied ships fired salvos at intervals of forty seconds. The operation had its origins in a Russian initiative. Confronted with invading Ottoman armies in the Caucasus, and hoping for relief, the Russian government raised, not for the first time, the idea of an Allied naval operation against the Straits.[57] In Istanbul, with fresh defeats at Sarıkamış and Suez and now the Allied fleet pounding the Straits, an acute nervousness set in among Ottoman leaders.

Despite the great number of books that have been written on the Gallipoli campaign, less known is the fact that just prior to the Allied attack, in early March 1915, the British government proffered a truce, of sorts, to the Unionists. The offer came at a time when the Ottomans were reeling from military debacles, dressing their wounds. Could the Unionists have bargained for their territorial integrity at this point, or was this offer simply an ultimatum, a last chance to surrender before the impending onslaught amassing at the Dardanelles? Coming before the mass deportation of Armenians, the Syrian famine, the Sykes-Picot agreement, the Arab Revolt, and the Balfour Declaration, a truce in spring 1915, it seems, might have averted the worst consequences of the war for the people of the region.

Speculation aside, on March 1, 1915, Sabahaddin's telegram, sent from Athens and addressed to Sultan Mehmed V Reşad, reached the desk of Grand Vizier Said Halim.[58] Sabahaddin, the opposition leader now in exile, reasoned that the empire's current political course would inevitably lead to the forcing of the Straits and the occupation of the Ottoman capital. "I beg your Majesty, in the name of the fatherland," Sabahaddin wrote, "to conclude peace with the Entente immediately." Sultan Reşad, formally the commander in chief of all Ottoman armed forces, should open the Straits and receive the Anglo-French fleet "as a friend and liberator." Only in that way could the double curse of the Unionists and the Germans be broken. Sabahaddin claimed that the Ottoman people had supported Britain and France, which stood for "justice, law, and the liberty of nations." He implored the sultan, "Let's make peace and make it fast."[59]

War Minister Enver seems to have done little to entertain the idea. He rejected the proposal categorically: "There is no need for the truce being proposed by the British."[60] Instead, Enver wrote to Berlin, on March 8, 1915, urging for a German-Habsburg breakthrough in Serbia. A military victory there would open the supply line to the empire. Securing supplies for the defense of Gallipoli was now "a matter of life and death," he said.[61]

Enver was not wrong. The first major attack came ten days later, on March 18, 1915. Two German planes had gone on early morning reconnaissance flights and returned immediately to warn the fortification installations to prepare for an assault. The Allied fleet was led by HMS *Inflexible*. The French *Bouvet* encountered a mine and sank with six hundred crew. About two hours later the *Inflexible* and the HMS *Irresist-*

ible struck mines. Of the eighteen ships, four were sunk. The fleet turned back, giving the Ottomans a huge triumph that is still commemorated in Turkey today. The mines had been laid some ten days prior, on a secret mission in the dawn hours of March 7, by the minelayer *Nusret*.[62]

Meanwhile, the Entente powers decided to put boots on the ground. They committed an initial five infantry divisions—four British, one French, some seventy-five thousand men in all—to occupy the Gallipoli Peninsula and, eventually, the Ottoman capital.[63] On March 24, 1915, Enver transferred command of the Fifth Army and defense of the Gallipoli Peninsula to Liman von Sanders. Relations among the German officers and within the German military mission were so tense, even openly hostile at times, that Liman did not appoint any German officers to his general staff; it consisted exclusively of Ottoman officers.[64]

Over the next eight months, tens of thousands of soldiers from Aleppo to Australia perished on both sides of the trenches. As if by a miracle, the Ottoman lines held through eight months of battle. On January 10, 1916, the day after the last Allied men had evacuated the peninsula, Enver appeared triumphantly in parliament to deliver the news of the enemy's final withdrawal. "When the General War began in Europe," he claimed, "the position of the royal dominions [*memâlik-i şahâne*] was such that staying out of the war would not have been possible. We were forced to declare general mobilization." Russia would only be satisfied when in possession of the Straits, Enver went on. Thus "even if we had opted to remain neutral, one day Russia and Russia's friends were going to corner us." He maintained the lie of the Russian attack in the Black Sea, which "dragged us, too, into this General War."[65]

Over the past century, in the collective memory of the war in today's Turkey, the Sarıkamış fiasco has been seen as a mirror image to the triumph of Gallipoli of 1915–1916. Sarıkamış, synonymous with imperial decay and failure, became personified by Enver. Gallipoli, synonymous with national triumph and salvation, became personified by Mustafa Kemal (later Atatürk), who ruled the Republic of Turkey from its founding in October 1923 to his death in 1938. Gallipoli stood for "the Turks' finest hour," Sarıkamış for its darkest.

Despite the triumph at Gallipoli, the Unionists, much like their allies, had launched offensives that failed. And like their German and Habsburg allies who turned on Belgian and Serbian civilians, respectively—including the collective punishment of entire villages and the burning of the Belgian town of Leuven—the Ottomans turned on civilians in the aftermath of failure. The next three chapters turn to the domestic consequences of the Sarıkamış, Suez, and Gallipoli campaigns.

4

Empire of Hunger

AS THE state vacuumed up men, food, and animals, famine became the Ottoman people's "invisible enemy," the deputy from Baghdad declared in the Assembly in January 1916. There was a war behind the war, he proclaimed, and in that war "we need food as much as we need munitions."[1] He demanded aid be provided to the people who had elected him. "Nothing has been sent to Baghdad," he said, "even though many of our residents have been conscripted" into the army. The massive locust plague, which appeared in March 1915, he continued, was wreaking environmental havoc: "Our crops have been destroyed by locusts, but we have not received any help" to mitigate the calamity.[2] Fifteen months into the war, the people of Baghdad, like those in all parts of the empire, were suffering from hunger.

Economic independence comprised one of the Unionists' main war aims. The actual war brought the opposite. Conscription moved men in their prime from villages to barracks, from farms to arms. The state thereby reduced the number of hands in the fields while simultaneously increasing the number of military mouths it had to feed. The lack of labor, and the lack of mechanization in its absence, caused agricultural production to plummet and markets to collapse. Hunger caused widespread social dislocation, fueling bitter condemnation of Unionist rule. The Anglo-French naval blockade, set up in August 1914, moreover, cut off foreign and domestic goods shipped to Mediterranean ports. The blockade's specific aim was to cause hunger and incite rebellion among the Arab population against the Ottoman state, a goal that would be accomplished in

1916.[3] For David Lloyd George, who replaced Kitchener as British war secretary, "potential famine was therefore the most powerful weapon in the army of the belligerents." It was understood that this type of warfare would target "men, women and children."[4] The Entente blockade played a crucial role in transforming the First World War into "total war," in which civilian deaths were not only acceptable but intended.[5]

Agriculture and the Ottoman Economy

The Ottoman economy was predominantly based on agriculture. Government estimates put the number of the empire's village or farm households (*zürra hanesi*) at some three million. Already by 1915, most of these agriculturalists required cash, seeds, and fertilizer, all of which the state proved unable to provide in all but negligible quantities.[6] Wartime hunger claimed over half a million lives in Beirut and Syria province alone—or one out of seven—but hunger became a fixed feature of daily life in all parts of the empire. It was also a defining aspect of the Unionists' deportation marches beginning in March and April 1915. Ottoman Christians—Arab, Armenian, Assyrian, Greek Orthodox—as well as Arab and Kurdish Ottoman Muslims were deported in large numbers, though the methods and underlying objectives varied significantly.

By early 1916, a register of children waiting to be admitted to orphanages listed some eight thousand names. An estimated forty thousand children empire-wide were living without family or permanent shelter. On the floor of the Senate, Ahmed Rıza, the former Unionist leader, cried out, "A government that gathers up orphans and leaves them hungry deserves to fail." He excoriated the government, which "should have thought of hunger earlier, not only now."[7] The Unionists' decision to bring the empire's agrarian society into an industrial war of attrition bore tragic consequences.[8]

Ottoman shortages appeared as soon as Europe went to war in August 1914. As the army mobilized and the war severed trade networks one by one, officials in the capital became inundated with requests for seeds, loans, animals, carts, and soldiers for agricultural labor. With the food supply shrinking and hunger growing, the state sought new ways of boosting production. It instituted agricultural conscription, requiring all those too young or too old, or otherwise deemed unfit for military service, to perform agricultural work. On October 19, 1914, the Interior Ministry decreed that "every individual between the ages of sixteen and twenty, and above the age of forty-five, in every village" must "plough and plant the fields." Any and all "verbal and written orders" issued by local police related to this regulation were to be followed "unconditionally."[9] In effect, the entire country was being conscripted, to take up either the gun or the plough. The ordinance was reaffirmed in September 1916, this time specifying that agricultural conscription applied to both "boys and girls."[10] As it pressed ever more men into military service, the War Ministry established a women's labor battalion that employed thousands.[11] In addition, large landowners could secure exemptions for their workers from military service.[12] Any household in possession of two draft animals was obligated to plough at least forty-five *dönüm* of land and work eight hours a day.[13] These measures would prove vastly inadequate to feed starving populations, however.

War and the mobilization of the Ottoman army in early August 1914 took an immediate toll on families. In Damascus, the young Nicola Ziadeh's father was conscripted when mobilization was first declared; by October, the family learned that he had fallen ill. As the family went from hospital to hospital in hope of finding their father, they were overwhelmed by the stench and unhygienic conditions they encountered. When they eventually found him, he was dead.[14]

The environmental differences across the empire and the specific features of local economies defined the intensity with which food shortages struck various regions. In peacetime, the government collected a percentage of a given year's harvest—mostly wheat and beans—in state depots (*emanet-i aşar anbarları*). In fall 1914 the Commerce and Agriculture Ministry distributed seeds from these reserves to farmers and peasants in need. In some provinces, including in Beirut, no such agricultural collection and therefore no such reserves existed. The absence of such stored reserves meant that Beirut and surrounding areas were especially at risk of hunger. The governor of the province, Bekir Sami, repeatedly and urgently reminded his superiors in Istanbul of Beirut's food precarity.[15]

As early as November 1914, he requested a loan of ten thousand lira to subsidize the purchase of seeds and draft animals. To make matters worse, a recent epidemic of "cattle plague [*veba-yı bakarî*] had wiped out 90 percent of animals in the villages" already prior to the war, the governor wrote emphatically.[16] By December 6, 1914, Governor Bekir Sami had received seven of the ten thousand lira of aid requested. He asked for the remainder to be disbursed immediately.[17] The "health" of the province "depended" on procuring seeds; Istanbul's "quick sending of the money" had become "absolutely necessary [*pek elzemdir*]."[18] Whatever the Unionist Bekir Sami thought about the political views held by the people of Mount Lebanon, he was ringing alarm bells in December 1914 and warning about the impending food shortages in Beirut province.

In Istanbul, the Commerce and Agriculture Ministry agreed with Bekir Sami's assessment: the situation in Beirut was turning grave, and fast. But the ministry had no cash to spare. It relayed the request to the Interior Ministry and insisted that the loan must be paid out "as a matter of utmost importance and great urgency for securing the fall [1915] crop" in Beirut.[19] At this point, the sowing season for wheat in Syria was already closing. Typically, wheat in Syria is sown from October to December and harvested sometime in June and July. Other crops, like chickpeas and lentils, could be planted later, in January and February, but wheat was the main staple crop and provided much of the population's nutrition. Thus, various parts of the central government in Istanbul already in December 1914 were discussing an impending food crisis in Beirut province for the following year. Beirut's Unionist governor, the evidence suggests, worked tirelessly to secure aid for his province.

For those wielding the levers of state power in the capital, hunger was not a far-off, easily ignored occurrence. To the contrary, food lines began forming in the capital as early as July and August 1914, when war in Europe cut wheat and other imports to the city in half.[20] In an "urgent and secret" meeting on December 2, 1914, the cabinet discussed Istanbul's bread shortages. Most bakeries (*fırıns*) had run out of flour (*dakik*); others were in short supply. Reserves in depots and on the market would be depleted within four days.[21] Eventually, the government distributed an ersatz bread,

TABLE 1. Ottoman Wheat Production, 1913–1918 (in million tons)[a]

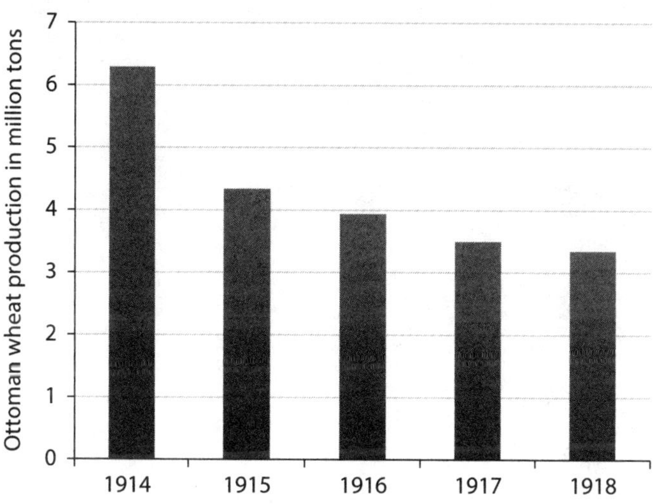

[a] Eldem, *Harp ve Mütareke Yıllarında*, 37.

widely referred to as "dark" bread for its color; it was comprised of barley, oats, and beans. A loaf weighed about 320 grams. Its nutritional value was as poor as its taste.[22] The Interior Ministry proposed importing flour from neighboring Bulgaria, still neutral at the time.[23] Wealthy families could purchase meat in the capital through much of 1915, after which point it became nearly impossible to obtain anywhere in the empire.[24]

The 1914 harvest had been unusually strong. The wheat crop exceeded that of the previous year's by 39 percent. Imports also exceeded prior figures, causing government wheat depots in many locations to be full when the fighting began.[25] It is possible that the strong prewar harvest emboldened Unionist politicians in the face of war in 1914, though no direct evidence demonstrating such a link has come to light.

In March 1915 the Assembly set aside special funds for distributing seeds to farmers and peasants for the upcoming planting season. The Armenian delegate from Muş, in southeastern Anatolia, asked where exactly the relief aid was to be sent. When told the aid was for the entire empire, he replied, "Then this money is completely insufficient." He argued that in "the war zones [*muharebe mahallerinde*] in Van, Bitlis, Diyar-ı Bekir,

FIGURE 5. Orphan boys. Original caption: "Waiting to be admitted to the orphanage." Harput/Kharberd, present-day Elazığ. *Source*: Parmelee Collection, box 6. Hoover Library and Archives, Stanford University

Erzurum, Harput—the people have paid three times the usual amount of the tithe tax [*öşür*]." As a result, the inhabitants in those provinces had "nothing left to eat." The allocated funds "should be sent there; no other area has this kind of need. This aid is not enough for the entire Ottoman Empire," he maintained.[26]

FIGURE 6. Orphan girls. Original caption: "Waiting to be admitted into the orphanage." Harput/Kharberd, present-day Elazığ. *Source*: Parmelee Collection, box 6. Hoover Library and Archives, Stanford University

"A Real Disaster in Syria and Palestine"

In early 1915, as Cemal Pasha's columns of some twenty thousand men, accompanied by over twenty-five thousand camels, marched south from Palestine on the Suez Canal, a vast sea of locusts swarmed north. Blanketing the skies along the Syrian coast from Jerusalem to Aleppo, immense locust populations devoured every green shoot in sight, adding environmental destruction to wartime suffering. Until March 1915, while living conditions had steadily worsened, death caused by hunger had remained rare. Beginning in March, those who had little to eat before—the poor—now had nothing. By the end of the war, hunger had claimed the lives of hundreds of thousands.[27] As the government's attempts to mitigate the crisis proved inadequate, shortages and hunger turned into widespread starvation and mass death, especially in Mount Lebanon and Beirut. The onset of the locust plague coincided with the loss of many lives to diseases that malnourishment caused.

In Syria, the 1915 harvest at first appeared promising but was largely destroyed by "terrifying swarms of locusts that, like a deluge, flooded all of Syria from Gaza to the Taurus Mountains."[28] In addition, military authorities were losing control over some of the rich producing areas of the Hawran and the Druze regions. On January 30, 1915, Saadeddin Efendi, the delegate from Hawran, brought to the floor of the Assembly a request for relief from village taxes (*kura vergileri*) for the people of Hawran because of the prevailing conditions of "famine (*kaht*)," a plea the Assembly approved immediately.[29]

On March 21, 1915, Governor Bekir Sami reported the sighting of "large locusts [*iri çekirgeler*] in great numbers from Tulkarm" in Palestine.[30] While locusts destroyed much of the summer harvest that year, disaster might have been averted: allocating transportation for supplying food from producing areas of the interior to coastal towns and villages could have limited if not prevented mass hunger. British Cyprus also endured the locusts during the war, but here food aid brought into the island saved its inhabitants from the worst effects of hunger.[31]

Eye-witness accounts of the locusts are terrifying. Observing the locusts wreak their havoc, the Spanish consul in Jerusalem jotted in his diary:

> Yesterday I marveled and was convinced of how small we are despite our pretensions. I made this reflection while contemplating the passing of a cloud of locusts. I was in my office when I was surprised by the strange color of the sky, with a light similar to that of a solar eclipse. Upon peeking out from the balcony I saw that an immense cloud had completely obscured the light of the sun. The ground, the balconies,

> the roofs, the entire city and then the countryside, everything was covered by these wretched little animals. At least it lasted less than an hour, but the unfortunate fields of Jericho, from whence the plague proceeded, must have been left without a blade of grass. As a consequence of all of this, the price of wheat has risen enormously. Just what we needed.[32]

By April 1915 desertion rates among conscripts began rising at a steady rate. "They don't give them food," Ballobar noted.[33] As the locust plague claimed more and more agricultural land, the food crisis deepened. "The olive trees, the vineyards, the sown fields and orchards, they have eaten everything," Ballobar exclaimed. "I ask myself what we will be able to eat this summer."[34] He thought that "only by seeing it can one believe the ravages these little creatures have done."[35] As hunger spread, Ottoman teachers and doctors, like their counterparts in Europe, measured and recorded the stunted growth rates in children, in most cases causing permanent, long-term consequences.[36]

In June 1915 Cemal Pasha reported from Damascus that the invasion of locusts had already caused "a real disaster in Syria and Palestine." He had tried, he claimed, to prevent it: "All the strong measures" that had been taken against the locusts had achieved only "partial success." If the Agricultural Bank (Ziraat Bankası) did not provide quick relief, he warned, conditions "will become catastrophic for the people of Syria and Palestine." In making his request for aid, Cemal acknowledged that the "disaster" was not the doing of the locusts alone. His military rule, which had sucked up large numbers of men and vast quantities of food, had contributed to the dire conditions. His "Egyptian campaign" against the Suez Canal, launched in January 1915, had, as Cemal himself noted, meant the levying of heavy "extraordinary taxes on the people of Syria and Palestine" throughout the fall and winter of 1914.[37]

Beirut province and the self-governing district of Mount Lebanon were particularly vulnerable to the breakdown of markets and trade networks. In the middle of the nineteenth century, Mount Lebanon's economy had relied primarily on silkworm cultivation. Following the opening of steady steamship traffic servicing Beirut, demand and export of silkworms only

FIGURE 7. Original caption: "Locust plagues in Palestine. Methods of fighting the locust plague. A flame-thrower." March–June 1915. *Source*: Matson Photograph Collection, Digital ID: matpc 02948, Library of Congress Prints and Photographs Division, Washington, DC.

intensified, causing Mount Lebanon's population to nearly double over the span of just a few decades. In the 1870s, however, silk prices collapsed, and much of the population found itself weighing emigration. Shifting back to agricultural production often did not appear promising, as the onset of the 1873 Great Depression, which lasted into the 1890s, meant that food prices dropped sharply and Ottoman markets could hardly compete with cheaper imports such as American wheat and other products. Despite the government's attempts to protect domestic markets by raising import duties, that endeavor proved unsuccessful.[38]

Going back to the nineteenth century, the central state had sought to bring land use and agricultural production under its direct authority.[39] Local elites across the empire proved highly successful at maintaining control over land and production, however. This process continued through the Hamidian period and into the aftermath of the 1908 Ottoman Revolution.[40] From the 1880s onward, much of the most fertile lands in Syria and Palestine was registered to powerful agricultural businesses based in Beirut.[41] When Cemal Pasha arrived in Syria in November 1914, he sought to coopt local business elites rather than to coerce them.[42] While he established friendly relations with many of them—relations that at times were cultivated over lavish banquets held in his honor—no adequate mechanism for distributing food to hungry and starving populations in Beirut and Mount Lebanon materialized. The authorities were not necessarily or primarily concerned with feeding hungry civilians.[43]

By 1914 Mount Lebanon's single largest source of income, some 40 percent, came from remittances sent from the United States.[44] Trade comprised the second key pillar of the economy of Beirut and its surroundings. Both sources of income were cut off abruptly in August 1914.[45] As food became scarce, military requisitioning in Mount Lebanon dropped noticeably after November 1914. At the same time, migrants from Lebanon in the United States grew convinced that Ottoman authorities were starving the people of Mount Lebanon and Beirut intentionally.[46] Given the tension that arose from Mount Lebanon's self-governance under French protection and the Unionists' centralism, it is not surprising that such assumptions arose readily, or that they were easily stoked by Entente propaganda.

In Beirut a new governor came to the helm, but the replacement of Bekir Sami by another Unionist leader, Mustafa Azmi Bey, did not improve conditions on the ground. In early September 1915, Azmi told the Interior Ministry to forget about any anticipated food deliveries to the military from Beirut province. Because of the locusts, no food could be secured for the army, "neither by purchasing it, nor by collecting it as war tax [*tekalif-i harbiye*]." Surrounded by a starving population, he reported that any troops in Beirut "must be supplied from elsewhere."[47]

As Syria's famine was unfolding, the French consul in Cairo alerted his government that tens of thousands had starved to death and suggested providing relief. The British response made clear that causing hunger was the blockade's very purpose: "His Majesty's Secretary of State for Foreign Affairs expresses his earnest hope that the French Government will not encourage any such scheme. . . . The Entente Allies are simply being blackmailed to remedy the shortage of supplies which it is the very intention of the blockade to produce." The French concluded that their British allies "consider the famine as an agent that will lead the Arabs to revolt."[48] The effects of Ottoman state policies, the Entente blockade, and environmental destruction caused by the locusts swept like a tidal wave over Syria's population.

By 1916 Beirut had become the epicenter of massive hunger. Unsurprisingly, hunger raged first among the poor. In November 1916 one eyewitness recorded in their diary that in Mount Lebanon "all the poor people have died."[49] Some bread was available but unaffordable for all but the wealthiest. The French foreign minister, Jules Cambon, in July 1916 noted that famine in Beirut and Damascus would prove useful in the long run, as the Ottoman Empire would become "hated in all of the Arab countries."[50] French and British decision-makers were intent on turning hunger to their advantage. Indeed, the provisioning of food and the birth of modern "humanitarianism" became the cornerstone of implementing French colonial rule in Lebanon in the war's immediate aftermath.[51]

The fact that hunger appeared early in the war and in all parts of the empire suggests that Cemal, who arrived as the commander of the Fourth Army in Damascus only in November 1914, did not bring about the shortages single-handedly. By 1916 the army had conscripted twenty-eight thousand men from Aleppo province, twenty-six thousand from Damascus province, and another twenty thousand from the Jerusalem district—a total of seventy-four thousand men. A high percentage of these conscripts had previously worked in agriculture. The requisitioning of animals further reduced the acreage of land under cultivation.[52] If Cemal did not orchestrate the food crisis, neither did he mitigate, or succeed in mitigating, the terrible wartime conditions for civilian populations under his rule, despite clear warning signs.

When the Assembly returned to session in November 1915, it immediately turned to the hunger crisis. The delegate from Çankırı, located in north central Anatolia, had just completed a three-month journey on foot visiting many villages and towns of Anatolia. He found the health of the people he encountered "extremely dreadful [*pek acınacak*]" and concluded that "the actual great war" and "the actual threat to the future of our people [*milletin*]" resided in the "seeds of illness and disease that continue to attack us." And he added that "for a people to be happy," they must first be healthy. But "from the standpoint of health," he proclaimed, "we are headed towards the abyss."[53] Beyond Mount Lebanon and Beirut, hunger quickly became a scourge felt in all parts of the empire.

Hunger Everywhere

Within just a few months into the war, hunger gripped the entire country. The governor of Yemen province, Mahmud Nedim, in April 1915 demanded funds "with the next possible courier." Without additional resources, "a grave disaster" would befall the province as a result of "famine and the locust plague."[54] In Yemen, no food was available locally to feed the troops stationed there. In the Jabal Tihame region, locusts had destroyed "eighty to ninety percent" of the crops. In early September 1915, few markets in the province had any produce to sell. Those who did have goods on offer demanded sky-high prices. Governor Mahmud Nedim urgently requested the government send money in order to provision "all soldiers and officials in the province."[55] They could not be fed from local sources.

Earlier that year, the governor—born and raised in Yemen himself—had engaged in a bureaucratic tango with the imperial center to exempt his province from conscription. Istanbul had raised the possibility of instituting military conscription in Yemen, but the governor shot back that conscripting anyone in Yemen now, "at this crucial moment [*şu mühim zamanda*]" and after decades of armed resistance there to Ottoman rule, would seriously "upset the sensitivities of this region."[56]

Military commanders in Yemen province also reported the plight of the civilian populations around them and asked that troops be supplied from elsewhere. In fall 1915 the Assembly sought to relieve civilian populations by cutting taxes in half or dropping them altogether. This specifically included taxes on oranges in Jaffa and Gaza, and also tariffs on bringing food to Yemen across the Red Sea. Exemptions for East African imports to Mecca and Hijaz followed shortly thereafter. The deputy from Karesi demanded all tariffs and fees on wheat (*buğday*), barley (*arpa*), and flour (*un*) be removed for the entire empire immediately, noting the sky-high prices of such foods. "Conditions in our country are extremely dire [*memleketimizin hali de pek fenadır*]," remarked the deputy from Karesi, an area just south of the Sea of Marmara.[57]

Until August 1914, 75 percent of Ottoman imports arrived via the Mediterranean Sea. These imports came to an end almost immediately with the beginning of the war. Land shipping routes with Germany and Austria-Hungary reopened only after the bloody defeat of Serbia in December 1915.[58] By that time, sugar, tea, coffee, and textiles had disappeared from the open market.[59] How the government allocated shrunken resources was determined as much by logistical as by political considerations.

The people of Istanbul, too, were hungry. In the Senate, the Meclis-i Ayan, the Greek Orthodox senator Legofet Bey noted that hunger had become the never-ending topic discussed in every home, from the wealthiest to the poorest. According to Legofet, a diplomat and statesman who had served in the Ottoman government for decades, parents were asking whether they will "have enough bread for our children?"[60]

A close look at the empire's best-supplied battlefront, the Gallipoli Peninsula, is revealing. Here too, at Gallipoli, hunger ravaged civilian life. The inhabitants of the Kale-i Sultaniye district—near the southern mouth to the Dardanelles, about one hundred and seventy miles southwest of Istanbul—held about "one month's worth of provisions" in September 1915. When that food ran out, the people would turn to the seed supply set aside for the planting season. Once those, too, were consumed, nothing would be left to eat, in the middle of winter, when bringing any supplies to the area would become "difficult and perhaps even impossible." Thus, the district governor (*mutasarrıf*) requested that steps be taken immediately to ship food and additional seeds by railway from the southern agricultural region around Izmir to Bandırma. These provisions should arrive by mid-October, the district governor reiterated, "when rainfall tends to become very heavy." From Bandırma, "the people" would have to transport the food "with their own carts." Getting the provisions there on time, the district governor warned, was "a matter of vital importance for the entire country."[61]

On October 10, 1915, the district governor wrote with a desperate request for food. He had "seen the people [of his district] in deep distress (*ahalinin pek büyük bir müzayaka içinde bulunduklarını gördüm*)." He found them "truly bewildered [*cidden muhayyer*]," their bewilderment "increasing by the day." Steady rains and winter were in the offing, meaning that impassable roads would soon keep any food from reaching his district. Hundreds, even thousands of soldiers, he said, had passed through the towns and villages and either had bought up or taken all the bread. "Having no bread," rendered "the lack of all other vital necessities [*havayic-i hayatiyenin*] meaningless." He therefore pleaded that the government send the requested provisions immediately.[62]

How had it come to this? On top of the collection of the general grain tax (*öşür*), the army's Purchasing Commission (Mubayaa Heyeti) had visited the area and bought foodstuffs at government set prices that "of course intensified further" the region's scarcity. The head of the Purchasing Commission had crisscrossed the district and found the lack of food "extremely deplorable." However, he felt he had to go ahead with the mandated purchasing "because of the army's own needs for provisions." Situated adjacent to the Gallipoli Peninsula, the region was "practically part of the theater of war." And therefore, the exasperated official continued, such conditions as existed in his district could not be tolerated, especially as much of "the army's food and matériel" was being "supplied and transported by means of the inhabitants' own carts and wagons." Soon, he argued, the army itself would suffer these logistical problems because of the prevailing conditions. Without relief arriving soon, "god forbid, the probable outcome will be the dispersion and dislocation of the population." To prevent this outcome, the district governor demanded the following amounts of food: two hundred and fifty thousand *kile* wheat, two hundred thousand *kile* barley, sixty-five thousand *kile* oats, ten thousand *kile* rye, five thousand *kile* corn, and ten thousand *kıyye* potatoes. In addition, if the seeds were to be planted with any success, the region desperately required workers: the head of the commission demanded a labor battalion totaling some twelve hundred men, reminding the government that the state could not exist without its people and that the support of each and "every individual" was required. The people of Kale-i Sultaniye, he assured the government, had been "fulfilling this sacred task" under the most difficult circumstances "since the very declaration of the war."[63]

For those conducting the war, feeding soldiers took priority. In early 1915 the Commerce and Agriculture Ministry tasked a special commission with drawing up a comprehensive picture of the empire's food supply and formulating new policies "according to the particular conditions prevailing in each locality at different times."[64] All provinces (*vilayet*s) and independent districts (*sancak*s) were to report the amount of beans and legumes collected as tithe tax (*öşür*), stored, and available to be turned over to the army.[65] Table 2 shows the results of this survey. It lists a total of 6,991,623 kilograms, or 6.9 tons, of stored beans and legumes (*kuru sebze*) in March 1915 by location. In comparison, the legumes yield for 1913 amounted to roughly 170 million kıyye.[66] The total wheat production came to some 162,443,509 *kile*, with 37,312,027 *dönüm* of agricultural land.[67]

Like Beirut province, Istanbul had no stored food reserves in state depots.[68] But while Istanbul, as the imperial capital, was left off the list as a supplier of food to the army, Beirut was not. Despite Governor Bekir Sami's repeated calls for relief to his province, Beirut was expected to provision troops nonetheless.

Equally striking was the projected capacity of Aydın province to provide 61.5 percent of the army's supply of beans and legumes in spring 1915. Located in Western Anatolia, Aydın Province was famous for its agricultural plenitudes, a kind of Ottoman California. But Aydın's abundance was by no means guaranteed. Before 1915, locusts (*çekirge*) had appeared "as an epidemic" in "certain parts of the Ottoman domains," and "in particular in Aydın province."[69] The voracious insect, moreover, threatened to have the same detrimental effect on Aydın that it would wreak soon

TABLE 2. Beans and Legumes Stored in Imperial Facilities Available for Military Use, March 1915[a] (in kilograms)

16,980	Edirne Province (*vilayet*)
6,400	Adana Province
4,303,341	Aydın Province
3,283	Baghdad Province
53,860	Beirut Province
298,696	Aleppo Province
1,540	Hüdavendigar Province
~~49,528~~ 88,374	Diyar-ı Bekir Province
216,682	Sivas Province
403,410	Trabzon Province
75,964	Kastamonu Province
164,048	Konya Province
69,174	Mamuretülaziz Province
9,137	Mosul Province
20,000	Urfa District (*sancak*)
983	İzmit District
35,000	Bolu District
473,600	Canik District
333,027	Karesi District
148,280	Kale-i Sultaniye District
80,964	Menteşe District
55,027	Teke District
68,649	Karahisar-ı Sahib District
65,204	Bitlis Province
6,991,623	**Total**

[a] BOA, DH.İ.UM 93-1/1-4, Interior Ministry, "Table Showing Available Foods Such as Beans [*fasülye*, *bakla*, and *bezelye*], Chickpeas [*nohud*], and Lentils [*mercimek*]," undated table [13 Cemaziyülevvel 1333; March 29, 1915]. On this copy the addition total appears incorrectly as 6,091,623 kilograms.

upon Syria. To prevent the wide-scale destruction of Aydın's crops, its governor requested an emergency measure: he wanted the sixteen thousand men in labor battalions assigned to road construction in Aydın to be immediately reassigned to collecting and destroying locust eggs before the eggs could hatch. In a cabinet meeting on February 28, 1915, War Minister Enver Pasha, Interior Minister Talat Bey, and five other ministers approved the request. Reassigning Aydın's labor battalions now, the cabinet's decision said, "will save the people [*millet*] and government from great harm."[70]

The effort significantly mitigated the locust attack. The state's intervention there contrasted with the absence of a comparable effort in Mount Lebanon and Beirut.

Encouraged by the strides made in Aydın, the Interior Ministry decided to allocate special funds to subsidize the major cotton producing region of Adana, in southeastern Anatolia. The ministry also resolved to invest in potato production—because of the plant's sturdiness and high nutritional value. Ankara, Çatalca, Edirne, Istanbul, Hüdavendigar, Konya, and Sivas—all predominantly Turkish-speaking areas located in Anatolia, not Arabic-speaking regions of the empire—were targeted for increased potato production and received special allotments of potato seeds. Lacking sufficient manpower, the Commerce and Agriculture Ministry sought to procure machinery to enhance production. In early 1915 the Commerce and Agriculture Ministry applied to Washington—technically still neutral in the war—"for two hundred and fifty reapers" from the United States, and for "as many as possible threshers from Hungary." To protect crops against fungi and other diseases, the ministry sought to purchase "three hundred thousand kilos of copper sulfate [*göztaşı*]" from Germany and "three million kilos of sulfur [*kükürt*]" from Italy, then also still a neutral power.[71]

In 1915 there were some eight million Ottoman lira in circulation; by 1918, this volume had risen to some 161 million—more than a twentyfold increase—causing prices to spike and purchasing power to plummet.[72] Banks took measures to increase the volume of available goods. In the Senate, the request by the Bank of Agriculture (Ziraat Bankası) to import tariff-free sulfur and copper sulfate "from Europe" for fungicides and herbicides was approved. Cemil Bey, speaking for the Commerce and Agriculture Ministry, reported that millions of kilograms of locust eggs had been collected and destroyed so far. The previous year locusts had swarmed from Sudan to Syria and were terribly destructive, he claimed. Now in the current year, in 1916, large swarms were appearing in Aydın and Aleppo provinces. Because of the anticipated destruction, according to Cemil, the people of Ankara Province had planted only some 10 percent of fields.[73] He urged the Senate to take additional measures to stop the locusts and increase production. One attempt by the government to increase grain production sought to convert some of the historically rich cotton-producing areas of the Cilician plain around Adana to cereal production. The central problem, however, was the lack of workers. The spring 1916 harvest fell 60 percent short of expectations because of the lack of skilled labor and the repeated attacks of large locust swarms.[74]

In January 1916, the government appealed to the Assembly for additional allocations of food to the military. Ahmed Rıza admonished the government for making such a request, warning that "hundreds of thousands" were "going hungry" and that "desperate women" and workers were everywhere. He saw "stark contradictions between what the City Prefect [*şehremini beyefendi*]" previously had "promised and the actual reality of living conditions." Senator Reşid Âkif noted that "the food situation today" was "for us a matter of life and death."[75] The senate demanded that the state act and improve conditions urgently.

The following week, Ahmed Rıza reminded the Senate that on August 22, 1915, Prefect Cemil had stood in front of them and declared there would be no bread shortages in the city, but now the ration in Istanbul was one *dirhem* per person, one *okka* for a family of six, and even these amounts were very difficult to obtain. The price of rice, a staple, was unaffordable for most. Ahmed Rıza went on to say that the people's support was essential for any government. "Nothing good will come if the government abuses the people's patience and resilience." And he reminded everyone, though it may have been news to some, that the Ottoman Empire did not enter the war "with the agreement and desire of the people" but rather that "the government entered the war based on its own judgement." He continued that "therefore it was the government's greatest duty to consider and ensure the people's necessities and needs before the war" and that "a government that does not think of its people does not have the right to expect its support and its sacrifice." Talat was present to respond personally, saying, "the conditions under which we entered the war and the degree to which both assemblies approved it is well known." Senator Ahmed Rıza objected: "The Interior Minister has said that the parliament approved the government's decision" to enter the war. "I do not recall such an approval. Your humble servant certainly did not offer approval. I want my words to be entered into the record." Talat went on to say that imports had stopped with the war but that this was not the real problem: lack of roads and transportation made it impossible to distribute available food to all areas, but not for lack of effort, he claimed: "Today and for some time the government's biggest concern is the question of provisions and food. We are working on this day and night."[76]

On February 15, 1916, Commerce and Agriculture Minister Ahmed Nesimi appeared before the Assembly. He sought to assure the deputies. His ministry was deploying the latest technology to combat the plague. The deputies were far from convinced. Ibrahim Efendi, from Kütahya, had seen with his own eyes the great damage the locusts had caused in his district. Wherever there were locusts, he declared, there were hunger and famine. Baghdad's deputy, Cemil Zehavi (known to his constituents as Jamīl Zahāwi), agreed. In Baghdad, locusts had wreaked havoc, and they continued to do so. There were locusts in areas where there were no state officials, where the state had no presence at all. What did the state plan to do, he asked, to prevent eggs from hatching and descending on plants and crops? A special budget of twenty million *kuruş* was approved for fighting locusts, but the outlook for success remained bleak.[77]

The Assembly continued to adopt measures and allocate funds for the mitigation of the locusts' destruction. On March 20, 1916, it approved a Locust Law, expanding on earlier legislation from 1912 and 1913. The law required immediate reporting to local authorities if locust eggs were sighted anywhere on Ottoman soil and promised a reward for such reporting (from 250 up to 1000 *kuruş*). When eggs were discovered, all villagers over the age of fifteen were obligated to destroy them, either by ploughing or collecting and delivering them to military authorities for incineration. The law stipulated punishment for discovering eggs and not taking action. If an area was affected beyond the ability of the population of the village to destroy or collect all eggs, then all surrounding villages within a three-hour travel time were required to assist in egg collection; these workers were promised a daily wage.[78] Given the hungry and weakened condition of village populations, however, these stipulations must have seemed preposterous in the eyes of the people.

Some four months later, on July 13, 1916, the government adopted a "Regulation for the Designation of Areas Infested with Locust Eggs" that required all villages and local governments to work with newly created special units designated Locust Combat Officers (Çekirge Mücadele Memurları) and report any locust eggs. These officers in the war on locusts were to draw up maps of infested areas, which local governments were to submit to Istanbul "by September," ahead of the hatching season. Here too, failure to comply was punishable by law.[79] As late as 1918, the Commerce and Agriculture Ministry informed the government of locusts that had appeared "in unexpectedly great many places," suggesting, perhaps unsurprisingly, that many infestations went unreported. In "Anatolia and Syria" the locusts had returned "in vast numbers." In July 1918, it was once again the season for "the swarming locusts to lay and bury their eggs." The Commerce and Agriculture Ministry sent inspectors and provided funds for egg eradication, but, it maintained, the process depended heavily on the vigilance of the villagers. Should the egg eradication fail again, the ministry warned, the country would find itself "facing even greater difficulties next year," and it would be very unlikely that the "plague could be extinct once and for all."[80]

But by far the greatest obstacle to achieving higher levels of production was the lack of workers. "In order to bring in the spring harvest" successfully, the empire had to solve "the vast problems of procuring the necessary labor." The Commerce and Agriculture Minister implored Talat to contact War Minister Enver immediately to tend to this "critical" problem.[81] As war minister, Enver oversaw conscription. Rather than reduce the number of men in uniform and allow the country's workers to remain in the fields, however, Enver did the opposite. The War Ministry continuously sought to expand conscription rather than to reduce it.

Already by April 1915, the state had lowered the military service age from twenty years to eighteen, and by March 1916 it raised it from forty-five to fifty.[82] The army began calling up those born in the year 1315 (March 1899–March 1900). A popular folk song known as "Onbeşli," that is, "Fifteeners"—after the year in which they were born—mourned their conscription. Senator Ahmed Rıza railed against the measure: "If they, too, are taken, who will be left? For whom will we be defending the country when no one is left in it?" He turned to his colleagues, imploring, "At least we should save these youths. What can seventeen-year-old children do? How will they be able to survive?" "They have just left their mother's bosom." Salih Pasha agreed; he wanted to know whether there existed any evidence that sixteen- and seventeen-year-olds could contribute effectively to the war effort. Ahmed Rıza added that if all were considered capable, then "women, too, ought to be conscripted." Salih Pasha added that "after two or three months they [the sixteen- and seventeen-year-olds] will either all be clogging up the hospitals or they'll all be dead."[83] By June 1917 the manpower problem had become so acute that the war ministry requested information from the provinces about the number of twelve- to seventeen-year-old boys.[84]

Speaking in the Assembly, Ali Galip Efendi, the deputy from Karesi, stated there was hunger back home in his district. In Balıkesir, the people could no longer feed themselves. He explained that "we go to the War Ministry with our pockets filled with telegrams [of petitions from the people]," to no avail. "The people tell us they are starving." He acknowledged that 1915 was a difficult year: "No rain this summer between March and October. Then there were locusts, and mice, everywhere."[85] But now, in January 1916, for most people life had become unsustainable.

The deputy from Erzurum, Seyfullah Efendi, insisted that "all parts of the Ottoman Empire need food, but Erzurum is more desperate than all." It needed seeds and animals.[86] Feyzi Bey, from Diyarbekir, believed the government was privileging certain regions of the empire and neglecting his province, even though the people of Diyarbekir were housing and provisioning the Third Army. He noted that crops had fallen to 30 percent of the usual amount. He called on the War Ministry to intervene, since it was the military commanders who held authority and power, not the officials from the Commerce and Agriculture Ministry. He added that women would plant the spring crop of white corn, but that they must be given incentives: there would be no motivation for them to plant and work if authorities simply requisitioned whatever was harvested. Şakir Bey from Yozgat stressed that to fill the void of conscripted men, women and the elderly were working in the fields day and night.[87]

To this, Commerce and Agriculture Minister Ahmed Nesimi responded that no transportation existed to send seeds to Diyarbekir or Erzurum and that he had impressed this on the war minister. Baghdad, too, was a

FIGURE 8. Refugees in Jerusalem, 1917. *Source*: BA-MA, PH 10-III, 80, Bundesarchiv-Militärarchiv, Freiburg/Breisgau.

priority, but there was no means of getting aid there. Supplemental funds of fifteen million *kuruş* for the Commerce and Agriculture Ministry were approved unanimously without further discussion.[88] The distribution of food was as much a problem as its availability. Wheat sat along railway stations but could not be transported to places where it was needed. At Rayaq station near Beirut, wheat was rotting. While wheat stored in dry conditions can last for months or even years, wet wheat spoils quickly. During heavy rains in late 1915 and early 1916, "great quantities of food and provisions, exposed without protection to the elements at train stations, were destroyed."[89]

The Commerce and Agriculture Minister, Ahmed Nesimi Bey, was called to the Assembly to answer questions about the food situation. He explained that the ministry would be distributing seeds even though it was cash strapped but pointed to the critical need for railway transportation to deliver any seed. He added that the War Ministry was supporting this effort, and that the largest amounts of cash had gone to the provinces of Konya and Syria and the districts of Eskişehir and Jerusalem. Production in Beirut was anticipated to drop by another 25 percent. Seeds were being transported to plant corn, summer wheat, and potatoes.[90]

"No Grain and Provision Reserves Left in Military Depots": March 1916

The War Ministry was not about to surrender supplies or men, however. To the contrary, Enver was furious that his army in 1915 "did not receive the majority of its requests for provisions [*iaşenin kısm-ı âzâmı alınamamış*]." He acknowledged some of the reasons behind the shortages, including consideration for "the needs of the people and [securing their] seeds [*ahalinin ihtiyac ve tohumlukları*]." For that very reason, the army "until now" had been fed from the military's own reserves, but this had been possible only "with great difficulty." Now, in March 1916, there were "no grain and provision reserves left in military depots (*askerî anbarlarında*)."[91] When Enver submitted the military's projected requirements for 1916, he underscored that the provisioning of the "mobilized imperial army" had entered "a very grave stage" and demanded prompt fulfillment of its needs.[92]

By March 1916, military depots holding provisions for the army were depleted. As a result, military authorities increased requisitioning of civilian food supplies.[93] The War Ministry pressured the government to adopt stronger measures in securing the necessary collection of food for the army: "We are unable to provide our soldiers with even a quarter of their meat ration. Their physical strength is melting away. Our doctors are reporting this daily. The disastrous effects of these conditions on the

TABLE 3. Provision Requirements of the Imperial Army for 1916 (1332)[a] (in kilograms)

	First, Second, & Fifth Armies: Provinces of Istanbul, Edirne, Hüdavendigar, Konya, Ankara, Kastamonu, Aydın; Districts (*sancaks*) of Çatalca, Biga, İzmit, Karahisar, Kütahya, Karesi, Teke, Manisa, Niğde, Bolu, Kayseri, Eskişehir	Third Army: Provinces of Sivas, Erzurum, Trabzon, Elaziz, Diyar-ı Bekir, and provinces east; District of Canik	Fourth Army: A. Mobile Inspectorate From provinces of Adana, Aleppo, Damascus, Beirut, and Districts of İçil, Urfa, Maaş, Jerusalem	Sixth Army: From Provinces of Baghdad, Basra, Mosul, and District of Zor	Total
Flour	204,000,000	51,000,000	51,000,000	10,300,000	321,300,000
Or flour equivalent: wheat, spelt, rye, corn and millet	255,000,000	63,750,000	63,750,000	19,125,000	401,625,000
Meat	42,500,000	10,625,000	10,625,000	3,187,500	66,937,500
Bulgur, rice	25,500,000	6,375,000	6,375,000	1,912,500	40,162,500
Clarified butter and olive oils	6,800,000	1,700,000	1,700,000	510,000	10,710,000
Dried legumes: beans, fava, chickpeas, black-eyed peas, lentils, green peas, potato etc.	40,800,000	10,200,000	10,200,000	3,060,000	64,260,000
Salt	10,880,000	2,720,000	2,720,000	816,000	17,136,000
Onion, garlic	6,800,000	1,700,000	1,700,000	510,000	10,710,000
Soap	3,060,000	865,000	865,000	229,500	4,819,500
Gas	10,200,000	2,550,000	2,550,000	765,000	16,065,000
Olives	2,560,000	640,000	640,000	192,000	4,032,000
Tea and Coffee	1,020,000	255,000	255,000	76,500	1,066,500—corrected 1,606,500
Sugar	6,800,000	1,700,000	1,700,000	510,000	10,710,000
(in units of Kiyah)	184,875,000	76,500,000	102,000,000	25,500,000	388,875,000
Hay	123,250,000	51,000,000	68,000,000	17,000,000	259,250,000
Feed: barley, oat, wild oats	277,312,500	114,750,000	153,000,000	38,250,000	583,312,500
Wood	436,000,000	109,000,000	109,000,000	32,700,000	686,700,000
Charcoal	24,000,000	6,000,000	6,000,000	1,800,000	37,800,000

[a] BOA, DH.İ.UM 94-4/1-48, War Ministry to Interior Ministry, "Ordu-yu Hümayun'un 332 senesinde muhtac olduğu mevadd-ı iaşe listesidir," 2 Mart 1332 (March 15, 1916).

war have already become apparent. Please take urgent measures for the securing of our meat supply."[94] Even the better-supplied German officer, Kress, leading troops in Palestine, lost one-third of his body weight. "Not a single green leaf was left," he noted. The "supply crisis" caused the "destitution" of the Ottoman soldier and led to "catastrophe in this theater [in Palestine]," he concluded.[95]

The War Ministry demanded an annual supply of sixty-seven million kilograms of meat, "requiring 4,666,000 [*sic*: 4,466,000] head of sheep, at fifteen kilos each." Because of the scant supply available, "these sheep will be difficult to secure by purchasing them." The War Ministry proposed collecting 15 percent of all sheep immediately as a war tax and then transferring them to military garrisons.[96] A week later, the War Ministry repeated its demand, reminding the Interior Ministry that the previous year the "army's needs went unmet."[97]

Just when Enver pressured the Interior Ministry to raise provisions for his army, the Interior Ministry was receiving urgent cries from the provinces of starving populations and reports that no food existed for collection. The governor of Baghdad province, Haydar, balked at the War Ministry's demands. Baghdad's harvest was expected to fall below that of the previous year's; he saw no way for his province to meet the army's demands.[98]

Hunger ravaged all corners of the empire. From Western Anatolia, the people of Emrudabad village, near Ayvalık, pleaded with the government. "For over a year," they wrote in a telegram in December 1916, "95 percent of our people" had been living in desolate conditions. Emrudabad's crops had been "destroyed in their entirety by the locust plague." While they had been receiving some food, including flour, from surrounding areas, this supply had now ceased, plunging them into utter despair and forcing them to survive "on things like acorns, chestnuts, and wild pears [*palamut pelitleri, kestane ve ahlat gibi şeylerin*]."[99] The consumption of grass, dirt, and orange peels became commonplace.[100]

5

Empire of Atrocity

WHEN THE deputies of the Assembly gathered on January 20, 1915, their first item of business was a seemingly ordinary one: excusing the absence of members not present in the Assembly that day. One such request came from Vramian, an Armenian deputy from Van, a city and province in eastern Anatolia. Van province was home to a large Armenian population and a centuries-old center of Armenian culture and political life.[1] In the telegram, Vramian apologized for his absence. He was in eastern Anatolia, acting "as mediator between the government and the Armenian people in the aftermath of the events that had taken place in the city of Van on November 20, 1914, in Ziyüstan and Keçen on December 8, 1914, and in Dehaş, Gevaş, Karcıgan, and Şıtak just one week ago." He asked for the Assembly's support at "this dangerous moment." The Assembly voted to excuse Vramian's absence, although it is unlikely that they were familiar with the specific events to which Vramian was referring. The government controlled the news; bad news it suppressed. Vramian's message must have raised the anxiety level that day in the Assembly considerably.

Vramian's fellow Armenian deputy from Van, Papazian Efendi, had also telegrammed the Assembly requesting to be formally excused. Ohannes Vartkes, an Armenian deputy present in the Assembly that day, explained that his colleague Papazian was currently in the city of Muş, and that "for the Armenian people his [Papazian's] presence in Muş" was "an absolute necessity." The deputy from Muş, İlyas Sami Efendi, objected; his colleague had used the phrase "elements [*anasır*]" of the nation, often employed in the Ottoman context to describe the empire's various ethnic populations. İlyas Sami, one of the few Kurdish members of the Assembly, argued that "Armenians and Muslims are fully united in the face of the enemy. They have always stood hand in hand; and yet here [in the Assembly] we are still talking about 'elements.' I beg you! Let us stop using such designations. Ottomans have formed a true unity under a single name and are now fighting to defend themselves."[2] The mundane exercise of excusing absent deputies had turned into a debate about the very character of the empire itself.

İlyas Sami's vision of the empire's "true unity" would not survive the First World War. Presuming disloyalty to the Ottoman state, the Unionist government between 1915 and 1918 ordered the destruction of nearly the entire Armenian population of Anatolia.[3] Greek Orthodox Ottomans, also presumed to be supporting the Entente war effort, were subjected to massive and, in most cases, permanent displacement. Dozens of Arab leaders were publicly hanged, while Arab populations—both Christian and Muslim—were deported, along with hundreds of thousands of the empire's Kurdish subjects. Jews, primarily those residing in Palestine without Ottoman citizenship, were deported to Alexandria.

Civilians, Atrocity, and the First World War

The First World War saw atrocities committed against civilians on a massive scale. Germany's occupation of Belgium and Austria-Hungary's of Serbia occasioned terrible violence, as did Russia's treatment of its Jewish, Muslim, German, and other non-Russian, non–Orthodox Christian populations. The Anglo-French naval blockade of the Syrian coast, moreover, fully intended the starving of the civilian population. The waging of "total war" was anticipated not only by the United States Civil War, the scorched earth policies of the Boer Wars in South Africa, and the Balkan Wars but also by the brutality of the colonial wars waged in Africa, Asia, and the Americas in the decades leading up to the First World War.[4]

A young British officer, Winston Churchill, described a campaign in India's northwestern corner at the end of the nineteenth century rather matter-of-factly: "We proceeded systematically, village by village, and we destroyed the houses, filled up the wells, blew down the towers, cut down the great shady trees, burned the crops and broke the reservoirs. . . . At the end of a fortnight the valley was a desert, and honour was satisfied."[5] This attitude was far from episodic, incidental, or temporary, and the lethality increased over subsequent decades with new technologies. Two years after the Armistice, descriptions of the British use of airpower in Iraq, in what was referred to as "policing," still sounded much like Churchill's description above: "The village where he [a rebel] resides will be destroyed; pressure will be brought on the inhabitants by cutting off water [and] power, the area being cleared of the necessaries of life. . . . Burning a village properly takes a long time, an hour or more according to size."[6]

There is no doubt that the world of global violence the Unionists inhabited shaped their worldview. Publications calling for the extermination of Armenians—in the way that California newspapers called for the extermination of Native Americans in the nineteenth century—had no Ottoman equivalents.[7] And yet by the era of the First World War, Fuat Balkan, a member of the Unionists' infamous Special Organization (Teşkilat-ı Mahsusa), a secret association of irregular military and intelligence forces, tasked with propaganda campaigns, covert operations, and political assassinations, declared that "when the homeland and nation demanded it," he and his comrades "burnt, destroyed, razed!" They left "no stone on stone, no head on shoulders."[8] Fuat's chilling candor reveals just how much the Unionists became like the very powers whose influence and control they sought to escape. The fact that their rule during the years of the First World War fit into a global culture of violence does not reduce the Unionists' culpability in the atrocities they directed against civilians.

Locating causes and origins of genocide anywhere but squarely with the perpetrators themselves should not be seen as obfuscating "key questions of responsibility."[9] Nor should it result in shifting "attention too far away from the actual agency of killing."[10] When it comes to groups or regimes implementing mass death, "the choice to commit genocide within this structure has been theirs alone."[11] But neither can there be a soft-pedaling, if not outright exoneration, of the crucial role played by European (and, to a lesser extent, US) imperial interests in the nineteenth and twentieth centuries.

One of the first actions taken by the Russian government in August 1914 was to order the deportation of some five hundred thousand to one million people for their potential loyalty to Germany. These deportations were aimed at Baltic Germans, residing primarily in Russian-ruled Latvia and Estonia.[12] Already by October 1914, Russian forces had occupied much of Eastern Prussia, causing some 350,000 civilians to flee their homes.[13] The Russian commander in the Caucasus, Vorontsov-Dashkov, proposed revoking the citizenship of all Russian Muslims, though the measure was dropped. Instead, Georgian-speaking Muslims were deported to internment camps in the Caspian Sea.[14]

We know little about the extent to which Ottoman leaders between August 1914 and April 1915 were influenced by wartime atrocities in the battlefields beyond Ottoman borders. What is certain is that they were well-versed in the imperial practices of the Great Powers in Africa, Asia, and Latin America, as well as the practices of the United States from North America to the Philippines. The Ottoman press reported on European "wars of pacification" and the so-called small yet incredibly brutal wars the Great Powers waged worldwide. In France's invasion of Algeria, about one-third of the Algerian population, or one million people, starved to death.[15] The Algerian conquest was marked by the deliberate targeting of civilians by "razing their villages" and implemented policies of "scorched earth."[16] The violence of European colonialism was covered widely in Ottoman publications.

Contemporaries, too, could see the Armenian genocide in global terms: Dr. Johannes Lepsius, a German Protestant pastor, was perhaps the most active and best-informed international observer of Ottoman Armenians and the violence visited upon them. In 1921 in Berlin, he served as a key witness at the trial of Talat's assassin, a young Armenian man named Soghomon Tehlirian. Lepsius's testimony was calculated to incriminate Talat of mass atrocity and to exonerate Tehlirian, Talat's traumatized murderer. Lepsius testified that the decision to deport the Armenians was taken in April 1915, and that "according to the Turks, it was the English precedent in the Boer Wars in South Africa that gave them the idea for the concentration camps."[17] Lepsius estimated that some 1.4 million Ottoman Armenians had been deported and believed that Talat had issued the orders personally.[18] Addressing the horrific acts against the Armenian population, Lepsius pointed to the atrocities' international roots: "The Armenian question is not an autochthonous development. It is the creation of European diplomacy. The Armenian people have become the victim of the political interests of Russia and England." He then added: "The humanitarian cause, the 'protection of Christians,' were pretexts."[19]

Contingency and Mass Violence

The state violence that began in February 1915 and initially was directed against suspected Armenian revolutionaries within a few months encompassed the entire Armenian Christian civilian population. After dispossessing them of their property and land, the Ottoman army marched Armenians southward in a trail of tears on which tens of thousands of the deported, women, children, and the elderly, starved to death, died of exhaustion, or were murdered. Troops, irregulars, marauders, and gangs of criminals raped women and girls. Some Kurdish and Muslim neighbors sought to save deportees by hiding them and providing shelter, especially children. Over a million and a half Armenians were uprooted from their homes; seven hundred thousand of them perished. A century later there is a considerable number of survivors' accounts describing the horrific suffering they endured.[20] The grandson of one, "born in a squalid Armenian refugee camp near Beirut," asked "what it would sound like" and if "the world would hear them" if all the "murdered souls arose from the dead and screamed all at once."[21]

In retrospect there appears to have been a myriad of factors that contributed to the near-wholescale destruction of the Ottoman Armenian world during the First World War. Like the subterranean world of an old tree, a complex system of interwoven roots sustained the violence. Among such roots, scholars have pointed to the arrival of millions of Muslim refugees from the Crimea, the Caucasus, and the Balkans. They stress the "land" or "agrarian question" that this in-migration created in the provinces of eastern Anatolia. A second set of roots sprang from the predatory imperial and colonial objectives of the Great Powers. Some roots ran deep and far, others shallow and near. They converged in 1915 to produce the terrible violence that destroyed Anatolia's Christian population.

And yet, scholars have also noted the absence of a government plan to remove or destroy the empire's Christian populations from Anatolia prior to the First World War. Nor, for that matter, did such an intention begin to crystallize until six months into the fighting. The Unionists' response to the pressures presented by war in 1915 were shaped by the dynamics of the prewar years, but they did not predetermine them.[22]

It is true that the 1908–1914 constitutional period had been a time of intense contestation among the empire's rival political parties, many of whom had their origins in revolutionary politics of the Hamidian period. The prewar years were marked by episodes of mass violence and political assassination. Beginning in August 1914, war conditions rendered these political antagonisms into military confrontation. Unionist leaders and their supporters questioned non-Muslims' and non-Turks' loyalty to the empire: Armenians and Kurds were cast as Russia's potential allies; Jews as Britain's; Arab Christians as France's; Arab Muslims (associated with Sharif Husayn of Mecca) as nationalist separatists and British allies; and Greek Orthodox Christians as willing partners in the *Megali Idea*, a Greater Greece that extended from the Greek peninsula to Asia Minor. And yet, these dynamics alone did not produce the violence; these forces existed between August 1914 and January 1915 without resulting in the mass deportation and mass death of the following year.

Because the Ottoman state's violent measures against its non-Muslim and non-Turkish citizens during the First World War are now relatively well-known, it is tempting to read much of the Ottoman Empire's final decades as an escalation toward this inevitable conflagration. Ussama Makdisi has challenged such a view and argued that in the Arab lands of the empire, a robust and sturdy "ecumenical frame" of Christian, Jewish, and Muslim life was being constructed well into the twentieth century.[23] But an interreligious culture also continued to thrive in the Anatolian and Balkan provinces of the empire, if more fragile, contested, and subjected to intense external pressures.

While some Ottoman Armenians in August 1914 joined Russian forces, others such as Yervant Alexanian and Kalusd Sürmenyan enlisted in the

Ottoman army and served willingly, even enthusiastically, at least initially. Both Yervant Alexanian from the city of Sivas and Kalusd Sürmenyan from the city of Erzincan, some one hundred and fifty miles apart, served until the end of the war. Both became officers. They represent a group whose experiences have remained little known. Yervant was born in 1895, not yet at the age of conscription when the war began. In fall 1914 he entered the final year of the Jesuit-run French high school as the student considered most likely to finish at the top of his class. In November 1914, the school was closed, its building requisitioned by military authorities. The next year, in 1915, Yervant became a private in the very army that, around the same time, deported his family. Yervant later attended the Military Academy (Mekteb-i Harbiye), earning the rank of second lieutenant in 1916. His fellow Ottoman Armenian officer, Kalusd Sürmenyan, meanwhile, had graduated from the Military Academy in June 1912, in time to serve in the Balkan Wars as a second lieutenant. Like Yervant Alexanian's, Kalusd Sürmenyan's family was deported in 1915. Yervant lost fifty-one members of his family. Kalusd lost his mother to the deportation but was able to save the rest of his family. After the war Kalusd settled in Baghdad, Yervant in the United States.[24]

The two men depicted prewar conditions in surprisingly optimistic terms, not as galloping toward mayhem. Yervant spoke in glowing terms of the 1913 "pan-Sivas 'Olympic' games," a competition among several youth scouting organizations across the region. He recalled how his Armenian Bertevagoump (Bartev Club) "took the most medals, gaining the admiration of all." He then told the story of how during the medal ceremony "all Armenian athletes stood and sang the Turkish anthem when the flag was raised." Yervant wanted his readers to know that singing the anthem was not a matter of formality but a moment when the Armenian athletes were "demonstrating again how loyal they actually were to the country in which they lived." He was not a member of Bertevagoump, and he did not mention whether or how well he knew the athletes or their political views. His point was that prior to 1914 "Armenians were very much part of the fabric of Sivas," and that, even more crucially, "nobody would have believed" that the Armenians of Sivas or Erzincan "could be annihilated so quickly." As Yervant put it, "Nobody would anticipate what was to befall us, even those who had survived the many pogroms and massacres, such as the Hamidian massacres, that preceded the Genocide of 1915."[25]

Kalusd Sürmenyan recalled that young Armenians eagerly joined the colors after the promulgation of the 1908 Constitution and the opening of military careers to them. He characterized the military authorities of Erzincan, his hometown, as welcoming and "accommodating," allowing Armenian men to attend church and observe religious holidays. And he added that Muslim Turkish officers respected Armenian soldiers and considered them "talented and capable."[26] After 1908, Kalusd recounted, the Muslim population treated Christian peoples and especially the Armenians "with sincerity and friendship," noting that "in all areas, all doors were open to Armenians within the military." Some, perhaps most, historians would accept these statements only with important qualifications, if at all. And yet, the warm, optimistic way in which Kalusd—fully aware of what had happened to the empire's Armenians by the time he penned his memoir—chose to portray the Ottoman Armenian world before the war is a crucial reminder that the pre-1915 Ottoman world was far from monochromatic. Once Armenians became subject to military service, Kalusd and several of his friends decided to become officers, saying that "if Armenians are going to serve in the military, let's also enter the military and defend the rights of these Armenian soldiers [by becoming officers]." Kalusd and four other Armenians enrolled in the Military Academy in 1910 (several others applied but performed poorly on the written entrance exam). Of the twelve hundred students at the Military Academy, there were ten Armenians, a few Greek Orthodox, and one Bulgarian.[27] According to Kalusd, when the state declared mobilization on August 3, 1914, "everyone" rushed to the enlistment stations to register.[28] Surprisingly, some Armenians were being conscripted into the Ottoman army in an orderly fashion—or what then passed as such—even as late as May 1915.[29]

In his study of "Greek Christian experiences" in the Ottoman Empire, Nicholas Doumanis argued that "until 1912, much of the empire was flourishing and stable, particularly western Anatolia and the Levant."[30] To be sure, stable coexistence was far from even across the empire, but relations did not collapse suddenly with the First Balkan War. That war brought to power an aggressive leadership and offered a spectacular reservoir of experiences of victimization. Perhaps, as Uğur Ümit Üngor has put it, "had some form of justice been delivered to Ottoman Muslims in 1913, there might not have been a vindictive Young Turk dictatorship that launched the later genocide. The idea of the Ottoman-Turkish state as victim granted many a necessary moral certainty that enabled mass murder."[31] It was this sense of victimization that opened the way to the subsequent victimization of non-Muslims, and also of non-Turks—the empire's Arab and Kurdish populations in particular.

Effects of Conscription and Requisitioning

As soon as war commenced in Europe, the offices of the Armenian patriarch in Istanbul, Zaven Der Yeghiayan, filled with urgent telegrams from the provinces. As the center of the Third Army with tens of thousands of troops, Erzurum quickly turned into a site of intense requisitioning. The Armenian prelate of Erzurum/Garin reported in August 1914 that "all the needs of the cavalrymen and their horses—feed, grass, barley," and "fuel, meat and furnishings, bread, rice, bulghur, and tea" were "being met entirely by the local population."[32] By September, some thirty thousand troops were "spread in the villages of Pasen. In the city of Garin and on its Plain there are at least forty thousand soldiers." Another thirty thousand men were due to arrive the next day. "In the single village of Mudurga there are stationed more than two thousand soldiers, and the other villages, too, contain similar numbers."[33] By October, the Erzurum prelate had become desperate: "We no longer know how to console the Armenian people."[34] The region had "already periodically supplied wheat, barley, oil, sheep, oxen, horses, tools, onions, beans, felt cloaks, rugs, socks, grass, hay etc.," but a new decree had just been announced "for another tithe to be exacted."[35] Conditions in Erzurum were not the exception.

In Diyarbekir province, too, requisitioning exhausted and demoralized the people. In late September 1914, the population had been "brought to such a point" that it was "almost impossible for them to continue living."[36]

Diyarbekir's prelate depicted a dire scene. There was little to stop requisitioning commissions from excessive collection:

> Sheep are needed for meat, wheat for making bread, barley, hay, and grass for the horses, oil, sugar, underwear, shoes, sandals, riding harnesses for the troops, etc. All of these are needed, and they have to be provided by the people. If it could only be done in an orderly manner! If only each village's and each person's ability to contribute could be taken into account and [the army's needs] communicated to the villagers through leaflets. Supposedly this was done, but the villagers have not seen any leaflets.[37]

Officials conducting the requisitioning at times "beat and torture[d] villagers." The prelate's letter described how the district governor "personally beats and dishonors several men—Turks, Armenians—in the center [of the *sanjak* (military-administrative district)] every day."[38] The requisitioning proceeded in chaotic and heavy-handed fashion and, at times, against both Christian and Muslim populations. In December, merchants from Van/Vaspurakan wrote to say that authorities would cause them to "soon become bankrupt—we will be sitting on ashes, unable to pay our debts."[39] Van's prelate reported that the wheat crop had been excellent in the current year, but that only some of it could be harvested and threshed. Many of the fields could not be planted for the following year.[40] Conditions in Anatolia's eastern provinces, as in the empire's other regions, were turning dire.

Effects of requisitioning were compounded by the effects of conscription. In towns and villages across Erzurum province, all between the ages of twenty and forty-five, "everyone," even schoolteachers, were "being taken away to the army with much severity and under stern threats." Hence the prelate's office "was under siege by women." Conscription added to the economic hardship of the authorities' requisitioning campaigns: "Homes and hearths are shut down; commerce is at a standstill; fields, threshing floors, and the harvest are all abandoned." While "these cruelties and worries" were still "partially bearable," the rapidly growing number of roving gangs of deserters exposed the people to the constant threat of robbery.[41] As the vicar of Bayezid put it, he was "living the crisis of unexpected developments."[42]

By late 1914, civilians' responses to these crushing wartime conditions blurred with the activities of political groups and revolutionaries. To defy conscription, some Armenian men took up arms and disappeared into the mountainous countryside. On occasion, groups of Armenian deserters linked up with established gangs whose actions dated back to the prewar period. In September 1914, in the town of Zeitun—situated in the Maraş district of Aleppo province—locals, including the mayor, considered rebellion. The news of a possible rebellion at Zeitun circulated widely enough for Armenian leaders outside the province to make calls against such a plan, as it would endanger Armenian communities elsewhere. Ottoman authorities intervened; they discovered ten Mauser guns and a number of Martini rifles. Weapon searches in surrounding villages produced some fourteen hundred firearms. The Zeitun mayor was arrested and executed in custody.[43]

At this point, in fall 1914, there were still attempts to prevent the state's collective punishment of the entire Armenian population. On October 23, 1914, a group of Zeitun's Armenian Christian and Muslim notables signed a letter, addressed to the central government in Istanbul, assuring officials that order prevailed in Zeitun and the region generally. They noted that some deserters had taken to the mountains and were committing robberies but, they stressed, the matter was being settled locally.[44]

Two days after the notables' letter, Patriarch Zaven, in Istanbul, met with members of the Armenian National Assembly and with Armenian members of the Ottoman parliament. They decided that Patriarch Zaven would cultivate friendly relations with the Unionists and reassure them of Armenian loyalty. In addition, they pledged that Armenian notables would raise funds to set up a hospital as a charity contribution to the war effort. The patriarch met with Interior Minister Talat, to give assurances of support and express his concern for the safety of the country's Armenian population. Bedros Halajian, a Unionist, elected deputy from Istanbul, and former minister of commerce and agriculture, was designated as a special Armenian liaison to the government. In November, the Constantinople

Armenian Physicians' Union organized events to train medics and nurses in treating wounded soldiers. Patriarch Zaven was doing all he could to affirm Armenian patriotism and loyalty to the Ottoman war effort. He believed he had been successful in calming both the anxieties among government officials and among the Armenian population. Articles appeared in the press that pointed not to the intensification but to the de-escalation of tensions.[45]

Requisitioning and conscription became sites of tense confrontation. Social fissures grew as feelings of desperation among civilians spread. By December 1914, four Armenian volunteer battalions had been set up under the command of General Andranik, an Ottoman Armenian who had led Armenian volunteers on the side of Bulgarian forces in the Balkan Wars.[46] The Ottoman embassy in Sofia reported that some one hundred and ten Armenians from Bulgaria had joined the Russian army as volunteers.[47] And yet, as the historian Donald Bloxham has put it, "Despite threats, increasing violence against Armenians in eastern Anatolia, including sporadic boycotts, and the deterioration of [Unionist]-Armenian relations from 1909, there is no evidence that a policy to physically destroy the community was forged prior to World War I, not least because the deportations only began after seven months of war."[48] Such a policy began to emerge only in March 1915, when Ottoman domestic life became a world war within.

The First World War in Eastern Anatolia

In November 1914, Boghos Nubar Pasha, the head of the Armenian National Delegation, sought to mobilize British support for an invasion of some fifteen thousand Armenian volunteers at Alexandretta.[49] The highest ranking British military official in Egypt, John Maxwell, found such an undertaking to be much more promising than the campaign to force the Dardanelles. The British vessel HMS *Doris*, accompanied by several warships, had conducted a reconnaissance tour of the coastal area, anchoring not too far from the city of Alexandretta itself. The fact that HMS *Doris* could do so relatively undisturbed, according to Maxwell, confirmed that there would not be much resistance to an invasion. Once on the ground, the British could count on reinforcements from the surrounding areas. Nubar had pledged support:

> Boghos Pasha Nubar, and other prominent Armenians, assured me that once we landed there [in Alexandretta in February 1915], we could count on the assistance of at least ten thousand Armenian mountaineers from the Zeitoun and Cilicia districts. Good fighting men, conversant with all the Passes in the Taurus and Armanus mountains, who had only to be armed to keep these secure from any Turkish advance.[50]

Meanwhile, Ottoman authorities in Adana province had arrested Armenian revolutionaries in contact with British warships just off the coast. In February, military authorities issued orders in areas with large Armenian populations, such as Sivas, for all firearms to be surrendered to local officials. According to Zaven, some believed that officials added from their own arsenal to the piles of weapons and photographed them, as evidence to demonstrate the Armenian population's plans for armed rebellion.[51]

On February 25, 1915, War Minister Enver ordered all Armenians already in uniform to be disarmed immediately and placed into labor battalions.[52] Confronted with defeats at the front, on the one hand, and hunger, disease, and displacement at home and facing fierce opposition in the Assembly and the Senate, the government invoked Article 7 of the constitution, suspending both houses of parliament on March 1, 1915. Justice Minister Ibrahim read out the statement shutting parliament until September of that year.[53] Thus the war's most traumatic and horrific moments took place in 1915 at a time when the Assembly and the Senate, perhaps the only institutions that could act as a check on government, were in abeyance.

Also on March 1, 1915, in one of the first instances of a deportation policy, Adana's governor suggested relocating the population of Dörtyol, a town of some ten thousand in the vicinity of Alexandretta. Dörtyol had been the scene of bloody massacres in 1895 and 1909, but despite those tragedies the people of Dörtyol maintained a vibrant economy of orange groves and artisanal manufacturing. In Istanbul, Interior Minister Talat approved the deportation on March 2, 1915. The objective of the deportation, according to the officials, was to demonstrate to the entire population that defiance or subversion of the Ottoman state would be heavily punished.[54] That same day, news reached Patriarch Zaven of the first cases of deportations in Erzurum/Garin province.[55]

Even at this juncture, however, there was no push for deporting the entire Armenian population. In late March 1915, when Cemal learned that some Armenians in Aleppo had grown afraid for their safety and were taking precautions, he wrote to Aleppo's governor that he must assure Armenians and the entire population that the government was pursuing and punishing any crimes, including those committed against Armenians. Cemal also stressed to the governor that "the majority of our Armenian compatriots are aggrieved by the actions of an insignificant few. Their devotion to the fatherland is beyond any doubt."[56] His comments suggest that at least some members of the Unionist elite remained committed to safeguarding the entire civilian population.

In early 1915 a sense of panic crept into the capital. In addition to the possible invasion of the Gulf of Alexandretta, Allied forces were preparing a naval campaign to pry open the Dardanelles and invade the Gallipoli Peninsula. The objective was to capture the Ottoman capital and reopen transportation routes between the Russian Black Sea and the Mediterranean, and between Russia and Russia's alliance partners. Watching this development, the Unionists took measures to evacuate the city and relocate the government to the Anatolian city of Konya.[57] In mid-February 1915 Kitchener informed Maxwell of a change in plans. There would be a major Anglo-French naval campaign against Gallipoli, and the invasion of Alexandretta was on hold.[58] The planned campaign and the Armenian volunteers' support for it in no way justify the Unionists' later policies of destroying an entire, centuries-old Ottoman Armenian world. It does show, however, the way in which the war put these policies in motion.

The Unionist government further tightened their grip on speech and the unfolding narrative about the war. The government declared Ottoman Turkish the only acceptable language in official communication and business affairs, legally disqualifying other languages spoken in the empire.[59]

These political goals predated the outbreak of the First World War. On February 20, 1915, the Assembly debated a proposal for charging a special tax on store signs using a foreign language, but the discussion clearly blurred the lines between "foreign" languages and languages spoken in the Ottoman Empire other than Ottoman Turkish. In the Assembly, Vartkes suggested the law should explicitly include Armenian, Greek, Arabic, Ladino, Hebrew, and any other language spoken by Ottomans as acceptable languages. When a colleague responded that there was only one "official language," Vartkes grew irate: "You cannot prevent me, an Ottoman Armenian, from writing in Armenian. And you cannot tax me for it."[60]

Perhaps to hide news about the Sarıkamış disaster, the government sought further legislation to curtail the flow of information in the empire. Emmanouil Emmanouilidis, the Greek Orthodox deputy from Izmir, rose in objection. Given the censorship regime in place already, there was no need for additional legislation, he argued. "The press can't write anything." Interrupting Emmanouilidis, a deputy asked, "What country does not have censorship right now?" Emmanouilidis replied, "Am I permitted to speak in this Assembly? Until now we have always had freedom of speech here, and mutual respect." He continued, "Our censorship doesn't just touch military operations; it is affecting everything, all aspects of life. It touches the very rules of speech." The Assembly president, Halil, issued a reprimand to Emmanouilidis for openly challenging the policies of the government.[61] Throughout the war, the Unionists continued their repression of all forms of dissent.

With the bitter military failures at Sarıkamış and Suez behind them and anticipating an Allied naval attack on the Straits in April 1915, the Unionists declared the empire's Armenian population in rebellion. Both Cemal and Enver felt personally humiliated by their military defeats; Cemal suppressed the news, and later, in 1917, said of Enver, "Whatever he touches, he fails at it. The two offensives in the Caucasus were a crime. The troops simply starved to death."[62] Upon his return to the capital, Enver gave orders to keep two locomotives permanently "on steam" starting on January 29, 1915. The first of these was designated for taking the sultan and his entourage, if the situation turned critical, to Konya "as a military measure." The second train would transport the grand vizier and the ministers if evacuating the capital became necessary.[63]

On April 24, 1915, the government began arresting Armenian political leaders, businessmen, and intellectuals in the capital. The following month, on May 24, the governments of Britain, France, and Russia, on the latter's initiative, declared that the Ottoman Empire was committing "crimes against humanity and civilization" and that they would "hold personally responsible members of the Ottoman government."[64] Three days later, on May 27, 1915, Interior Minister Talat issued the infamous order to deport any individuals or groups deemed to endanger Ottoman military operations.

That same month, in May 1915, the government issued a series of regulations pertaining to the confiscation of Armenian property. The regulations added a veneer of legality by stipulating that the owners would be compensated, but no such compensation ever took place.[65] As the Assembly was not in session, regulations were adopted as "temporary laws," without parliamentary deliberation or approval. When parliament reopened in September 1915, Ahmed Rıza immediately submitted a request (*takrir*) in the Senate for an investigation into the deportations and reports of mass killings of Armenians. He demanded permission to read his request in the chamber, but was denied, on the grounds that it pertained to the conduct of war and broached military matters.[66] The following week, he admonished his colleagues and the government, "The Armenians today in their mountains are wandering, roaming aimlessly, impoverished and bewildered. Before the winter season arrives, they must be returned to their homes or to wherever their safety can be ensured. I expect that from the government's sense of justice and fairness . . . ('hear, hear', from the Assembly delegates)."[67]

In a session of the Senate on October 11, 1915, Ahmed Rıza proposed a law that protected Armenian property and prevented the homes of deported Armenians from being sold.[68] When the bill came up for deliberation, in December 1915, he challenged the slew of temporary laws the government had adopted during the parliament's suspension over the preceding months. He insisted his proposed bill be passed immediately. Otherwise, if the Assembly took its time, "there won't be any property or possessions left" and that "there won't be anything for us to debate." He argued there were "no legal grounds for designating the property under discussion as abandoned property," as the government's temporary laws had done. "The owners of this property, the Armenians," Ahmed Rıza continued, "did not leave behind their property willingly. They were removed from their place by force." And now "the government's officials are selling their property." Ahmed Rıza urged his colleagues, "Our state," as opposed to the government, "never permits or wishes for tyranny and cruelty [*gadr ve zulmü*]." Therefore, "if I don't want to sell my property no one can force me to." He reminded his colleagues, "Article 21 of the constitution forbids this. If there exists a constitution and constitutional rule in this country, then this cannot be. This is oppression. Drag me by the arm, expel me from my village, and then sell my property: this is never lawful. Neither the Ottomans' conscience nor any law allows this." Others in the Assembly defended the bill, saying the constitution allowed for the adoption of temporary laws. Ahmed Rıza responded that temporary laws were constitutional, but this law violated the constitution. He urged them not to postpone debate: "The Armenians' property has been plundered in part already. By the time the legislature rejects the [governments' temporary] laws, nothing will be left. All the damage will already have been done." Citing procedure, Aristidi Pasha, a Greek Orthodox member of the senate who had served as forests, minerals, and commerce minister in 1909, opined that the law could not be considered in the senate but must originate in the lower house, the Assembly; Ahmed Rıza objected, noting that the Senate's hands were not tied. "Why can't we make a law and send it to the government?"[69] The meeting moved on to the next item of business.

Ahmed Rıza was right that any intervention would arrive too late. By June 1915 the government had already begun the process of resettling Muslim refugees from the Balkans and the Caucasus in the villages and homes of deported Armenians.[70]

That same month, on June 15, 1915, Interior Minister Talat told Hans Humann, a political officer at the German embassy, that "we are now ridding ourselves of the Armenians in order to be better allies to you." By "better allies" Talat said he meant "allies without the liability of an internal enemy." Relaying the conversation back to Berlin, Humann added, "The Armenians are now more or less being exterminated [*ausgerottet*] for their conspiracy with the Russians! This is a harsh but useful policy." Born in Izmir/Smyrna, the son of an archaeologist, Humann was a childhood friend of War Minister Enver and was charged with keeping tabs on the German ambassador, Hans von Wangenheim. Wangenheim clearly disapproved of Talat's Armenian policy, to Humann's dismay. "Unfortunately, to our great detriment," Humann noted, "Ambassador Wangenheim won't stop complaining [about the Unionists' violent measures]."[71] Humann's remarks reveal both Talat's coldblooded determination to carry out ethnic cleansing and the fact that the German government was willing to tolerate her Ottoman ally's horrific policies. Ambassador Wangenheim's complaints in Berlin fell largely on deaf ears. In October, the ambassador died of a heart attack.

Talat repeated the point in a conversation two days later with the chief translator at the German embassy, Dr. Johannes Heinrich Mordtmann. Born and raised in Istanbul, Mordtmann after the First World War became a professor of Ottoman Studies in Berlin. Mordtmann also reported that Talat had shared his intention to use the war to "finish up thoroughly [*gründlich aufzuräumen*] with its internal enemies—the domestic Christians—without being disturbed by diplomatic intervention from abroad." Repeating what he had told Humann, Talat sought to convince Mordtmann that this policy "is also in the interest of Turkey's ally Germany, because Turkey in this way will be stronger."[72]

After the war, Talat talked about this decision in the memoir he began writing in his hideout in Berlin in 1921. He claimed that he had initially opposed deportation, because "I knew," he wrote, that the process of relocating the entire Armenian population "would have appalling consequences." Police and gendarmerie forces had been conscripted into the army, Talat explained, and therefore irregular forces, so-called militias, had to be tasked with evacuating Armenian village populations.[73] If Talat ever had such hesitations, he had cast them aside by early 1915.

In August 1915 Kress, the German commander so influential in the Syrian theater, traveled across Anatolia to Damascus. On his journey he saw "some seventy thousand" Armenians languishing in large camps, "the misery impossible to put into words." The deportees were being held for further transport, waiting "in the worst possible state of hygiene." Kress found the deportations he witnessed appalling beyond belief. He was not alone: "Not only all the Europeans, but also many Turks and Arabs," according to Kress, "were outraged by these cruelties being visited upon the Armenians."[74] Upon returning to Jerusalem on October 14, 1915, Kress reported what he had just witnessed to Cemal, who promised to order the delivery of food to the deportees Kress had seen.[75]

Cemal's pledge to send provisions notwithstanding, by the following month conditions had worsened. At the end of November, Enver summoned Cemal and Kress to a meeting in Istanbul. Traveling in one of the country's few automobiles, the two men saw the "streets still jammed with Armenian deportees. Countless Armenian corpses unburied along the side of the road. Shocking scenes." Cemal stared in silence, shaken to the core, according to Kress. When Cemal finally spoke, he sought to distance himself from the tragedy unfolding before his eyes: "My colleagues in Istanbul issue their orders without much worry; they don't have to witness the horrible consequences of their orders."[76]

In the capital, the government moved full steam ahead. On December 14, 1915, War Minister Enver ordered that all non-Muslims still employed in any branches of the military be removed "within twenty-four hours." These measures were necessary, the order said, because "recently captured documents" gave evidence of "our enemies' espionage operations within our own borders." Sent to all ministries in the capital and all the armies in the field, the orders required that all "non-Muslims (Armenians, Greek Orthodox, Jews) be dismissed from their positions immediately, even if considered indispensable, and sent to places outside of Istanbul, away from points of defense or the front." Each office was to report the names of the deportees and the locale to which they had been sent.[77] After the war, Kress concluded that "we Germans—soldiers and civilians alike," and the German government and public, "which had knowledge of these events in all their detail," were "morally just as culpable" as their Ottoman counterparts.[78]

In late 1915 another German officer, Captain Wilhelm Busse, accompanied Cemal back to Syria. Rolling out of Haydarpasha station at 4:05 p.m. on December 16, 1915, the train arrived thirty-five hours later at Pozantı in "a very good performance of the Anatolian Railway." Until Konya, the train had run on coal, then switched to wood for the rest of the journey. The passengers crossed the unfinished parts of the railway through the mountains by car, then reboarded and continued by train to Aleppo. Once in Syria, Busse traveled extensively and prepared three detailed reports. The Aleppo headquarters of Cemal's Fourth Army operated out of the Hotel Baron, whose owner, an Armenian, had "avoided deportation by providing this service," according to Busse. The city had been hit by waves of disease. "For months, Armenian deportees were marched through rather than around the city, as is the practice now." Still traveling with Cemal, Busse was just as horrified by what he witnessed as his colleague Kress earlier: "I saw an orphanage and a camp and found the horrible stories I have heard confirmed." Busse was told that deportees were now being provided with food. He believed that "without German pressure and German aid the misery would have been much greater than it is undeniably now." He also saw how "the police retrieved two hundred and fifty children from the orphanage and attached them to an Armenian deportee caravan headed east." And he knew that "since the temperature fell to eight degrees Celsius at night and the children's clothes were very scant, this measure amounted to a death sentence." Busse felt his and his government's hands were tied, because this was a "purely" internal affair.[79]

Poisoned Relations: War as Personal Experience

Surrounded by a crowd of weeping wives, mothers, and children, twenty-seven-year-old Ali Rıza reported for duty following the mobilization orders issued on August 3, 1914, at his birthplace near the eastern Anatolian city of Erzincan. Within a few weeks, he was surrounded by snow and freezing cold, infected with dysentery and discharging blood "in my urine and from my bottom," and, a few days later, through his mouth. He had seen the first victims among his comrades succumb to dysentery before ever encountering the enemy. "The poor wretches," he noted in his diary on October 3, 1914. The empire was not yet at war, but Ali Rıza and the other soldiers were on their way through the mountains to Sarıkamış, where in January about 80 to 90 percent of the Third Army would perish. Ali Rıza was a common soldier; because his older brother was a doctor and officer, Ali Rıza was assigned to the medical corps as an assistant to the battalion doctor. His brother's position also meant that, unlike many of his peers, Ali Rıza had cash to purchase food and clothing during the initial weeks of mobilization. As Ali Rıza's unit marched east, bread was produced in the bakeries of villages they passed, in ovens fueled by cow dung, which greatly slowed down the process of baking bread. Four days into his unit's first engagement, on November 11, two of his comrades froze to death in what would become a common end for many soldiers.[80]

In most accounts their tragedy is glossed over with the Ottoman triumph of Gallipoli or ignored given the brutal Ottoman policies toward Christian populations that culminated in the destruction of Anatolia's Assyrians and Armenians. Yet the extreme deprivation, poverty, exposure to disease, and lawlessness enabled such policies of destruction. Already in the fall of 1914, as Ali Rıza saw, many of his peers had already deserted—at least half a million by the end of the war, or one out of every six men conscripted.[81] Deserters were shot on the spot to keep anyone else from contemplating flight. Desertion, already significant, and certainly understandable, was in fact the first charge levied against Armenians. By December 1914, Armenians in the ranks were being singled out as potential defectors to the Russian side and being shot preemptively—"accidentally," as the saying went. Ali Rıza was filled with anger at Armenians, swearing, on January 17, 1915, after the Sarıkamış campaign had taken the lives of tens of thousands (from disease and winter conditions as much as Russian action), to "poison and kill 3 or 4 Armenians in the hospital." He could not believe that Armenians and Turks would be "brothers and fellow citizens" once again after the war; the campaign to invade Russian territory at Sarıkamış had been too much.[82] Ali Rıza's sense that the war was irreversibly severing the ties that had held together the empire's ethnic and religious groups for centuries would prove devastatingly accurate.

Many Ottoman men, whether Christian, Jewish, or Muslim, sought to evade conscription. The Ottoman army had the highest desertion rate of any First World War army. Conscription and war requisitions, therefore, often proceeded at gunpoint. In Van province, for example, troops surrounded Ararots Church and "took to the garrison all the Armenians" coming out of the service.[83] The same authorities took with them "Armenians and Turks engaged in commerce on the square, without regard to age or size."[84]

The greatest danger facing Kalusd and Yervant, the two Armenians who had served in the Ottoman army and whom we encountered earlier, was not foreign troops but the military in which they served. They both narrowly escaped deportation. Kalusd was perhaps saved by the intervention of an officer in Erzurum, Fuad Ziya Bey. Yervant survived thanks to a benevolent commander who used Yervant's rudimentary sewing skills and then his ability to play the bugle to keep him employed. Yervant eventually converted to Islam, after which he was known as Zia. Both Kalusd's and Yervant's survival depended to a great extent on their status as officers, a status few Armenians could claim.

A few weeks after Yervant's school was shut down in early November 1914, the governor, Ahmet Muammer and the police commissioner led a "bloodthirsty mob" to the school and "violently removed the cross that sat atop the small chapel and replaced it with a crescent." Shortly thereafter, in late 1914, Kalusd noted, the government had the priest Sahak Odabashian killed, sending shockwaves throughout the Armenian population. Odabashian had been traveling from Bursa to assume his new post at Erzincan when he was murdered. Another worrying sign, according to Kalusd, was the fact that Armenian conscripts were being employed as porters, carrying military matériel on foot across long distances such as the road through the mountains between Erzincan and Erzurum.[85]

On May 18–21, 1915, the Armenian notables of Erzincan were put on notice that they would have to leave the city. The next day, Kalusd was dispatched to Erzurum, leaving behind his family. The roughly "40 Armenian villages of Erzurum" had already been deported, and Kalusd found the roads crowded with deportees.[86] A month later, the authorities issued instructions for the deportation of Armenians in Yervant's city of Sivas. He heard the announcement in church from his priest, Father Kalemkerian: "The government has been told that some people have stashed weapons in this Church. I'm to stay here while they tear it down and look for them."[87] In Yervant's case, conscription came as a savior, "just weeks before my family was forcibly made to take the road of deportation." "The only Armenians left in Sivas" were "soldiers, apostates, and [those] who knew crafts that were valuable to the Ottoman government."[88]

Officials in Sivas issued a formal deportation order on June 15, 1915. As Yervant put it, "the Bezia neighborhood, the first to be deported, went on the death march" on June 22, 1915.[89] His use of the phrase "death march" raises the question as to whether Sivas deportees thought of their removal in these terms or if he applied that designation retrospectively. According to Yervant, the deportees knew what lay in store: "Eventually came the turn of my neighborhood, on July 3, 1915. Like everyone else, the Armenians were told they would be taken to a peaceful, stable region, where they would be able to establish their own communities. They were told to leave their belongings behind [and] that they would be sent after them. However, we all knew what was going on, so most Armenians sold most of their belongings at dirt cheap prices."[90]

Yervant lost fifty-one family members in the deportations. Aware of the charges brought against Armenians as revolutionaries, he noted in his memoir that "none of these innocent victims were a member of any political party or were involved in any type of political activity." They had not done anything to undermine the Ottoman war effort, and "their only crime was being Armenian."[91] Kalusd saw the immediate cause behind the deportations as Enver's defeat at the Battle of Sarıkamış in January 1915. Upon his return to Istanbul, Enver ordered all Armenian soldiers and officers into positions away from the front but, as Kalusd noted, most were killed before reaching their new assignments. Enver and Talat, Kalusd wrote, planned the destruction of the Armenians and put Governor Muammer of Sivas, District Governor Memduh of Erzincan, and Bahaeddin Şakir, a prominent Unionist, in charge of this policy. Then, Kalusd continued, "from jails they released murderers and robbers [*haydut*] to form gangs to carry out this 'holy business.'"[92] In fact, as a high-ranking officer (and later war minister) recorded in his diary, the army had already begun to form "a militia and a national organization [*teşkilât-ı milliye*] against Armenian gangs" in March 1915.[93]

Upon learning of the deportations in Erzincan, Kalusd rushed back to look for his family. The trip was harrowing. A man Kalusd encountered on the journey spoke "of rumors that all Erzincan Armenians have been deported and massacred in the valley and that none survived." Kalusd remembered that terrifying moment: "I sat down on a large rock and watched the sky and the sun, . . . I could not see anything around me. That day seemed like the last day of the world to me, nothing made sense."[94] Arriving in Erzincan, he found that his family had been deported two weeks prior. Entering his emptied home, he recalled the joyous celebration of his wedding just ten months ago: "It was as if the walls were going to collapse on me."[95]

Life became even more precarious for Kalusd and Yervant. Yervant was one of the last Armenians remaining in Sivas. He was summoned by his commander and told there were orders "from the top" that Armenians could no longer serve in the army, that they had to convert to Islam or be deported. Yervant thought he had to "choose between life and death." Yervant and six other Armenians initially refused to convert, while the majority of Armenian conscripts agreed to do so.[96] When Yervant eventually converted, he received training as an officer and learned how to operate machine guns. Promoted to second lieutenant, he served at Gallipoli and Izmir/Smyrna.[97]

Kalusd sought to hide his Armenian identity from his soldiers and fellow officers as the war went on. When he objected to his fellow soldiers boasting of attacking Armenians, they replied, "The sultan ordered the killing of the unbelievers—who are you to hold us back?"[98] Later, as he heard a fellow officer's account of how Armenians had been killed, Kalusd felt "as though the entire world had become a cemetery."[99] Among Kurdish fighters who had carried out raids on deportees, Kalusd felt himself "a sheep in wolves' clothes hiding in a pack of wolves."[100] Following the route of the deportees to locate his family, Kalusd feigned a toothache and bandaged his face, fearful that some deportees might recognize him and expose his Armenian identity.[101]

Abandoning his command to look for his family, Kalusd encountered hundreds of bodies at Kemah, near the Euphrates River, "swollen, disfigured, unrecognizable."[102] He finally found his family, alive, about a hundred miles south of Erzincan. His ethnicity revealed, Kalusd was immediately arrested, charged with distributing weapons to deportees and inciting rebellion.[103] He spent the next three months under arrest but through another officer secured a safe place for his family in Arapgir. The details of how he rescued his family and himself remain unclear. Once he was out of jail, his uniform, weapon, missed pay, and officer status were restored. He reunited with his family in Arapgir, except for his beloved mother, who had succumbed to illness.[104]

Both Yervant and Kalusd reported having been in close contact with high officials and experiencing the temptation to exact revenge. When General Liman von Sanders and Enver Pasha ate at the mess hall Yervant oversaw at Menemen, he considered poisoning them. "Oh, how I was anxious to serve them a good meal.... Perhaps their last one.... When I realized I would come into close contact with their food, I thought of poisoning the meal, and I almost put that plan into motion, but I had to remind myself that if I had assassinated Enver Pasha, I would not have been the only one paying the price for the act."[105] Similarly, Kalusd considered killing Memduh Bey, the district governor (*mutasarrıf*) of Erzincan. But he knew that acting on his desire would cost him his own life. Only the knowledge that if he killed Memduh he would not see his family again prevented him from going through with the plan.[106]

The "Sultanate of Turkey"

In early 1916 the Assembly once again took up legislation requiring companies to use Ottoman Turkish as the language of their business affairs. Interior Minister Talat was in attendance and intent on personally ushering it through. According to Talat, the law's purpose was to get foreign enterprises to use Turkish instead of French, Russian, Italian, or Spanish. The deputy from Damascus, Faris al-Khoury, suggested changing "Turkish" to "Turkish and local languages [*Türkçe ve lisan-ı mahallî*]," to include Arabic. Cemil Zehavi/Jamil Zahawi, the deputy from Baghdad, supported the change, saying that not allowing Arabic in Arab-speaking regions would impede economic development. He added that if the law pertained only to a company's direct correspondence with the government, this should be stated explicitly. Haralambidi, the deputy from Istanbul, thought the law was unconstitutional; the constitution declared Ottoman Turkish the official language but did not prescribe what languages people could or could not speak. Talat argued that the law did not violate the constitution. The Assembly voted in favor of the bill, sending it on to the Senate.[107]

In the Senate, too, the language question touched off a heated debate. As ever, Ahmed Rıza boldly took the stage: "For a while now there has been this Turkishness line, and the erroneous ways in which it has been pursued has brought distance and alienation to the peoples who are not Turks. Laws like these will give birth to ugly suspicions among the population. At a delicate and precarious moment such as this one, when what we need is for the population and all the various people to be united and to work together, it is wrong to adopt policies that might alienate them from the government."[108] Like the Unionists, Ahmed Rıza desired unity, but the methods he espoused were radically different.

Ahmed Rıza also requested that the government send its representatives before the parliament closed and that it offer "a general account of the state of the country" to the legislature and the elected deputies of the people. He demanded that the Unionists account for the temporary laws they had passed: "Everyone believes things are going badly and that, if things were going well, they'd be announced and proclaimed. Newspapers that are being received by German and Austrian officers do not depict our armies in an encouraging light. This kind of news is spread by word of mouth. The government should come and give us a clear picture."[109] Then Ahmed Rıza questioned the Unionists' conduct of the war altogether:

> A captain of a ship might be incredibly patriotic but might not know how to run their ship. Or this captain might get confused in a storm and run aground. It is possible that our government, too, without intending to, is in fact steering this ship of state into dangerous waters. Once we crash into the cliffs it will not do us any good to receive information here. We should all know that now.[110]

The Senate president noted that information could be requested from the government but insisted that the empire's military position was secure: "There is nothing to worry about, thank god."[111]

The Senate continued debating the language bill. Aristidi Pasha, the Greek Orthodox senator who had previously served in the lower house as the elected deputy from Aydın, defended the proposed law, saying, "This is Turkey [*Türkiye*], and we are Turks [*Türk'üz*]." Manuk Azaryan Efendi, an Ottoman Armenian senator, chimed in: "Everyone here knows that I am proud to be an Ottoman; I have been serving this state for forty-six years. From the bottom of my heart, I want our people and our country to make progress. There should be no doubt about that, not even for a second." Small companies, however, should be exempt from the language requirement, Manuk Azaryan Efendi noted. Nail Bey, a former education minister and teacher of Turkish, opposed the law: "Turkish isn't the only language spoken in our country. Why should we forbid some Ottomans from conducting business in their own languages? This would be a limitation on their personal freedoms." Bohor [Eskenazi], the Salonika-born Jewish senator, disagreed, saying, "Until now the state gave complete freedoms to the various peoples [*anasır-ı muhtelife*]; it says establish your own schools as you like, speak whatever language you prefer." Bohor argued that requiring Turkish as the common language would create Ottoman citizens: "We brought all the foreign languages to our private schools, but we rejected the Ottoman language." Manuk Azaryan objected, saying, "God forbid! I reject your words. I protest." He maintained that Turkish was being taught in all schools. Manuk Azaryan's words, uttered at a time when the Unionist government, in the name of its revolutionary aims, waged war on its own citizens, came rather unexpectedly. Perhaps the Armenian senator was dutifully performing his loyalty to the government and demonstrating his commitment to Ottoman unity, hoping to mitigate the Unionists' violent lashing out against members of his community. Or, perhaps, his rationale stemmed from a residual hope for postwar coexistence, or perhaps some mixture of both.

Then Musa Kazim, a member of the Unionist government, took the floor. He started by saying that "all the government is trying to do is to make sure everyone knows our official language within four years. I don't understand how this would limit anyone's freedom?" When Azaryan asked whether it could be "learned in four years," Musa Kazim could only reply that "everyone should learn it." But then he made clear what the government's motivation was: he noted that "this sultanate is a Muslim sultanate, and this is Turkey, and the official language is Turkish. Therefore, the adoption of this law is absolutely necessary." Musa Kazım's idea of establishing unity and a common language clearly had a different conception than that of Ahmed Rıza, Aristidi, or Bohor. Musa Kazım had nothing to say about what had changed that now demanded the push for a single language. Why did multilingualism no longer meet the empire's needs? Bringing the focus back to business affairs, Ahmed Rıza asked whether there was any evidence that the Ottoman economy would benefit from the Turkish language requirement. He himself did not think so. Then he added, "And this is not, as Musa Kazim Efendi has claimed, the Sultanate of Turkey [*Saltanat-ı Türkiye*]. As the constitution states clearly, this is the Ottoman Sultanate. The government's representatives are Ottomans. The Sultanate of Turkey is his own invention. To be clear once again, I, too, hope for the broader use of the Turkish language through suitable means, but this is not the time for that, and to do it now is harmful and dangerous."[112] Musa Kazım's arguments should not be read as expressions of nationalism but as an aggressive determination to put an end to multiethnicity. It was not a bid for popular support but a strategy to keep European power out of the empire.

"Because the Armenians Have Been Deported in Their Entirety and All the Muslims Have Been Conscripted"[113]

When Talat was telling Humann about his resolve "to rid" the empire of Armenians, in July 1915, governors from several affected provinces warned the Interior Ministry that local production and markets were collapsing. If there were to be a harvest, the army had to release soldiers for agricultural labor. Whether the governors were concerned about production or this was a way to resist Istanbul's Armenian policy, or both, is not entirely clear. Concerned about the disruption to agricultural work and the ability to feed troops and maintain morale, Talat ordered the commander of the Third Army, Mahmud Kâmil, headquartered in Erzurum, to release some eighteen thousand soldiers for work in the fields, "because the Armenians have been deported in their entirety [*kâmilen*] and all the Muslims have been conscripted."[114] Sivas province should receive fifteen thousand and Diyarbekir province three thousand soldiers. If these men were not made available, the harvest would be jeopardized and "dearth and famine [*kaht-ü-gala*]" would seize the country, endangering "the army's supplies" and thus potentially opening the road to military "disaster."[115] General Mahmud Kâmil assented to the request immediately, promising that he would have the men in place within a few days' time.[116] Requisitioning, conscription, and deportation had emptied the fields and caused agriculture to collapse. The army now returned to rebuild what it had destroyed.

Hilmar Kaiser has argued compellingly that "the notion of an empire-wide genocide of Ottoman Armenians perpetrated by a unified CUP [Unionist leadership] is untenable."[117] The Unionists' war aims were a consequence of their revolutionary fight against the international order. That fight had commenced in the nineteenth century and was full-blown by 1908. And yet the destruction of the empire's Armenians was not a long-term consequence of prewar dynamics but resulted from the dynamics of the war itself. It is true that issues of nationality, language, and multi-ethnicity remained unresolved in 1914. But it was the context of total war that moved some Unionists to enforce the radical policies of mass deportation and permanent uprooting of the empire's Christian populations. Unionist culpability and the deleterious effects of imperialism should not be viewed as mutually exclusive explanations. Minimizing the imperial and colonial context, however, leads to false conclusion, such as that ethnonational or ethnoreligious identities were the cause rather than the symptom and result of the Unionists' wartime mass violence.

The conflicts that resulted from the Unionists' wartime policies, together with four years of wartime hunger, disease, and famine, lit a match to the empire's social fabric. Although some imperial sinews remained, the war became a crucible of new political identities that profoundly transformed the region. Despite being cornered by the Great Powers, the Unionists had, of course, options other than resorting to mass violence in front of them. Such options were being aired publicly by prominent leaders such as Prince Sabahaddin Bey, grandson of Sultan Abdülmecid I and nephew of Sultan Abdülhamid II. Other prominent voices included the Armenian physician and deputy in the Assembly, Krikor Zohrab, and the Greek Orthodox intellectual and deputy Emmanouil Emmanouilidis. Arab leaders such as Ruhi al-Khalidi, Shakib Arslan, or even Sharif Husayn of Mecca, also proposed alternatives to the hyper-centralized imperial rule of the Unionists. It is to their disappointments and responses that we now turn.

6

Resistance, Rebellion, and Revolution

THE END OF THE OTTOMAN EMPIRE

UNIONIST RULE had led to war, famine, and genocide. Perhaps unsurprisingly, it generated a wide range of resistance movements, uprisings, and rebellions across the empire. All the participant countries of the First World War eventually saw mounting opposition to their governments' conduct, especially once conditions of hunger became widespread. Revolution and civil war toppled the Russian government in 1917, ending the Romanov dynasty and transforming the Russian world forever. Although the Ottoman dynasty, the House of Osman, survived until November 1922, the consequences of the war were no less transformative in the lands of the Ottoman Empire.

The deprivation brought on by war and the state's policies first enfeebled and then shattered the Ottoman state's legitimacy. In 1913 Ohannes Pasha, an Armenian Christian, assumed the post of governor of Mount Lebanon. He was deemed the right person for the job in part because of his well-known commitment to Ottomanism and the constitution. By war's end, his faith in the empire as a multireligious, multinational project was dead.[1] Private Ihsan, a Muslim Arab conscript in Jerusalem, expressed the feeling of many that the government had abandoned its people. He noted in his diary on December 17, 1915, that "if the government had any dignity, it would have saved wheat" in its wheat depots "for public distribution at a fixed price, or even have made it available from military supplies. If these conditions persist, the people will rebel and bring down this government."[2] Nazik Jawdat, born on the outskirts of Aleppo in 1903, voiced the transformation of so many Ottomans: "I had been brought up as an Ottoman patriot, and I was one, but now things had changed," she recalled. The "Ottomans were divided and killing each other. The war had forced us—Turks, Arabs, Kurds, Circassians—to question our identity. On which side did I belong and what was I expected to do?"[3] During the war, both Enver and Cemal visited Nazik Jawdat's school, the Teacher's Training College for girls, where a wartime decree had changed the school's language from Arabic, Nazik's mother tongue, to Turkish, as the sole language of instruction.[4]

Perhaps the most widely known instance of opposition to the wartime government is the revolt launched in June 1916 by Sharif Husayn of Mecca, made famous by David Lean's Oscar-winning 1962 film, *Lawrence of Arabia*. Leaning on British promises of an independent Arab state under his rule, Sharif Husayn mobilized a force against Istanbul. Another instance is the Armenian armed resistance against the state's deportation policies, most prominently at Van in April 1915 and Aleppo, the latter retold in the novel by the Austrian writer Franz Werfel, *The Forty Days of Musa Dagh*, published in 1933.[5] Throughout 1915–1916, moreover, armed uprisings along the Tigris River, from Mosul to Baghdad, contested Ottoman authority. A less known phenomenon was the opposition network that formed in European cities like Bern, Geneva, and Paris, where Entente governments provided opposition groups with cover and facilitated their work. The five hundred thousand men in uniform who deserted should be considered yet another avenue of massive resistance. Of the roughly three million men conscripted into the Ottoman army over the course of the war, one out of six deserted, a level unmatched in any of the armies fighting in the First World War.[6] The thousands of protest petitions sent to the government, especially by women on the home front, confronting hunger and state policies of requisition, represented another form of important resistance.[7] Finally, a small yet vocal opposition sat right in the heart of the empire's capital, in the Ottoman parliament, questioning the state's conduct of the war in nearly every single session.

This chapter examines aspects of these various forms of opposition. The bitter experiences of the war engendered widespread resistance that carried into the postwar period. When European powers concluded an armistice in November 1918, resistance, rebellion, and revolution continued in the Ottoman lands unabated. War-torn and defeated, the people of the Ottoman Empire rejected the new colonial rule set up by the Great Powers at the Paris Peace Conference and the League of Nations.

Resistance Groups Take Action

From north to south, the three Ottoman provinces of Mosul, Baghdad, and Basra comprised the empire's long southeastern border region with Iran. The provinces were tied commercially by the Euphrates, linguistically by Arabic, and religiously by Shia Islam; after the war they formed the basis of the future Iraq. Here, along the Euphrates, as in Anatolia, village criers and posters announced the army's mobilization and the commencement of conscription on August 3, 1914.

While the number of conscripts during the first year of the war remains unknown, the number of those who deserted in Baghdad alone reached twenty thousand. Large groups of deserters began crowding into Najaf. Situated on the eastern edge of the Arabian Desert, as the burial place of Ali ibn Abi Talib, the first Shi'i imam, Najaf was one of the region's spiritual centers and one of Shia Islam's holiest places. There, deserters—some aided by British agents—called for revolution and the end of Ottoman rule over the Euphrates region. A special Ottoman gendarmerie force arrived in the city in May 1915 looking for deserters, questioning the men, and searching the women on suspicion that deserters were hiding in female dress. On May 22, 1915, in a surprise operation, deserters and locals hit back, killing some twenty soldiers and forcing the entire unit's surrender. By the end of 1915, towns all along the Euphrates River—Karbala, Hilla, Kufa, Shamiyya, Tuwayrij—followed suit and took up arms, attacking telegraph offices and other official buildings.[8]

As if conscription and requisitioning were not enough to ensure the military's unpopularity, coercive and punitive measures taken by individual commanders rendered the state's footing among the populace infinitely worse. Government authorities believed that any form of popular resistance should be harshly suppressed for the purpose of deterrence. No signs of disloyalty could be tolerated: "The people of Iraq revolt when they are not subjected to force and violence. This has been proven by history," one official memorandum said.[9]

Baghdad's governor saw the solution in replacing the police force composed of locals with "men from Anatolia" because, according to the governor, local police units were joining the rebellion, especially at Najaf and Karbala. He asked for what he considered to be a modest unit of reinforcement, some two hundred men.[10] Two weeks later, the War Ministry denied the request.[11] With the Gallipoli Peninsula under attack, Eastern Anatolia ravaged by war and violent deportations, Beirut, Damascus, and Jerusalem under surveillance, and Sharif Husayn of Mecca increasingly restless, the army had no manpower to spare.

In Hillah, a city on the Euphrates some sixty miles south of Baghdad, authorities shot at deserters, sometimes in crowded places, with women and children huddling for cover, demonstrating the state's ruthless determination to suppress any resistance. These actions evoked colonial rule; Ottoman forces appeared to be an occupying army rather than defenders of the land. But the authorities' demonstration of power proved insufficient. In August 1915 Hillah's residents and a force of deserters ransacked the local army garrison and official buildings. When Ottoman reinforcements eventually arrived, the Hillah movement had joined forces with the surrounding region's tribal population. It took Ottoman authorities over a year to reassert control over the Euphrates region and required the dispatch of an additional force of some five thousand men, complete with artillery and airpower.

By December 1916 Hillah had become the site of an encounter "verging on a massacre."[12] Over fifteen hundred residents lay dead; the authorities had arrested and hanged some one hundred and twenty-six opposition figures and resistance fighters. An estimated fourteen hundred homes had been burned to the ground, and a large group of civilians, including women and children, was marched into exile in Diyarbekir, some five hundred and sixty miles to the north. The deportation prompted Richard von Kühlmann, who had replaced Wangenheim as ambassador after the latter's death in October 1915, to warn the Foreign Office in Berlin that "it is not desirable that the notorious Armenian migratory camps [*Wanderlager*] are revived in a new Arab edition." Kühlmann added that deportations only hurt the Ottoman war effort, because they eventually turned into "a source of epidemics which in effect kill masses of brave Turkish soldiers."[13]

Like Kühlmann, some Ottoman officials, too, worried about Istanbul's heavy-handed suppression measures and their effects. Officers in the Sixth Army, based in Baghdad, rebuked the Unionists' policies and rang alarm bells. In January 1916 Yusuf Ziya, second in command of the Thirteenth Army Corps, objected to the orders coming down from Istanbul. He had serious doubts regarding the effectiveness of the government's methods. The War Ministry demanded that deserters be shot, but Yusuf Ziya refused to follow such orders. Instead, deserters, the latest six hundred and sixty of them, had been arrested and put into labor battalions tasked with road construction. These deserters, "whose numbers are very large," should never be executed, Yusuf Ziya argued. Doing so would not deter others from deserting, which the policy was intended to accomplish. Yusuf Ziya added that a recent law calling for the families of deserters to be exiled from their homes should be rescinded immediately. And in any case, no means of transportation for such a removal existed. He proposed the government suspend conscripting the next class of recruits, those born in the years 1896 and 1897 (then turning twenty and nineteen, respectively): "I think we would lose much more than we would gain in Iraq through such a measure." Resentment of the Ottoman government and state was palpable everywhere, according to Yusuf Ziya. For this he blamed the Ottoman authorities themselves: "The officials who have been sent to Iraq so far have not understood how to rule the people here and have only attracted their hatred." Yusuf Ziya warned that "Iraq's population will turn away even further from the government and will attempt, if possible, to raise an internal rebellion against the government." He pointed to the recent rebellions at Karbala and Najaf as dangerous signs. "May god prevent any further rebellion," he prayed, and asked "what consequences did the punitive expeditions have in the Hawran and in Yemen and in Albania! Here, too, we would only suffer the same bitter consequences," by which he meant armed resistance and rebellion.[14] Yusuf Ziya's warnings, however, went unheeded.

From Kut on the Tigris, south of Baghdad, the renowned German general Colmar von der Goltz wrote to War Minister Enver that while he was using whatever men he could get, he "urgently [needed] good Anatolian troops."[15] Following the uprisings at Hillah and other towns, Goltz expressed fears of relying on local conscripts, deeming Arab recruits "useless." He claimed they "posed a danger" to the Ottomans' success because such units were "contaminated [*verseucht*] through their proclivity toward England for hope of material advantage." In contrast, he gave praise to the "Turkish soldier," who "deals with any unusual and unfavorable circumstances with the greatest calm."[16] Before arriving on the Ottomans' eastern front, Goltz had been the military governor overseeing the brutal German occupation of Belgium. The idea that "Anatolian troops" were preferable to men conscripted in the Arab lands was not an uncommon attitude among Turkish-speaking officers. It is clear from the sources that young men in the Sixth Army region around Baghdad were resisting conscription. Whereas mutual respect and even deep bonds existed between Arab and Turkish officers, the views of some German and Turkish officers of Arab conscripts often were laced with bigotry and contempt.[17]

In Istanbul, the Assembly of Deputies continued to be a thorn in the government's side. Having failed to muzzle or shut down parliament altogether, the Unionists took a different tack. In March 1916 they proposed a constitutional amendment that would reinstate the sultan's prerogative of dissolving parliament and calling new elections, a sultanic privilege that had been abolished in the aftermath of the 1908 Revolution. A second amendment would alter election rules by allowing candidates to run for parliament from any district, even if they had never set foot in it. In theory, the argument for the amendment went, any deputy elected to the Assembly represented all Ottomans, not only those from a particular district. In practice, however, the change would allow the Unionists to pack the Assembly with candidates loyal to the government. Rising in opposition, Senator Ahmed Rıza argued that deputies must possess a deep understanding of the districts they represent. The "Ottoman banner," he went on, included all the people of the empire. "In many places there are Arabs,

Kurds, Armenians, Rum [Greek Orthodox] who have not even yet learned the Turkish language." These populations could not be represented by a person from outside of their community, Ahmed Rıza argued. Furthermore, among local populations across the empire, there existed "a spirit of communal honor and dignity [*haysiyet-i kavmiye*], just as the people of a particular city possess a kindred bond and pride." Thus, Ahmed Rıza continued, "assigning to these groups a representative from places outside their district is to offend such feelings, and to inflict great damage." After all, "no matter how ignorant the people of the provinces might be considered to be in comparison to the people of Istanbul, a deputy from Yemen or Konya will know the conditions and needs of Yemen and Konya better than a person from outside those places, like say from Salonika." But everyone in the chamber understood the true purpose of the proposed amendment, and Ahmed Rıza did not mince words: "Would the government ever abuse this power? It [the government] is human, so of course it would. Those who don't think so should ask our fellow Armenians and find out." He closed by saying, "I hope that the Senate will not surrender to the government the power to dissolve the Assembly at its pleasure and thereby facilitate this move toward authoritarian rule."[18]

Ahmed Rıza's comments—his elitism notwithstanding—are noteworthy in several respects. In March 1916 Ahmed Rıza was keeping alive a vision of the Ottoman Empire as a multiethnic and multireligious society. He was not the only one to do so, but as the longtime senior leader of the Unionist movement his voice as an intrepid critic of the government carried outsized weight. He declared openly that the Unionist government controlled the sultan, and that any powers granted to the sultan meant granting them to the government—a truth widely known but rarely spoken.

Like Ahmed Rıza, Gazi Ahmed Muhtar Pasha, the former grand vizier whose Savior Officers had ousted the Unionists following the rigged elections of 1912, also rose in opposition to the amendment. Allowing districts to be represented by politicians from anywhere would result in "all local concerns to be completely forgotten." Rather, a representative "must be a person who has tasted the local water and breathed the local air."[19] Defending the government's proposed law, Foreign Minister Halil claimed that following the 1908 Revolution the adoption of many constitutional amendments had been rushed and required revision. In fact, Halil was saying that too much power had been allocated to the parliament after 1908, at a time when the Unionists enjoyed great popularity and dominated that body, and that the Unionists now fully intended to shift power away from it.

The attempt to change the constitution in the middle of war reveals how contested and significant the question of legitimacy remained even under the crushing conditions of war. It points to the deep transformation the war engendered, from real to sham representation. The Unionist revolutionaries of 1908 had seized power from the sultan and assigned it to the people's Assembly. Now, during the war years, they reversed course, shifting those same powers back to the palace.

"Arabness, Armenianess, and Other Unlawful Opposition Activities"

In 1915 the Unionists' expanded their war on opposition movements and on populations whose loyalty they suspected. That campaign amounted to a war behind the war, and it turned increasingly bloody. We saw the horrific consequences of this dynamic for the Armenian people in the eastern provinces of Anatolia and the Arab population of Iraq. In 1915 Cemal ordered the arrest and execution of prominent political figures and intellectuals in Beirut, Damascus, and Jerusalem and the deportation of their families, as well as the deportation of entire villages. One scholar has averred that "Cemal's actions in Syria were comparable in nature, if not in extent, to those policies pursued with respect to the Armenians in Eastern Anatolia." And while "both emanated from a fear that a nationalist uprising would come into being with encouragement from enemy powers," in both cases "the threat was more perceived than real."[20]

Over the course of the war, the Unionists' attacks on disparate opposition movements increasingly converged. In September 1916, at a banquet held in Jerusalem in Cemal Pasha's honor, guests took a seat "beneath a stately walnut tree to have an aperitif." Then Cemal "entertained" the attendees "with his pleasant conversation." When talk turned to the possibility of Greece entering the war on the side of the Entente, Cemal "began to attack the Greek consul," who was present, "and said he was going to produce three documents related to the revolutionary operations of the Greeks [i.e., the *Rum* or Greek Orthodox Ottomans] in Turkey, which would oblige him to take vigorous measures of security." Then Cemal "spoke of sending to Mesopotamia the three million Greeks that live in Turkey." Cemal's chief of staff, Ali Fuad Bey, chimed in: "We will treat them worse than the Armenians." Ballobar, the Spanish consul who recorded the conversation in his diary, noted that the Greek consul had been opposed to Greece's intervention in the war exactly because of fear of such Ottoman retribution. The Greek consul responded to Cemal and Ali Fuad's threats with the observations that there were "300,000 Muslim Turks in Greece," to which Cemal repeated, "And we have three million Greeks in Turkey."[21] Greece eventually entered the war the following year, in July 1917, after an Entente-supported coup dethroned King Constantine I and brought the allies' protégé, Eleutherios Venizelos, to the prime ministry.[22]

Before the war, Sabahaddin Bey, leader of the Freedom and Entente Party, had been one of the most vocal and public opposition figures in the empire. As early as February 1915, as we have seen, he sought to mediate a truce between the Entente and the Ottoman government. By the end of that year, the Ottoman ambassador at Athens, Galib reported that Sabahaddin was meeting with other prominent opposition figures, such as Şerif Pasha and Natık Pasha. They had gathered in Greece and were convening meetings in Athens and Salonika.[23] Şerif Pasha was one of the founders of the Kurdish Society for Mutual Aid and Progress (Kürd Teavün ve Terakki Cemiyeti). Before the war, the society had pressed for Kurdish rights within the Ottoman imperial fold.[24] Natık Pasha was the former military commander under Sultan Abdülhamid II and, to the Unionists, a senior member of the ancien régime. In Athens, Ambassador Galib had learned that British forces were about to take some eight thousand Greek Orthodox Ottoman refugees from the island of Mytilene/Midilli to Egypt to serve as volunteers; Şerif and Natık would accompany them to Egypt.[25]

On May 17, 1916, the Ottoman ambassador to Switzerland forwarded a pamphlet carrying the title *An Open Letter to Grand Vizier Said Halim Pasha*. Published in Geneva and dated May 1, 1916, the twenty-six-page letter was signed by a certain "Midhat Bey," who, according to the ambassador, was "obviously none other" than Sabahaddin Bey himself. The ambassador had demanded a meeting with the Swiss foreign minister, Monsieur Hoffmann, and expressed his dismay about the fact that "neutral Switzerland" was permitting this type of propaganda against the Ottoman government and that it was providing shelter to "individuals convicted of murder in our homeland."[26] Despite these efforts, the opposition in Entente and neutral countries remained beyond the Unionists' reach.

Like Natık, former officials who had lost power in the ouster of Sultan Abdülhamid II had joined the opposition. ʻÜryanizade Cemil Molla, a legal expert and close personal friend of the former sultan, was in Istanbul but according to intelligence reports maintained regular contact with opposition forces in Bucharest and Geneva.[27] İzzet Holo ül-Abed (Arabic, Izzat Hawlu al-Abed), Sultan Abdülhamid II's former second secretary (*ikinci katib*), had participated in meetings in Switzerland but now had gone to Paris.[28] On July 11, 1916, the consul-general at Geneva, Yusuf, told the Foreign Ministry that for over a year now they had received reports that the British government was encouraging and supporting a planned uprising led by Sharif Husayn of Mecca. Intelligence agents reported that the son of the former sheikh ul-islam, the highest ranking Ottoman official of religious affairs, Cemaleddin Efendi, and Kamil Paşazade Said in Cairo also were in talks with Sharif Husayn Pasha.

From Geneva, Yusuf reported that Sharif Husayn claimed as his mission the well-being of all Muslims. But Yusuf believed Sharif Husayn's goal was the overthrow of the Unionist government. In support of Sharif Husayn's activities, the French air force would be sending a plane to drop leaflets written in Arabic over Syrian towns and cities, calling on the people of Syria to rise up in rebellion. The plane would also drop a letter signed by Sabahaddin Bey himself.[29] In other words, beyond the borders of the Ottoman Empire, a multiethnic opposition network including Arab, Kurdish, and Turkish leaders had taken shape. Sabahaddin was in close contact with the movement around Sharif Husayn and his sons—Abdullah, Ali, and Faysal. After the war, the latter would go on to become rulers of Jordan (King Abdullah I), the Hijaz (King Ali), and Iraq (King Faysal I), respectively.

On July 19, 1916, the consul-general at Geneva reported back to Istanbul that the French government had called İzzet Pasha and "a number of other Syrians" to Paris from Nice. Prominent Muslims from Syria, Egypt, and India were to gather in Cairo and anoint Sharif Husayn as the new caliph, with the seat of the caliphate moving from Istanbul to Mecca. After some hesitation, Sultan Husayn Kamil of Egypt (r.1914–1917) had approved the plan.[30] Two days later, on July 21, 1916, the consul-general reported that the Arab Society had met in Paris. At the gathering, its members decided that this coming Thursday [July 27; 27 Ramadan 1334 Hijri], which coincided with the holy day of Laylat al-Qadir—*leyle-i celile-i kadire*, marking the night the Quran was first sent from heaven—Sharif Husayn would accept and proclaim the caliphate.[31] Sabahaddin, who had been in Geneva for a while, would now go to Paris to attend the Arab Conference, which, as previously reported, was being organized by the French government.[32]

Talat followed the various opposition movements closely and—as the tone of his telegrams suggest—nervously. He had learned that the former director of the Istanbul police, Yusuf Rasih, and the writer and poet Hüseyin Sîret were both in Switzerland engaged in opposition work. Only scant information had reached him on the matter, he complained. Officials in Bern and Geneva should be reporting in detail about any and all activities, which were so "intimately linked to the state's domestic and international security."[33] In September 1916 Talat repeatedly expressed anxiety about opposition groups organizing in France and Switzerland.

Talat asked specifically for evidence that incriminated Armenians in activities undermining the state. From Bern, Ambassador Fuad Selim responded in a strongly worded telegram on September 29, 1916, stressing that no heed should be paid to rumors that Armenians were working with the opposition in Switzerland. He objected to suggestions that individuals could simply enter Austria-Hungary and make their way all the way to Galicia or Istanbul with the goal of sowing revolution and overthrowing the government. He assured Talat that should any evidence "worth communicating" materialize, the embassy would report so immediately.[34] From Vienna, Ambassador Hüseyin Hilmi confirmed the same, reassuring the Foreign Ministry that no members of the opposition would be able to enter Austria-Hungary from Switzerland, let alone make it to Galicia and contact Ottoman troops there.[35] Talat demanded evidence showing that Armenians were conspiring, but the ambassadors could not track down any such information. On November 27, 1916, Talat again requested information from the embassy at Bern, this time linking Arab and Armenian opposition groups. He insisted that "because Switzerland is a neutral power, some individuals there" were pursuing "Arabness, Armenianess, and other unlawful opposition activities."[36]

As he widened investigations into opposition groups abroad, he ordered the publication of documents intended to prove the culpability of opposition at home. Talat claimed the documents proved the widespread treason that allegedly targeted the Ottoman state. The publication is yet another illustration of how the Unionist regime saw itself at war not only with foreign powers but with all opposition groups, domestic and abroad. In 1916 Talat set up a Special Committee (*heyet-i mahsusa*) within the Interior Ministry to counter mounting charges of atrocity. He tasked the Special Committee with gathering photographic and written material documenting the activities of Armenian revolutionary groups since the war's start. Published in 1916 and known as the Red Book (*Kırmızı Kitab*), these documents were intended to prove Armenian treachery and justify their deportation.[37] Talat's interior ministry then published a second volume on Arab revolutionary groups to legitimize the state's suppression of Arab organizations.[38] In 1916 the Unionist government was claiming that it had incontrovertible evidence to justify and legitimize its policies of deportation and arrest of Armenians, Arabs, and anyone involved in revolutionary opposition movements.

For Talat, political opposition amounted to treason. He said so himself, in a newspaper interview he gave in August 1916. Asked about Ottoman policy toward non-Muslims, "specially Armenians," he replied, in broken English, that non-Muslims have "the same rights" as Muslims "in this country." He claimed that after the 1908 Constitutional Revolution, Armenians had enjoyed equality, but that "instead of changing their bad attitude, the misleading element tried to make use of them. Secret Societies, Anarchist organisations, arms and explosives were prepared for revolution." Referring to the Armenian volunteers, he noted that "those who were near the Russian Frontier, threw [in] their fate with Russia and rebelled." He claimed that more Armenians had been ready to join them. When the Entente launched the attack on Gallipoli, he continued, "we were prepared to ruin Constantinople and remove our Government to Askishehr [Eskişehir]." The decision to deport Istanbul's Armenians, he claimed, was in response to the Anglo-French naval attack on the Dardanelles. Talât acknowledged that Armenians had "suffered from this and some of our officials have mis-used their authorities." Nonetheless, he justified such abuses: "As the Empire was in danger, we were obliged to take such steps." Unsurprisingly, he denied any responsibility. He claimed to have sent commissions to investigate and punish any abuses, but no such system of supervision was ever put in place. "I am sorry that some inhuman acts" had been committed, he added callously. "But our official [*sic*] are also human beings not an angel [*sic*] and the guilty has suffered for his sin."[39]

In the Senate, Ahmed Rıza questioned the death sentence that had been issued for Senator Abdülhamid Zehravi (Abd al-Hamid al-Zahrawi), insisting that the verdict, signed by Grand Vizier Said Halim, be read out loud in the Senate. Abdülhamid Zehravi had been found guilty of membership in "the Society for Decentralization that had been founded in Egypt" and of working to "establish in Syria an independent Arab kingdom and an Arab caliphate based in Egypt." He was charged with attempting to "bring Syria under the protection of the French and the English, having gone to Paris after the Balkan Wars to meet with the said Society," organizing revolutionary gangs (*çetes*) in Syria and all of Arabia (*Arabistan*), and issuing statements in support of these efforts. His own writings and additional documents, it was claimed, proved this involvement and activity. Signed on November 19, 1916 (6 Teşrin-i sani 1332), the sentence carried the signature of Grand Vizier Mehmed Said.[40] The following week, Ahmed Rıza told his fellow senators that he had obtained a copy of the *Aliyye Divan-i Harb-i Örfisinde Ruyet Olunan Mesele-i Siyasiye Hakkında*

FIGURE 9. One of the numerous public executions during the war years, with death sentences displayed on the bodies of the executed. *Source*: Cornelius Van H. Engert Papers 2, box 19, folder 7, Lauinger Library, Booth Special Collections, Georgetown University.

İzahat, published under Cemal's aegis and that it included a quote attributed to Ahmed Rıza that was a "calumny" and a "lie." He added that he would like to write about this false attribution and the volume generally but that the prevailing censorship prevented him from doing so. Therefore, he noted, unable to write about the matter in the newspaper, he at least wanted to have this comment recorded in the Senate minutes, demonstrating once again how some senators and deputies made the parliament a subversive space, a forum in which they voiced their opposition in order to have it recorded into the minutes of the parliament.[41]

"Yes, We Rebelled"

On June 27, 1916, Sharif Husayn issued a proclamation, citing the executions of Arab leaders at Beirut and Damascus as one of the reasons for his break with the Unionists. Husayn charged the Unionists with mismanaging the empire since coming to power in 1908. The numerous wars since the Revolution were impoverishing the people, especially those in the Hijaz, Husayn argued. Even worse, according to the sharif, the Unionists were not following the path of Muhammad. The caliph no longer enjoyed his traditional role of authority, and the empire was no longer ruled by the sultan but by Enver, Cemal, and Talat. None of these developments benefited the empire and its people, Husayn asserted. Sharif Husayn's call to rebellion is searing in its criticism of the Unionists. It described how first the Italian and then the Balkan wars had devastated the empire's economic life and torn apart families. Just when "the artisan and the porter" returned "to their families and their villages in order to once again secure their food and provide for them, they once again were called up to go to war [in 1914]."[42]

Husayn's movement was hardly inspired by Arab nationalism or even the idea of Arab independence. The declaration highlighted his claim that the Unionist leaders had committed grave errors and crimes, including leading the Ottoman people into further wars after the Libyan and Balkan wars. All Muslims had been opposed to this, Husayn claimed, and he accused the Unionists of acting out of personal greed. Sharif Husayn insisted that the Unionists were guilty of "murdering Greek Orthodox and Armenians," who were "the equals to Muslims" and "without distinction among the Ottoman people [*arasında fark bulunmayan Osmanlı ahalisinin*]." They had "committed the same crimes in Syria, Iraq, and the other Arab lands." The statement concluded by admitting that, "Yes, we rebelled." It insisted that "our rebellion" and "our enmity and hatred" were directed at "Enver, Cemal, Talat, and their supporters," not against the empire itself. Husayn went on, "All Muslims of sound mind, including even the members of the royal family and the Ottoman dynasty, share these views with us."[43] This was not a national or an "Arab" revolt, according to Husayn, but the rising of citizens against the injustices of their government.

Shakib Arslan, the Druze leader from Mount Lebanon who in the war's aftermath became a prominent Arab voice internationally, acted as a critical liaison between Cemal and the Arab population under Cemal's rule. Shakib Arslan also knew both Enver and Talat well. In his account of his time as Cemal's assistant, Shakib Arslan claimed that he tried at great length to change Cemal's mind about the arrests and deportations of Arab leaders and their families. He strongly objected to the deportations and especially the public hangings of prominent Arabs in August 1915 in Beirut and in May 1916 in Beirut and Damascus, warning Cemal that the executions "will be the reason for the separation of Arabs and Turks."[44] Many Arab memoirs and histories record May 6, 1915, the day of the hanging, as the turning point in how they related to the Ottoman state.[45]

In Palestine, Private Ihsan Turjman noted in his diary, "Rebellion. Sherif Hussein Pasha declared rebellion against the state. There were demonstrations in Medina, and some of the Hijazi rail lines were destroyed. But the rebels' numbers were few, and they were dispersed. Could this be the beginning?" Then his thoughts turned to the causes of the rebellion:

> Every Arab should be pleased about this news. How can we support this state after it killed our best youth? They were hanged in public squares like common criminals and gangsters. They were executed for demanding their rights and for questioning their fate in the general conscription. They died, and not one voice was raised in protest in this miserable Arab nation. Not one Palestinian or Syrian voice. May God bless our Hijazi leader and strengthen his hand.[46]

Despite Ihsan's sentiments, Husayn's movement fell short of inspiring large segments of society, whether in Palestine and Syria, the Hijaz, or in Baghdad. Husayn secured British supplies and money. He also entered into an agreement with the British, in writing, for the establishment of an independent Arab state, which would extend from Mecca to Damascus, ruled by Husayn himself. The British pledge was a wartime measure to rally the Muslim world behind the Sharif and thus, indirectly, behind the Entente. It was an attempt to counter the Ottoman sultan's proclamation of jihad. Once the Ottoman Empire was defeated in October 1918, however, London quickly discarded this agreement for Arab independence and imposed colonial rule.[47]

As Ottoman authorities stepped up suppression of the rebellion, they further undermined the state's legitimacy in the eyes of the people. On August 22, 1916, the governor of Beirut province, Mustafa Azmi, arrested the deserter Umar Raf'i, who had attended the "revolutionary committee" meeting in Damascus. According to the governor, Raf'i was in contact with Sharif Husayn and had been attempting to recruit supporters in Tripoli. But Governor Mustafa Azmi spoke confidently; there was nothing to worry about. "This region," he reported, was "quiet and secure." He expressed concern about the Sharif's possibly winning over the Nusayri tribes of Latakya, the Syrian coastal region southeast of Aleppo, but thought that this could be prevented by presenting them with gifts. About two hundred lira were set aside for this purpose.[48]

Similarly, acting on the idea that Bedouin participation in war against the Ottoman state was driven not by nationalist ideology but by hunger, Ottoman leaders sought to buy a truce with the two largest and most influential tribal formations along the Euphrates and Tigris rivers, the 'Anizah and Shammar organizations. Brigadier General Mustafa Kemal, the hero of Gallipoli and commander of the Seventh Army at the time, conducted extensive negotiations and meetings with Arab tribal leaders in the summer of 1917. In September, he hosted several Bedouin leaders in Aleppo, won the pledge of their support, and decorated them with medals. They agreed on a number of points, but, as Mustafa Kemal noted, "only time will tell to what extent they will carry out the above duties."[49]

Then, just as revolution threatened to undermine the empire, revolution in Russia afforded the Ottomans a reprieve. The Russian Revolution allowed Ottoman forces to retake the important cities of Erzurum and Trabzon and to push all the way to Baku on the Caspian Sea the following year. In the empire's southern provinces, however, Ottoman forces could not match the Entente's superiority in manpower and matériel.

Ottoman Defeat and the Arrival of the Middle East

From the Sinai Peninsula, Mustafa Kemal watched the advances of the British forces. Along the Syrian coast, they marched on Gaza, laying waste to the city in two successive attacks. Despite the strong presence of German artillery and an Austro-Hungarian aircraft squadron, Mustafa Kemal had little hope for the defense of Palestine. He had even less faith in his German alliance partners' intentions. In his view, Germany was using the war "to colonize us" and "to gain control over all the resources of our land."[50] It would not come to that, of course. Neither Berlin nor Istanbul would play a role in the future of Palestine and Syria in the war's aftermath. In December 1917, British imperial forces, including significant contingents from Australia and New Zealand, captured Jerusalem.[51]

The occupying forces of the Entente knew well the conditions of famine that had ravaged populations in Palestine and Syria. They now distributed food they had previously prevented from entering the region.[52] Nicola Ziadeh, the young boy from Damascus who had lost his father so early in the war, remembered British forces distributing "Australian wheat" and "Egyptian rice." By then Nicola was living in Jenin, in Palestine, where his mother had found work in the German hospital.[53] The Entente strategy of establishing control in Syria, Lebanon, and Palestine through food was successful—at least in the short-term—as starving populations embraced the end to hunger and war.[54]

To the east, in Baghdad, too, British forces presented themselves as "liberators." A British army, this time containing many Indian troops, captured the city in March 1917. In front of a large crowd of men and women, the commander of the British forces, Lieutenant-General Stanley Maude, delivered a "proclamation" addressed "To the People of Baghdad." Maude declared that "our armies do not come into your cities and lands as conquerors or enemies, but as liberators." The people of Baghdad, Maude went on, "for 26 generations" had "suffered . . . at the hands of those alien rulers, the Turks."[55] For now, the war had come to an end for the people of Baghdad. It would resume, as it did for all the people of the Ottoman Empire, shortly after the armistice, when the war's victors began imposing colonial rule over them.

FIGURE 10. Original caption: "Ruins of Gaza at the time of the Great Attack." April 1917. *Source*: Digital ID: ppmsca 13709, Library of Congress Prints and Photographs Division, Washington, DC.

FIGURE 11. Funeral for an empire. Unionist dignitaries at the funeral procession of Sultan Abdülhamid II, who died on February 10, 1918. Looking at the camera, Rifat Bey, a former finance minister and president of the senate. To Rifat's right, Talat Pasha. Standing in front of Talat, Said Halim Pasha. To Rifat's left, Enver Pasha. Standing behind Enver, General Kâzım Karabekir. *Source*: Cornelius Van H. Engert Papers, box 10, folder 8, Lauinger Library, Booth Special Collections, Georgetown University.

FIGURE 12. Funeral procession of Sultan Abdülhamid II, 1918. The picture shows Talat, Enver (second and third from the right, second row). On the bottom left, Said Halim and Halil Bey. Cornelius Van H. Engert Papers, box 10, folder 8, Lauinger Library, Booth Special Collections, Georgetown University.

The following year, Entente forces reached Aleppo in northern Syria. In the Balkans, a British army broke through at Salonika and moved toward the Ottoman capital. In Europe, Germany suffered one final, decisive defeat. The Ottomans, and their allies, were defeated.[56] On October 30, 1918, Ottoman representatives signed an armistice aboard a British battleship anchored off the island of Lemnos. Two days later, on November 1, another group of Ottomans, including Cemal, Enver, and Talat, escaped Istanbul for Europe, aboard a German ship. On November 5 the Ottoman Committee of Union and Progress, meeting in Istanbul, dissolved itself.

In the days following the Ottoman entry into the war in 1914, the prominent Ottoman writer Ömer Seyfeddin had spoken of war as a liberating and unifying experience for the people of the empire. But the war became the very opposite. The Unionists had not only failed to make the war about a common goal but also taken the war to the people. Their conduct of the war alienated the empire's populations and engendered the birth of radically new political identities.[57] Rid of the Unionists and devastated by war, the people of the empire embarked on picking up the pieces.

Conclusion

DISMEMBERED EMPIRE, REMEMBERED PAST

THIS BOOK has treated the empire's end not as a foregone conclusion but as an outcome of the First World War. Not to recognize this may lead to false conclusions: that it was the empire's ethnic and religious diversity, or the nationalities—the "races" of the empire, to use the language of the time—that destroyed it. But the Ottoman Empire was not dead on arrival in 1914. It was war and defeat, and the occupations that followed, that destroyed the empire as a multiethnic, multireligious polity. That polity had held empire-wide elections in 1908 and formed an imperial parliament, gathering representatives from all regions of the country, Christians, Jews, and Muslims; Arabs, Armenians, Greek Orthodox, Kurds, and Turks.

Interpretations of the late Ottoman period and the history of the First World War are fraught with deep political implications. Maintaining that the various people of the empire could not have managed their future together presumes the existence of differences that could not be overcome by political means. It presumes that intercommunal violence and the dissolution of the empire were simply a matter of time. Cast in this way, the history of the Ottoman Empire normalizes division—whether "achieved" by nationalists from within or by imperialists and the League of Nations from without.

The First World War altered the terms of political contestation in the Ottoman Empire in a pivotal and far-reaching way. Whereas before the war political groups vied for greater participation in the Ottoman state, after the armistice, political groups contended largely to establish their own state projects.

The Greek Orthodox deputy from Izmir, Emmanouil Emmanouilides, known as Emanuelidis Efendi in the Assembly, had been a staunch defender of the Ottoman Empire's multiethnic unity. In spring 1914, in the aftermath of the Second Balkan War, the Greek Orthodox population of Izmir faced violent expulsion, as we have seen. The Great Powers' announcement that the islands of Chios and Mytilene would be ceded to Greece had generated an intense wave of anger against the Greek Orthodox population on the shores of the mainland, just a few miles away. On the floor of the Assembly, Emmanouilidis rose to speak. "I am not a representative of Greece (*Yunanistan*) here. I am an Ottoman deputy. And you can be absolutely certain that I hold no other wish and hope than to remain Ottoman." Also in attendance that day was Interior Minister Talat. "But in order for me to remain Ottoman," he continued, "you must provide rule of law and safety from harm, so that no one may attack anyone else and so that justice is rendered equally among all the various peoples [*anasır arasında*]" of the empire. Emmanouilidis pleaded that "human society cannot be administered through force and violence." The government was accusing all of the empire's Greek Orthodox, collectively, of treason, Emmanouilidis argued. "You say 'this person's loyalty is to Greece [*yunan kafalı*]—hit them in the head!' This cannot be tolerated. Give that pro-Greece person justice and they will be pro-Ottoman." For Deputy Emmanouilidis, it was the government that was turning away from its people, not the people who were abandoning their government: "To accuse the entire Greek Orthodox population of supporting Greece is not an indictment [*itham*] of that population, but perhaps it is an indictment of the Ottoman government."[1]

Four years later, in 1918, it was Emmanouilidis's turn to abandon the Ottoman state. He was coauthor and signatory to the "Memorandum, Presented by the Greek Members of the Turkish Parliament, to the American Commission on Mandates over Turkey."[2] The document claimed that "any Greek of any social standing, whether young or old, man or woman" now "demand[ed] the total abolition of Turkish rule over the Greeks." They demanded unification with the Kingdom of Greece.[3] In a sharp departure from Emmanouilidis's own earlier writings, the memorandum depicted Ottoman rule over its Greek Orthodox population as "five centuries" of suffering: "enslavement, deportation, robbery, plundering, conversions to Mohamedanism by force." The list continued.[4] That the authors of this document put forward such claims is perfectly understandable, given the emotional and physical despair of the empire's Greek Orthodox population in the war's aftermath. The arguments articulated in the memorandum also served the political utility of winning over the support of the Great Powers. And the memorandum also illustrated the beginning of new national identities based on claims of centuries-old persecution by the Ottoman state and its Muslim subjects.[5]

These sentiments were echoed in a second memorandum delivered to Paris, "Greece before the Peace Congress of 1919: A Memorandum Dealing with the Rights of Greece," penned by Eleutherios Venizelos, the prime minister of Greece.[6] Venizelos reminded the Big Four gathered at Paris—Georges Clemenceau, David Lloyd George, Vittorio Emanuele Orlando, and Woodrow Wilson—"that in January, 1915, the Entente Powers promised my Government very important territorial concessions on the coast of Asia Minor."[7] These promises had been repeated subsequently, Venizelos went on, "with the assurance that the vilayet of Aidin was included in these concessions."[8] Playing to his audience's religious beliefs and Orientalism, Venizelos presented the Balkan Wars as a "crusade of the Christian states of the Balkans against Turkey." The memorandum argued that as "one of the most ancient nations of Europe," Greeks were entitled to Anatolian territory.[9]

A delegation headed by Boghos Nubar and Avetis Aharonian, moreover, submitted claims on behalf of Ottoman Armenians. Amid the trauma and devastation of genocide, the document depicted Ottoman rule as "six centuries of martyrdom."[10] The Ottoman state, according to the memorandum, had always sought "to exterminate the Armenian race."[11] As Tamari noted for Palestine, the war was writing its own history. The memorandum based its claims on "the historical rights of its racial elements."[12] Armenians deserved the Great Powers' support, it went on, because they were "an Aryan and Christian people." Moreover, "the Armenian is a westerner, but he lives in contact with the Turks and the Tartars, who are the most backward peoples of the Orient."[13] These comments grew out of the Unionists' wartime atrocities, but they were also intended to confirm European perceptions of Ottoman rule.

Armenian representatives at Paris demanded Great Power support to "bring about the evacuation" of "the Turks, Tartars and others of all the Armenian territories." They intended to "expel from the country all the disturbing elements and the lawless nomadic tribes." Finally, they requested the Great Powers' help to "return to their homes all the Mouhajirs [refugees from the Caucasus and the Balkans] who have been brought into the country during the Hamidian regime and by the Young Turks."[14] In a separate memorandum, Avetis Aharonian reminded the Entente powers of the Armenians' military contribution to the war effort "from the very first days of the War." They had fought in the Caucasus, in Syria, and in Palestine, and on the Western front. Aharonian then further reminded the allies of the promises they had made to the Armenians during the war, and he quoted back two such statements by Prime Minister Lloyd George and Arthur Balfour.[15]

A delegation led by Sherif Pasha, moreover, represented the empire's Kurdish population. The delegation presented a "Memorandum on the Claims of the Kurd People." The document laid out arguments in what they saw to be "excessively imperialistic claims of Armenia."[16] Sherif defined the extent of the geographical boundaries of Kurdish populations and the towns, villages, and mountains, and their "thirteen-hundred-years"-old Kurdish names that comprised it.[17] Addressing the Peace Conference, Sherif cited Western scholars and their work, such as Mommsen's *History of Rome*, and *Nutall's English Encyclopedia*. Sherif mapped a Kurdistan in which the Kurdish population formed the majority. He noted that:

> The national wealth of the Kurds being almost entirely derived from cattle-raising which requires, on account of the climate, Winter and Summer pastures, we urgently reguest [*sic*] that these pastures shall not remain outside the frontiers assigned to Kurdistan.[18]

Sherif proposed "the creation of a Kurd state, entirely free and independent," in accordance, as he stressed, with Wilson's Twelfth Point. He also felt the need to state in the memorandum that proposing a Kurdish state in no way suggested disloyalty to the Ottoman Empire: "Since the Ottoman Government has accepted Mr. Wilson's fourteen points without reservation, the Kurds believe that they have every right to demand their independence, and that without in any way failing in loyalty towards the Empire under whose sovereignty they have lived for many centuries, keeping intact their customs and traditions."[19]

At Paris, the war's victors laid out a vision of the world that, despite new language, was distinctly colonial. They declared the inhabitants of the Ottoman Empire to be "peoples not yet able to stand by themselves under the strenuous conditions of the modern world." These erstwhile citizens of the Ottoman state required the "tutelage" of European powers, meaning Britain and France, who divided the Ottoman Empire into several parts to be ruled as League of Nations mandates.[20] Unsurprisingly, former Ottoman citizens rejected this characterization, first by political and diplomatic means, then, once these efforts fell on deaf ears, through demonstrations and mass protests. They eventually rose up in armed resistance against Anglo-French, Greek, and Italian occupations and colonialism, from Anatolia to Syria and from Iraq to Egypt.

In Damascus in July 1919, a council of the people—the Syrian General Congress—gathered to establish Syria as "a democratic civil constitutional Monarchy on broad decentralization principles." Their Syria would be comprised of Christian, Jewish, and Muslim citizens with equal rights. They sought to claim the rights that the 1908 Ottoman Revolution had promised and that the Unionists—and now the British and French—had denied them.[21] The Congress at Damascus called attention to the League's double standards, and they declared their "protest against Article 22 of the Covenant of the League of Nations."[22] The members of the Congress were fully aware of Syria's military occupation, and that London and Paris held all the cards. For now, their weapon was the language of justice and international law. In his Fourteen Points speech delivered before the United States Congress in January 1918, President Woodrow Wilson had posited the "absolutely unmolested opportunity of autonomous development" to

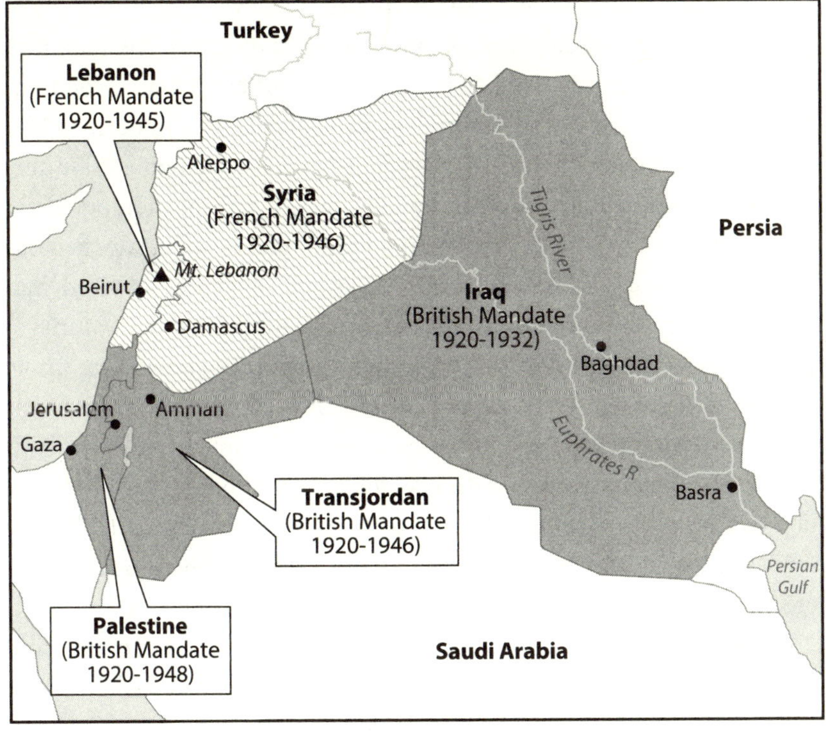

MAP 4. The Middle East, 1922.

the people "outside of the turkish portion of the Ottoman Empire." The Congress at Damascus, for "the event of the rejection" of their demand for independence, agreed to accept "technical and economical assistance from the United States of America" for a period of twenty years, "believing that the American Nation is farthest from any thought of colonization and has no political ambition in our country."[23] At the Paris Peace Conference of 1919 and, subsequently, the League of Nations at Geneva, both of these proposals were readily ignored.

Instead, over the course of the next months and years, and even decades, British and French military power put down any such demands for sovereignty with ruthless violence, including issuing orders to open fire on civilians, as was the case in Egypt in 1919, the bombardment of towns and cities, as in Damascus in 1925, and using ferocious, indiscriminate airpower, as in Iraq during the 1920s.[24] The League of Nations was, in fact, a league of empires.

It should come as no surprise, therefore, that even though the Ottoman Empire was defeated in 1918, Ottoman revolutionary aims to remove foreign control not only lived on but intensified. After the war, revolutionary ideas and goals became more relevant, not less. Ahmed Rıza, the former Unionist who emerged as the Unionists' most vociferous critic during the war years, railed against the injustices of European imperialism in the war's aftermath. Foreshadowing Frantz Fanon and a later generation of anti-colonialists, he demanded to know, "What has survived, materially or morally, from the colonial activity of the preceding centuries?" He answered his own question: "A massive, world-wide convulsion; whole races almost entirely exterminated; others transplanted from one continent to another in the fleets of the slave-traders; immense tracts of land utterly devastated; yesterday, slavery; today, wretched poverty. Civilization has in no way suppressed barbarism, it has simply refined it."[25] In the war's immediate aftermath, so-called Western liberalism was gaining little credibility in the Ottoman Empire.

Ahmed Rıza also called out the Great Powers' supposed humanitarian interventions. The policies of European powers and the United States, he went on, "[inspire] the Muslims with the most profound contempt, particularly as they are well aware that this concern for the interests and protection of the Christians in the East is in reality nothing more than a hypocritical mask hiding the real motives: the conquest and destruction of the Muslim powers." Ahmed Rıza, who had spoken up courageously on behalf of Armenians in 1915 and 1916, now decried the European liberalism that he previously had so cherished. For Ahmed Rıza, the Unionists and the Great Powers, together, had destroyed the Ottoman world.[26]

But if revolutionism and its corollary—the suppression of competing revolutionary ideas and movements—lived on, so did colonialism and its corollary, anti-colonialism. The new Republic of Turkey, proclaimed in October 1923 with its capital at Ankara, pursued an uncompromising centralism aimed at the full control over all administrative branches of government, political movements, and natural resources at home. It divided Anatolia into four regional "general inspectorates" (*umumî müfettişikler*) and ruled Anatolia from 1927 to 1952, in part, as a colonial realm. The inspectorates drew on the precedents of European colonial protectorates and reform proposals—especially the Armenian Reform Proposal of 1913–14.[27] The Turkish Republic's continuation, or adoption, of European colonial practices suggests the extent to which the late Ottoman and then the new Turkish state increasingly mirrored Western European and North American practices of statecraft.[28]

Enver and Talat, despite the empire's defeat and their own grave misdeeds, are often revered in Turkey today as warriors for their country against all odds. Mehmed Zeki, writing immediately after the war, insisted that Enver and Talat had been true patriots who entered the war to save the empire. But the remedies they prescribed proved more deadly than the disease. The German officer Lieutenant Colonel Friedrich Baron Kress von Kressenstein, who had worked closely with the commander of the Fourth Army, Cemal Pasha, described Cemal as "imbued with a glowing patriotism," like "all the leading Young Turks." Their "deepest desire" and "only objective," Kress believed, had been to achieve "complete independence" for their homeland and reclaim for the empire "its place in the community of nations."[29] Not unlike Mehmed Zeki, however, Kress raised doubts about their decisions and methods. Patriotism alone does not equip leaders with wisdom and skill, of course. Kress could not understand why Cemal, for example, "especially during wartime, under the heavy burdens brought on by an unpopular war," had sought, as governor of Syria, to push through "certain Turkification measures," thereby alienating "the greatly suffering Arab population."[30]

Others, too, were unwilling to make excuses for Unionist leadership. Kurd Ali, editor of the paper *al-Muqtabas* in Damascus, had been in close contact during the war with both Cemal and Enver, as well as other high-ranking officials and military officers. In his memoirs he recalls a conversation with Hulusi Bey, at the time the governor of Syria province. He recalls the governor saying, "May God's curse be upon the Unionists. I am not one of them, anyway. They are a lot who will ruin the country and it will be wrecked at their hands."[31]

One reason why the legacies of the Unionists generally and Cemal, Enver, and Talat, in particular, remain complicated and mixed is because the register shifts depending on whether the question is posed from the standpoint of foreign policy or domestic politics. The Unionists' war on

MAP 5. The Middle East today.

the Goliath of European imperialism has garnered sympathy and continues to do so, not only in Turkey but across the Eastern Mediterranean and far beyond. As a regime in control of the government and domestic policy, however, they proved incapable of living with dissent or tolerating opposition. They failed to make the empire's struggles a common goal for all Ottomans.

In Turkey, the principle that "sovereignty resides unconditionally with the people" became enshrined as the first article of the new republic's constitution. The dictum still stands today, carved into slabs of marble and shimmering on billboards across Turkey. At the end of the First World War, it functioned as a call to arms. It was at the center of Mustafa Kemal's resistance movement that fought to overthrow the Allied occupation of

Istanbul and to defeat the British-backed invasion of the Greek army of Western Anatolia in 1919. In those campaigns, the slogan was crucial in mobilizing popular support. As became clear after the establishment of the independent Turkish Republic in October 1923, however, the phrase did not amount to the empowerment of the people. Much like the Unionists, when Mustafa Kemal and the revolutionaries around him made this claim, what they were asserting was that sovereignty over Ottoman lands could not be ceded to foreign control.

As Turkey's citizens quickly discovered, however, "to the people" had, in fact, a myriad of meanings. In 1919 Anatolia, it meant that sovereignty belonged neither to the foreign, occupying powers of the Allied victors, Britain and France, nor to the sultan's palace on the Bosphorus. Once those enemies were defeated, it turned out that sovereignty did not "belong to the people" either. When the Unionists demanded that sovereignty belong to the people, they were making a claim that it did not belong to Sultan Abdülhamid II or the Great Powers of Europe. In fact, first the Unionists and then, after the First World War, Atatürk's Republican People's Party, claimed this sovereignty for themselves.

Still, the Ottoman intercommunality of the prewar years did not come to an end overnight. During the war between Greece and the Ottoman Empire in 1919–22, Demetra Vaka, a Greek Orthodox Istanbulite, met with Prince Sabahaddin, who had led the opposition against the Unionists. In 1923 Demetra wrote Sabahaddin a letter about their meeting. Among other things, she said,

> We met when the army of your race and that of mine were clashing on the battle-field; yet there was no prejudice, no antagonism, no hatred between us. You knew me to be a Greek by blood, and born in Turkey; yet you accepted me as Ottomans should accept each other—as children of the same empire.
>
> You refused to listen to the voice of calumny, which preceded our meeting. You knew me to be a lover and admirer of the best there is in your race, and we came together, not as a Turk and a Greek, but as two Ottomans, loving the Ottoman Empire, our birthland, with the same kind of love, wishing for it progress and civilization.

> Before we were many hours together, I felt you to be the man who might save what was left of the empire, because you believed that all Ottomans, be they Turks or Arabs, Greeks or Armenians, Syrians or Jews, be they Mohammedans or Christians, should look upon one another as compatriots, sharing in the government of their country and its benefits, shouldering its responsibilities, its burdens, its labors, and loving each other in the sharing.[32]

Demetra Vaka had seen the empire's potential, and she mourned its loss. A century later, that upheaval, from Kurdistan to Gaza to Baghdad to Libya, appears as unsettled as ever.

NOTES

Introduction: History as a Minefield

1. BOA, DH.EUM.AYŞ 47/17, 25 Teşrin-i evvel 1336 (October 25, 1920).

2. For a comparative study of civilian deaths in the First and Second World Wars, see Cormac Ó Gráda, *The Hidden Victims: Civilian Casualties of the Two World Wars* (Princeton University Press, 2024).

3. These are the words of Talat Pasha, the Ottoman interior minister and, after 1917, grand vizier; see al-Amīr Shākib Arslān, *Sīrah Zātiyyah* (Beirut: Dār al-Tāl'iyya lil'taba'a wa al-nashr, 1969), 238–39.

4. Salim Tamari, ed., *Year of the Locust: A Soldier's Diary and the Erasure of Palestine's Ottoman Past* (University of California Press, 2011), 5.

5. D[emetrios] E. Theodore, *The Sacrificials: Part of an Autobiography Depicting the Life of Minorities in a War Torn Country* (n.p, 1970), 47.

6. Nicholas Doumanis, *Before the Nation: Muslim-Christian Coexistence and Its Destruction in Late Ottoman Anatolia* (Oxford University Press, 2013), 43–87.

7. *Osmanlı İttihad ve Terakki Cemiyeti*, in Ottoman Turkish.

8. Frederick F. Anscombe, *The Ottoman Gulf: The Creation of Kuwait, Saudi Arabia, and Qatar* (Columbia University Press, 1997).

9. See Leyla Amzi-Erdoğdular, *The Afterlife of Ottoman Europe: Muslims in Habsburg Bosnia Herzegovina* (Stanford University Press, 2024); Edin Hajdarpasic, *Whose Bosnia? Nationalism and Political Imagination in the Balkans, 1840–1914* (Cornell University Press, 2014); Emily Greble, *Muslims and the Making of Modern Europe* (Oxford University Press, 2021).

10. On Iran, see Oliver Bast, "Les 'buts de guerre' de la Perse neutre pendant la Première Guerre mondiale," *Relations Internationales* 160 (2015): 95–110; on Morocco, Jonathan Wyrtzen, *Making Morocco: Colonial Intervention and the Politics of Identity* (Cornell University Press, 2015); on Afghanistan, Faiz Ahmed, *Afghanistan Rising: Islamic Law and Statecraft between the Ottoman and British Empires* (Harvard University Press, 2017); for a broad treatment from Iran to Morocco, see Jonathan Wyrtzen, *Worldmaking in the Long Great War: How Local and Colonial Struggles Shaped the Modern Middle East* (Columbia University Press, 2022).

11. Lauren Benton, *They Called It Peace: Worlds of Imperial Violence* (Princeton University Press, 2024); Jennifer Pitts, *Boundaries of the International: Law and Empire* (Harvard University Press, 2018); Lauren Benton and Lisa Ford, *Rage for Order: The British Empire and the Origins of International Law, 1800–1850* (Harvard University Press, 2017).

12. M. Şükrü Hanioğlu, *A Brief History of the Late Ottoman Empire* (Princeton University Press, 2008); James McDougall, "Sovereignty, Governance, and Political Community in the Ottoman Empire and North Africa," in *Re-imagining Democracy in the Mediterranean, 1780–1860*, ed. Joanna Innes and Mark Philp (Oxford University Press, 2018), 127–52; more broadly, Jürgen Osterhammel, *The Global Transformation of the World: A Global History of the Nineteenth Century*, trans. Patrick Camiller (Princeton University Press, 2015); C. A. Bayly, *The Birth of the Modern World, 1780–1914: Global Connections and Comparisons* (Blackwell, 2003).

13. Mahmoud Haddad, "Syria and Iraq as Proxy Colonies before Colonization: The Ottoman Vali versus the Western Consul in the Era of Capitulations," *Die Welt des Islams* 60 (2020): 3–30. The distinction between modern state-building and internal colonialism continues to be a matter of debate. On Ottoman internal colonialism, see Raoul Motika and Christoph Herzog, "Orientalism Alla Turca: Late 19th/Early 20th Century Ottoman Voyages into the Muslim 'Outback,'" *Die Welt des Islams* 40 (2000): 139–95; Ussama Makdisi, "Ottoman Orientalism," *American Historical Review* 107 (2002): 768–96; Selim Deringil, "'They Live in a State of Nomadism and Savagery': The Late Ottoman Empire and the Post-Colonial Debate," *Comparative Studies in Society and History* 45 (2003): 311–42; Thomas Kühn, "Shaping and Reshaping Colonial Ottomanism: Contesting Boundaries of Difference and Integration in Ottoman Yemen, 1872–1919," *Comparative Studies of South Asia, Africa, and the Middle East* 27 (2007): 315–31; Vangelis Kechriotis, "Postcolonial Criticism Encounters Late Ottoman Studies," *Historein* 13 (2014): 39–46; Chris Gratien, *The Unsettled Plain: An Environmental History of the Late Ottoman Frontier* (Stanford University Press, 2022), 75–93. For Egypt, see Omnia S. El Shakry, *The Great Social Laboratory: Subjects of Knowledge in Colonial and Postcolonial Egypt* (Stanford University Press, 2007.)

14. Mahmood Mamdani, *Neither Settler nor Native: The Making and Unmaking of Permanent Minorities* (Harvard University Press, 2020); A. Dirk Moses, *The Problems of Genocide: Permanent Security and the Language of Transgression* (Cambridge University Press, 2021).

15. See the works of M. Şükrü Hanioğlu, *The Young Turks in Opposition* (Oxford University Press, 1995) and *Preparation for a Revolution* (Oxford University Press, 2001). See also Nicholas A. Robins and Adam Jones, eds., *Genocides by the Oppressed: Subaltern Genocide in Theory and Practice* (Indiana University Press, 2009).

16. Rebecca E. Karl, *Staging the World: Chinese Nationalism at the Turn of the Twentieth Century* (Duke University Press, 2002), provides a fascinating discussion of Chinese perspectives on foreign control in the Ottoman Empire.

17. For China, see Anne Reinhardt, *Navigating Semi-Colonialism: Shipping, Sovereignty, and Nation-Building in China, 1860–1937* (Harvard University Asia Center, 2018); for Egypt, see Juan R. I. Cole, *Colonialism and Revolution in the Middle East: Social and Cultural Origins of Egypt's 'Urabi Movement* (Princeton University Press, 1993); for Iran, see Charles Kurzman, *Democracy Denied, 1905–1915: Intellectuals and the Fate of Democracy* (Harvard University Press, 2008); for a panoramic view, see Elizabeth F. Thompson, *Justice Interrupted: The Struggle for Constitutional Government in the Middle East* (Harvard University Press, 2013).

18. See especially the works of Hanioğlu, *The Young Turks in Opposition*; idem, *Preparation for a Revolution.*

19. Leon Trotsky, *The Balkan Wars, 1912–13: The War Correspondence of Leon Trotsky*, trans. Brian Pearce, ed. George Weissman and Duncan Williams (Monad Press, 1980), 4.

20. Y. Doğan Çetinkaya, "1908 Devrimi ve Toplumsal Seferberlik," in *II. Meşrutiyet'i Yeniden Düşünmek*, ed. Ferdan Ergut (Tarih Vakfı, 2010), 13.

21. Bedross Der Matossian, *Shattered Dreams of Revolution* (Stanford University Press, 2014), 19–22.

22. Michelle U. Campos, *Ottoman Brothers: Muslims, Christians, and Jews in Early Twentieth-Century Palestine* (Stanford University Press, 2011); Ilham Khuri-Makdisi, *The Eastern Mediterranean and the Making of Global Radicalism, 1860–1914* (University of California Press, 2010).

23. See Gökhan Kaya, *II. Meşrutiyet Döneminin Demokratları: Osmanlı Demokrat Fırkası (Fırka-i İbad)* (İletişim, 2011), 199.

24. Dikran Mesrob Kaligian, *Armenian Organization and Ideology under Ottoman Rule, 1908–1914* (Transaction, 2009), 1–42; Der Matossian, *Shattered Dreams of Revolution*.

25. The election system was two-tiered and granted voting rights to men over the age of twenty-five who met a minimum property requirement. The system, therefore, was far from uncontested.

26. For a comprehensive study of the 1908 Revolution's aftermath, see Nader Sohrabi, *Revolution and Constitutionalism in the Ottoman Empire and Iran* (Cambridge University Press, 2011).

27. Huseyin Yilmaz, "The Eastern Question and the Ottoman Empire: The Genesis of the Near and Middle East in the Nineteenth Century," in *Is There a Middle East? The Evolution of a Geopolitical Concept*, ed. Michael E. Bonine, Abbas Amanat, and Michael Ezekiel Gasper (Stanford University Press, 2012), 11–35, quote on 35. See chapters in the same volume, especially Roger Adelson, "British and U.S. Use and Misuse of the Term 'Middle East,'" 36–55.

28. Campos, *Ottoman Brothers*, 8.

29. British Foreign Secretary Arthur James Balfour to Lord [Walter] Rothschild, November 2, 1917. Published in the *Times*, November 9, 1917.

30. For an exception see Donald Bloxham, *The Great Game of Genocide: Imperialism, Nationalism, and the Destruction of the Ottoman Armenians* (Oxford University Press, 2005), and idem, "The First World War and the Development of the Armenian Genocide," in *A Question of Genocide: Armenians and Turks at the End of the Ottoman Empire*, ed. Ronald Grigor Suny, Fatma Müge Göçek, and Norman M. Naimark (Oxford University Press, 2011), 260–75.

31. BA-MA, N155/21, Firle papers, folio 106, October 31, 1914, Rudolph Firle diary, 1914–1918.

32. BA-MA, RM41/74 folio 19: "*Strictly Confidential!* Enver, Talat, and Cemal arrived on November 3 from Constantinople and continued incognito to Berlin in the evening." Handwritten marginalia instructions: "destroy original." The German *R01* was the captured Russian ship *Schastlivyi*, see Paul G. Halpern, *The Naval War in the Mediterranean, 1914–1918* (Naval Institute Press, 1987), 550.

33. He did so, briefly, after a meeting with Lenin in Moscow. He then switched sides and joined rebel fighters in Bukhara, only to perish at the hands of the Red Army in 1922.

34. al-Amīr Shākib Arslān, *Sīrah Zātiyya*, 238. Arslān (1869–1946) had completed this section of his memoir as early as 1923, see his note on page 6.

Chapter 1. An Empire's Revolutionary War

1. Horatio Herbert Kitchener (1850–1916), British colonial officer, held office in Sudan, South Africa, India, and Egypt. He became secretary of state for war in August 1914 and remained in that role until his death in June 1916. Kitchener made the statement on August 17, 1914. See Nicholas A. Lambert, *The War Lords and the Gallipoli Disaster: How Globalized Trade Led Britain to Its Worst Defeat of the First World War* (Oxford University Press, 2021), 69.

2. See Feroz Ahmad, "Unionist Failure to Stay Out of the War in October–November 1914," *Perceptions* 20 (2015): 23–38; for France, see L. Bruce Fulton, "France and the Ottoman Empire," in *The Great Powers and the Ottoman Empire*, ed. Marian Kent (Frank Cass, 1996; 1984), 154 and 163n83; see also G. P. Gooch and Harold William Vazeille Temperley, eds., *The Near and Middle East on the Eve of the World War*, vol. 10, part 1, *British Documents on the Origins of the War, 1898–1914* (H.M.S.O., 1927), 901–2, appendix, "Overture of Turkey to Great Britain, June 1913," for the renewed Ottoman offer in 1913, following British rejection in 1911.

3. Gooch and Temperley, *The Near and Middle East on the Eve of the World War*, Grey to Lowther, July 31, 1908, also quoted partially in Mesut Uyar, *The Ottoman Army and the First World War* (Routledge, 2020), 1, and in Mahmoud Haddad, "Syria and Iraq as Proxy Colonies before Colonization: The Ottoman Vali versus the Western Consul in the Era of Capitulations," *Die Welt des Islams* 60 (2020): 30.

4. T. G. Otte, *Statesman of Europe: A Life of Sir Edward Grey* (Allen Lane, 2020), 334–35. See the same work at 511, on Grey's fears as to the effects of successful constitutionalism in the Ottoman Empire on British Egypt and India.

5. Juan R. I. Cole, *Colonialism and Revolution in the Middle East: Social and Cultural Origins of Egypt's 'Urabi Movement* (Princeton University Press, 1993), 3–22; see also Elizabeth F. Thompson, *Justice Interrupted: The Struggle for Constitutional Government in the Middle East* (Harvard University Press, 2013), 61–88.

6. Keith Wilson, "Grey and the Russian Threat to India, 1892–1915," *International History Review* 38 (2016): 278, citing Grey to Lowther, August 11, 1908.

7. This was the basis on which Sir Edward Grey pitched an understanding to Russia in December 1905, the moment he became foreign secretary. See Wilson, "Grey and the Russian Threat to India," 277.

8. Wilson, "Grey and the Russian Threat to India," 275–84. See also Jennifer Siegel, *Endgame: Britain, Russia and the Final Struggle for Central Asia* (I. B. Tauris, 2002), especially 175–201.

9. For the intense rivalry between the Ottoman and British empires in the Hijaz, see Michael Christopher Low, *Imperial Mecca: Ottoman Arabia and the Indian Ocean Hajj* (Columbia University Press, 2020); Frederick F. Anscombe, *The Ottoman Gulf: The Creation of Kuwait, Saudi Arabia, and Qatar* (Columbia University Press, 1997); Lâle Can, *Spiritual Subjects: Central Asian Pilgrims and the Ottoman Hajj at the End of Empire* (Stanford University Press, 2020).

10. Milena B. Methodieva, *Between Empire and Nation: Muslim Reforms in the Balkans* (Stanford University Press, 2021); Leyla Amzi-Erdoğdular, *The Afterlife of Ottoman Europe: Muslims in Habsburg Bosnia Herzegovina* (Stanford University Press, 2024); Uğur Zekeriya Peçe, *Island and Empire: How Civil War in Crete Mobilized the Ottoman World* (Stanford University Press, 2024).

11. Peçe, *Island and Empire*, 21–28.

12. Yuval Ben-Bassat and Eyal Ginio, "Introduction: The Case Study of Palestine during the Young Turk Era," in *Late Ottoman Palestine*, ed. Yuval Ben-Bassat and Eyal Ginio (I. B. Tauris, 2011), 2.

13. Y. Doğan Çetinkaya, *The Young Turks and the Boycott Movement: Nationalism, Protest and the Working Classes in the Formation of Modern Turkey* (I. B. Tauris, 2014), 51; Murat Koraltürk, *Ekonominin Türkleştirilmesi: Erken Cumhuriyet Döneminde* (İletişim, 2011), 40–41.

14. Fatma Aliye, *Tercüman-ı Hakikat* (The Interpreter of Truth), October 19, 1908, quoted in François Georgeon, "Religion, Politics and Society in the Wake of the Young Turk Revolution: The 'Ramadan of Freedom' in Istanbul," in *The Young Turk Revolution and the Ottoman Empire: The Aftermath of 1908*, ed. Noémi Lévy-Aksu and François Georgeon (I. B. Tauris, 2017), 184. In 1908 Ramadan commenced on September 27.

15. Stefan Hock, "'Waking Us from This Endless Slumber': The Ottoman-Italian War and North Africa in the Ottoman Twentieth Century," *War in History* 26 (2019): 204–26.

16. Zaven Der Yeghiayan, *My Patriarchal Memoirs: Zaven Der Yeghiayan, Armenian Patriarch of Constantinople, 1913–1922*, trans. Ared Misirliyan, annotated by Vatche Ghazarian (Mayreni, 2002); originally published in Armenian as *Badriarkagan Hooshers, Vaverakrer yev Vgayutyunner* (Cairo, 1947). Boghos Nubar was the founder of the Armenian General Benevolent Union, founded in Cairo in 1906. His father served as prime minister of Egypt under the British.

17. Restoring land to their Armenian owners elicited strong resistance from local populations and, of course, their new owners. See Mehmet Polatel, *Armenians and Land Disputes in the Ottoman Empire, 1850–1914* (Edinburgh University Press, 2025), 142–53; in the second half of the nineteenth century, many Kurdish landowners were dispossessed of their land as a result of the Ottoman state's centralization policies, see Nilay Özok-Gündoğan, *The Kurdish Nobility in the Ottoman Empire: Loyalty, Autonomy and Privilege* (Edinburgh University Press, 2022), 177–279.

18. Cemil Koçak, *Umûmî Müfettişlikler (1927–1952)*, 3rd ed. (İletişim, 2016; 2010; 2003); W. J. van der Dussen, "The Question of Armenian Reforms," *Armenian Review* 39 (1986): 11–28.

19. The agreement carried the signatures of Grand Vizier Said Halim and the chargé d'affaires at the Russian embassy, Konstantin Gulkevich. The provinces were Bitlis, Diyar-i Bekir, Erzurum, Harput/Mamuretülaziz, Sivas, and Van. For further discussion, see chapter 2 of this book; for a different interpretation, see Hans-Lukas Kieser, Thomas Schmutz, and Mehmet Polatel, "Reform or Cataclysm? The Agreement of 8 February 1914 regarding the Ottoman Eastern Provinces," *Journal of Genocide Research* 17 (2015): 285–304.

20. Der Yeghiayan, *My Patriarchal Memoirs*, 28.

21. Der Yeghiayan, 29.

22. Der Yeghiayan, 33.

23. Yiğit Akın, *When the War Came Home: The Ottomans' Great War and the Devastation of an Empire* (Stanford University Press, 2018), 15–51; Çetinkaya, *Young Turks and the Boycott Movement*; Fikret Adanır, "Non-Ottomans in the Ottoman Army and the Ottoman Defeat in the Balkan War of 1912–1913," in *A Question of Genocide: Armenians and Turks at the End of*

the Ottoman Empire, ed. Ronald Grigor Suny, Fatma Müge Göçek, and Norman M. Naimark (Oxford University Press, 2011), 136–48; Ramazan Hakkı Öztan, "Point of No Return? Prospects of Empire after the Defeat in the Balkan Wars (1912–1913)," *International Journal of Middle East Studies* 50 (2018): 65–84.

24. TNA, FO 800/80, Mallet to Grey, December 9, 1913.

25. TNA, FO 800/80, Mallet to Grey, December 17, 1913.

26. A day after the Ottomans signed the Armenian Reform Agreement, Grey threw his weight behind Greek rule over Chios and Mytilene, believing that doing so might bring the Unionists' government to an end: there was "nothing for us to do but to wait upon events." And: "When a country has learnt by experience, it changes the rulers who have brought it to trouble." See TNA, FO 800/80, Mallet to Grey, February 4, 1914, and Grey to Mallet, February 9, 1914.

27. TNA, FO 800/80, Grey to Mallet, April 30, 1914; see also Rashid Ismail Khalidi, *British Policy towards Syria and Palestine, 1906–1914: A Study of the Antecedents of the Hussein-McMahon, the Sykes-Picot Agreement, and the Balfour Declaration* (Middle East Centre, St. Antony's College, 1980).

28. TNA, FO 800/80, Mallet to Grey, March 10, 1914.

29. David Todd, *A Velvet Empire: French Informal Imperialism in the Nineteenth Century* (Princeton University Press, 2021), 72–122 and 206–18, quotes on 206 and 215. Todd concludes that: "On the whole, France's conquest of the Ottoman Empire by money was successful." See the same volume, 217.

30. TNA, FO 800/80, Mallet to Grey, March 23, 1914.

31. See Foreign Office claims to the oilfields from Mosul to the Gulf. As Grey put it, the French government opposed only "a British oil monopoly over the whole of Turkey, or of Syria, which we have assured them was never in contemplation," in TNA, FO 800/80, Grey to Mallet, April 30, 1914.

32. Ronald Bobroff, *Roads to Glory: Late Imperial Russia and the Turkish Straits* (I. B. Tauris, 2006), 90–91.

33. TNA, FO 800/80, Grey to Mallet, December 23, 1913.

34. TNA, FO 800/80, Grey to Mallet, December 23, 1913.

35. Mustafa Aksakal, *The Ottoman Road to War in 1914: The Ottoman Empire and the First World War* (Cambridge University Press, 2008), 75.

36. Joseph Pomiankowski, *Der Zusammenbruch des Ottomanischen Reiches: Erinnerungen an die Türkei aus der Zeit des Weltkrieges* (Vienna: Amalthea-Verlag, 1928), 51.

37. PA/AA, R 2125, Jagow to Wangenheim, July 28, 1913, also in PA/AA, R 14524.

38. *Ahenk*, October 13, 1912, quoted in Zeki Arıkan, "Balkan Savaşı ve Kamuoyu," in *Bildiriler: Dördüncü Askeri Tarih Semineri* (Genelkurmay Basımevi, 1989), 176.

39. Ahmed Selahaddin, *Makedonya Meselesi ve Balkan Harb-ı Âhiri* (Dersaadet: Kanaat Matbaası, 1331 [1915]), Bismarck's quote is on the title page. See also Ahmed Selahaddin's *Berlin Kongresi'nin diplomasi tarihine bir nazar. Külliyati hukuk ve siyasiyat'dan birinci kitab* (1327 (1911/1912), and his magnus opus on international law, *Hukuk-i Beyneldüvvelin Mukaddimat-ı Nazariye ve Safahatı Tekamüliyesi* (Kanaat Matbaası, 1331 [1915]).

40. For anti-imperialism in Beirut and Cairo, see Ilham Khuri-Makdisi, *The Eastern Mediterranean and the Making of Global Radicalism, 1860–1914* (University of California Press, 2010).

41. These legal and economic provisions were known in Ottoman Turkish alternatively as *ahdnâmes* ("the agreements"), *uhûd-u âtika* ("ancient pledges"), and *imtiyazat* ("privileges").

42. İbnürrefet Mehmed Memduh, *Kapitülasyon-Capitulations: Yahud, memalik-i osmaniye'de ecnebilerin haiz olduğu imtiyazat* (Dersaadet: Matbaa-i Ahmet İhsan, 1327 [1911/12]), 5.

43. İbnürrefet Mehmed Memduh, *Kapitülasyon-Capitulations*, 3–4.

44. It is unclear how successful such ads were in convincing the public. For a discussion, see Yavuz Köse, "Between Protest and Envy: Foreign Companies and Ottoman Muslim Society," in *Popular Protest and Political Participation: Studies in Honor of Suraiya Faroqhi*, ed. Eleni Gara, M. Erdem Kabadayı, and Christoph K. Neumann (Istanbul Bilgi University Press, 2011), 283.

45. Köse, "Between Protest and Envy," 265: "Osmanlı parası Osmanlılara kalmalı."

46. Adam Block, "The Commercial Independence of Turkey," *Times*, December 14, 1908, quoted in Murat Birdal, *The Political Economy of Ottoman Public Debt: Insolvency and European Financial Control in the Late Nineteenth Century* (I. B. Tauris, 2010), 20. Block served for many years in the Ottoman Public Debt Administration.

47. Birdal, *Political Economy of Ottoman Public Debt*, 20; Birdal is referring to Charles Morawitz's article "Obstacles to Reform in Turkey," *North American Review* 179 (1904): 194–206, not that Morawitz had any sympathy for the Ottomans' web of debt, as his writings make clear; see also W. Morgan Shuster, *The Strangling of Persia* (New Century, 2012), and Mohammad Mosaddegh's 1913 dissertation on the Capitulations written in Switzerland.

48. Maurits van den Boogert, *The Capitulations and the Ottoman Legal System: Qadis, Consuls and the Beratlıs in the 18th Century* (Brill, 2005), 19–24.

49. Turan Kayaoğlu, *Legal Imperialism: Sovereignty and Extraterritoriality in Japan, the Ottoman Empire, and China* (Cambridge University Press, 2010), 43.

50. Kayaoğlu, *Legal Imperialism*, 5; Janice E. Thomson, *Mercenaries, Pirates, and Sovereigns: State-Building and Extraterritorial Violence in Early Modern Europe* (Princeton University Press, 1994).

51. In neighboring Iran, the Capitulations, too, were on the minds of government leaders, economists, journalists, and intellectuals. In 1914, Mohammad Mosaddegh, who in 1951 would be elected prime minister of Iran, had just completed a dissertation in law at the University of Neuchâtel and published articles on Iran and the Capitulations' infringements on the Iranian state and economy. The future revolutionary leader Ayatollah Khomeini was expelled from Iran in 1964 for suggesting that the special privileges granted to the United States in the twentieth century were akin to the Capitulations of the previous century. See H. E. Chehabi and Ali Gheissari, "Extraterritoriality and Capitulations in Qajar Iran," in *Unconquered States: Non-European Powers in the Imperial Age*, ed. H. E. Chehabi and David Motadel (Oxford University Press, 2024), 201 and 204.

52. Kayaoğlu, *Legal Imperialism*, 46–48, 104, 115. Few indicators revealed the military weakness of the Ottoman Empire, and its precarious place in the international landscape as much as the "Treaty Guaranteeing the Independence and Integrity of the Ottoman Empire: Austria, France, and Britain," signed in 1856. The treaty supplemented article 7 of the Treaty of Paris (1856), which also promised to safeguard the empire's integrity; yet the empire's

sovereignty was already substantially compromised and continued to be so until the era of the First World War. The signatories pledged to protect the empire's borders and independence militarily. The rationale behind the agreement was preventing Russia from expanding into the Ottoman Empire and maintaining a "balance of powers" in Europe, especially between Britain and Russia. It did not, however, keep the signatories from extending extraterritorial rights to Ottoman subjects and exploiting Ottoman resources economically and geostrategically. See Kayaoğlu, *Legal Imperialism*, 111.

53. M. Şükrü Hanioğlu, *A Brief History of the Late Ottoman Empire* (Princeton University Press, 2008), 72–108; James McDougall, "Sovereignty, Governance, and Political Community in the Ottoman Empire and North Africa," in *Re-imagining Democracy in the Mediterranean, 1780–1860*, ed. Joanna Innes and Mark Philp (Oxford University Press, 2018), 127–52; Richard E. Antaramian, *Brokers of Empire, Brokers of Faith: Armenians and the Politics of Reform in the Ottoman Empire* (Stanford University Press, 2020); Ussama Makdisi, *Age of Coexistence: The Ecumenical Frame and the Making of the Modern Arab World* (California University Press, 2019).

54. Deniz T. Kılınçoğlu, *Economics and Capitalism in the Ottoman Empire* (New York: Routledge, 2015), 45–47; Şevket Pamuk, *Uneven Centuries: Economic Development of Turkey since 1820* (Princeton University Press, 2018), 127.

55. Pamuk, *Uneven Centuries*, 127.

56. At the face value of 3 million and 5 million British pounds, respectively. See Ali Coşkun Tunçer, *Sovereign Debt and International Financial Control: The Middle East and the Balkans, 1870–1914* (Palgrave Macmillan, 2015), 55.

57. Jonathan Grant, "The Sword of the Sultan: Ottoman Arms Imports, 1854–1914," *Journal of Military History* 66 (2002): 9–36; Edhem Eldem, "Ottoman Financial Integration with Europe: Foreign Loans, the Ottoman Bank, and the Ottoman Public Debt," *European Review* 13 (2005): 431–45.

58. Pamuk, *Uneven Centuries*, 161.

59. Pamuk, *Uneven Centuries*, 131.

60. Birdal, *Political Economy of Ottoman Public Debt*, 7.

61. Birdal, *Political Economy of Ottoman Public Debt*, 6–8; Kılınçoğlu, *Economics and Capitalism*, 43; Tunçer, *Sovereign Debt*.

62. Elkins refers to this process as "predatory banking," see Caroline Elkins, *Legacy of Violence: A History of the British Empire* (Alfred A. Knopf, 2022), 9; Todd, *Velvet Empire*, 206–18; Giampaolo Conte, "Unholy Alliances: Disentangling the Economic Relations between Italy, the Holy See and the Ottoman Empire," *International History Review* 43 (2021): 1142–59; Giampaolo Conte and Gaetano Sabatini, "The Ottoman External Debt and Its Features under European Financial Control (1881–1914)," *Journal of European Economic History* 43 (2014): 69–96; idem, "Debt and Imperialism in Pre-Protectorate Tunisia, 1867–1870: A Political and Economic Analysis," *Journal of European Economic History* 47 (2018): 9–32. The governments of Egypt, Greece, Iran, Serbia, Tunisia, and countries further afield such as Argentina also found themselves entangled in a web of debt and defaulting on their payments.

63. The government hired Sir William Willcocks, a renowned irrigation engineer. See also Elizabeth R. Williams, *States of Cultivation: Imperial Transition and Scientific Agriculture in the Eastern Mediterranean* (Stanford University Press, 2023); Chris Gratien, *The Unsettled Plain: An Environmental History of the Late Ottoman Frontier* (Stanford University Press, 2022).

64. Birdal, *Political Economy of Ottoman Public Debt*, 91–92, 96–98, 113–15, 121; Williams, *States of Cultivation.*

65. Birdal, *Political Economy of Ottoman Public Debt*, 131–35. Birdal notes, "Throughout its operation the Régie always remained a focus of public opposition, regarded as a symbol of Western imperialism and exploitation, mostly due to its controversial methods in dealing with the cultivators and its infamous surveillance agents, the *kolcu*, who were regarded as responsible for the deaths of thousands" (163); see also Can Nacar, *Labor and Power in the Late Ottoman Empire: Tobacco Workers, Managers, and the State, 1872–1912* (Palgrave Macmillan, 2019), 127.

66. Nacar, *Labor and Power*, 3 and 24. Nacar estimates the number of private tobacco factories in the empire for the year 1883 as between 300 and 450.

67. Elkins, *Legacy of Violence*; Todd, *Velvet Empire.*

68. Kemal Karpat, *The Politicization of Islam: Reconstructing Identity, State, Faith, and Community in the Late Ottoman State* (Oxford University Press, 2001), 97; Pamuk, *Uneven Centuries*, 130; see also Bedross Der Matossian, *Shattered Dreams of Revolution* (Stanford University Press, 2014); Alexandre Toumarkine, *Les migrations des populations musulmanes balkaniques en Anatolie (1876–1913)* (Editions Isis, 1995).

69. İbrahim Hilmi, *Milletin kusurları* (1913/14), 13, also quoted in Eyal Ginio, *The Ottoman Culture of Defeat: The Balkan Wars and Their Aftermath* (Oxford University Press, 2016), 191–92.

70. Fuat Dündar, *İttihat ve Terakki'nin Müslümanları İskân Politikası (1913–1918)* (İletişim, 2001), 56; Ella Fratantuono, *Governing Migration in the Late Ottoman Empire* (Edinburgh University Press, 2024); Methodieva, *Between Empire and Nation*; Amzi-Erdoğdular, *Afterlife of Ottoman Europe*; Emily Greble, *Muslims and the Making of Modern Europe* (Oxford University Press, 2021).

71. Mediha Kayra, *Hoşça Kal Trabzon, Merhaba İstanbul: Bir Kız Çocuğunun Günlüğünden I. Dünya Savaşı'nda Anadolu*, ed. Cahit Kayra (Istanbul: Tarihçi Kitabevi, 2013), 247–48, see also 241.

72. Vladimir Hamed-Troyansky, *Empire of Refugees: North Caucasian Muslims and the Late Ottoman State* (Stanford University Press, 2024); see also Benjamin C. Fortna, *The Circassian: A Life of Eşref Bey, Late Ottoman Insurgent and Special Agent* (Oxford University Press, 2016).

73. "By 1864, the north-western Caucasus had been emptied of its indigenous population almost in entirety." See Stephen D. Shenfield, "The Circassians: A Forgotten Genocide?" in *The Massacre in History*, ed. Mark Levene and Penny Roberts (Berghahn Books, 1999), 154; see the works of Vladimir Hamed-Troyansky, Alexandre Toumarkine, Isa Blumi, David Gutman, and Ella Fratantuono.

74. Cem Behar, ed., *Osmanlı İmparatorluğu'nun ve Türkiye'nin Nüfusu, 1500–1927* (Ankara: Devlet İstatistik Enstitüsü Matbaası, 1996), 62; Onur Yıldırım, *Diplomacy and Displacement: Reconsidering the Turco-Greek Exchange of Populations, 1922–1934* (Routledge, 2006), 89.

75. Hamed-Troyansky, *Empire of Refugees*, 72–75.

76. Erik Jan Zürcher, "The Young Turks—Children of the Borderlands," in *Turkology Update Leiden Project Working Papers Archive* (2002): 1–9, and idem, "How Europeans Adopted Anatolia and Created Turkey," *European Review* 13 (2005): 379–94.

77. Enver Pascha, *Um Tripolis* (Munich: Hugo Bruckmann, 1918).

78. Çetinkaya, *Young Turks and the Boycott Movement*; Khuri-Makdisi, *Eastern Mediterranean and the Making of Global Radicalism.*

79. Çetinkaya, *Young Turks and the Boycott Movement*, 49; Koraltürk, *Ekonominin Türkleştirilmesi*, 40–41.

80. Çetinkaya, *Young Turks and the Boycott Movement*, 52, 100, 119, 126; see also Emre Erol, *The Ottoman Crisis in Western Anatolia: Turkey's Belle Époque and the Transition to a Modern Nation State* (I. B. Tauris, 2016).

81. Çetinkaya, *Young Turks and the Boycott Movement*, 116, 165; for the quotes see 166 and 171.

82. Çetinkaya, 177–78; for the quote, see 225.

83. Koraltürk, *Ekonominin Türkleştirilmesi*, 30–35. One privilege, for example, exempted foreign companies from paying any taxes on profits earned. A subsequent law, dated March 8, 1915, required that non-Ottoman citizens be subject to the same regulations as Ottoman citizens for providing legal, medical, pharmaceutical, or engineering services, and to open schools or publish journals and newspapers. See also Semih Gökatalay, "Economic Nationalism of the Committee of Union and Progress Revisited: The Case of the Society for the Ottoman Navy," *Nationalities Papers* 48 (2020): 942–56.

84. Bishop Nighogos also spoke of Ottoman rule as that of "the heathen Turkish khanate" and deemed Ottoman rule the "lesser of two evils" in comparison to European rule. Nonetheless, the overall vision conveyed is that of a strong, united Armenian community among other Ottoman communities. For an astute, insightful discussion of the memoir see Nora Lessersohn, "'Provincial Cosmopolitanism' in Late Ottoman Anatolia: An Armenian Shoemaker's Memoir," *Comparative Studies in Society and History* 57 (2015): 548, which cites Lessersohn's great-grandfather's memoir: Hovhannes Cherishian (1886–1967), *Testimony* (unpublished, Brooklyn, NY, 1966), 24–25. For the divisive effect of American and European missionaries on Ottoman Armenians, see the writings of the famous Armenian writer Raffi (ca. 1835–1888).

85. Lessersohn, "Provincial Cosmopolitanism," 548–49; see also Julia Phillips Cohen, *Becoming Ottomans: Sephardi Jews and Imperial Citizenship in the Modern Era* (Oxford University Press, 2014); Campos, *Ottoman Brothers.*

86. BOA, DH.ŞFR 43/127, Talat to Hacı Adil, Governor of Edirne Province, encoded telegram, *Very Urgent* [*Gayet Müstaceldir*] 15/16 Temmuz 1330 (July 28/29, 1914).

87. BOA, DH.ŞFR 43/127, Talat to Hacı Adil, Governor of Edirne Province, encoded telegram, *Very Urgent* [*Gayet Müstaceldir*] 15/16 Temmuz 1330 (July 28/29, 1914).

88. Hans-Lukas Kieser, *Talaat Pasha: Father of Modern Turkey, Architect of Genocide* (Princeton University Press, 2018), 41. The family returned to Edirne after the end of that war.

89. The psychological impact of the Balkan Wars on Ottoman society and especially on the Committee of Union and Progress leadership has been examined in Erik J. Zürcher, *The Young Turk Legacy and National Building: From the Ottoman Empire to Atatürk's Turkey* (I. B. Tauris, 2010); for a diverging view, see Öztan, "Point of No Return?"

90. Serhat Güvenç, *Birinci Dünya Savaşına Giden Yol: Osmanlıların Drednot Düşleri* (İş Bankası, 2009), 74.

91. A. Warren Dockter, "'A Great Turkish Policy': Winston Churchill, the Ottoman Empire and the Origins of the Dardanelles Campaign," *History: The Journal of the Historical Association* 102 (2017): 78.

92. Nadir Özbek, "Defining the Public Sphere during the Late Ottoman Empire: War, Mass Mobilization and the Young Turk Regime (1908–18)," *Middle Eastern Studies* 43 (2007): 795–805.

93. Kayra, *Hoşça Kal Trabzon*, 21 and 197.

94. In May 1914, Mallet had learned that the Greek navy was considering "sinking the 'Sultan Osman' and 'Rechadieh' on their way out" on the voyage from England to Istanbul. Mallet observed that such a step would be regrettable, but that nothing could really stop Greece. "If anything of that kind happened," he noted, "it would of course put the Greeks in the wrong, but that would be a matter of secondary importance, as it would probably not deprive them of the moral sympathy of Europe." See TNA, FO 800/80, Mallet to Grey, May 17, 1914. The Russian government, too, in early 1914, actively tried to prevent or delay the completion and transfer of the dreadnoughts the British companies were building for the Ottoman navy. Saint Petersburg successfully sought to prevent the sale of two additional dreadnoughts originally ordered by the Brazilian and Chilean governments. Even before the July Crisis, therefore, there were second thoughts about handing this additional sea power to the Ottomans, given the hostility between the empire and Greece. London was in no mood to arm their protégé's enemy with state-of-the-art dreadnoughts, see Bobroff, *Roads to Glory*, 89–90.

95. Özbek, "Defining the Public Sphere," 795–809; Güvenç, *Birinci Dünya Savaşına Giden Yol*, 22. The medals consisted of various metals such as copper and nickel and a green and white banner; for an image see Güvenç, 25.

96. Güvenç, *Birinci Dünya Savaşına*, 37–54.

97. For the Ottoman military attaché's reporting from Berlin of the German emperor's approval, see ATASE, BDH, Klasör 243, Yeni Dosya 1009, Fihrist 7–2, Cemil to Enver, August 3, 1914; for Enver's initial request, see PA/AA, R 22402, Wangenheim to Auswärtiges Amt, August 2, 1914, no. 407; for Enver's orders to admit any German or Habsburg ships into the Straits, see ATASE, BDH, Klasör 4611, Yeni Dosya 10, Fihrist 4, 1–4, Enver to the Commander of the Southern Dardanelles, *Very Confidential and Urgent*, 22 Temmuz 1330 [August 4, 1914]; ibid., Fihrist 1–61, *Very Confidential*, 22 Temmuz 1330 [August 4, 1914]; for the Ottoman "purchase," see BA-MA, RM 40/671, 4 and reverse, Wangenheim, August 10, 1914, and Aksakal, *Ottoman Road to War*, 117–18. Klaus Wolf, moreover, has suggested the British navy "allowed" the two German ships to reach Istanbul, because it saw them as a potential buffer to Russian ambition to seize the Straits, see Klaus Wolf, *Gallipoli 1915: Das deutsch-türkische Militärbündnis im Ersten Weltkrieg* (Report Verlag, 2008), 36–37; BA-MA, RM40/184, "Kritische Stellungnahme des Admirals Souchon zum türkischen Operationsplan Herbst 1914," 22, folio 58, says it was Wangenheim, who, on August 1, 1914, suggested to Said Halim to make the request, and that the request was approved only on August 4, after the bombardment of Bone.

98. Cavid Bey, *Meşrutiyet Ruznâmesi*, ed. Hasan Babacan and Servet Avşar (Ankara: Türk Tarih Kurumu, 2014), entry for August 2, 1914, vol. 2, 615–16.

99. Bobroff, *Roads to Glory*, 101, citing Leontiev to Saint Petersburg, August 13, 1914, reporting conversation from August 5; also, Aksakal, *Ottoman Road to War*, 127–28.

100. Aksakal, *Ottoman Road to War*, 4, citing Giers to Sazonov, August 5, 1914.

101. Aksakal, *Ottoman Road to War*, 127–28; Bobroff, *Roads to Glory*, 102.

102. The *Goeben* was renamed the *Yavuz*, after the sultan who had conquered Egypt back in the sixteenth century; the name signaled that Egypt, occupied by Britain in 1882, remained Ottoman. The renaming of the *Breslau* as the *Midilli* (Mytilene/Lesbos) after the Aegean island had two rationales: Cemal, the navy minister, had been born there, and it was one of the islands Greece had captured in the First Balkan War in 1912. The names of the famous new ships were meant to serve as constant reminders of these wounds and symbols of the government's life-and-death reassertion.

103. Cavid, *Meşrutiyet Ruznâmesi*, August 10, 1914, vol. 2, 618.

104. Cavid, *Meşrutiyet Ruznâmesi*, August 10, 1914, vol. 2, 618; this part of the original Cavid diary, Notebook 14, is missing, see editor's note on vol. 2, 613. The editors have used the serialized Cavid diary appearing in *Devrim* newspaper in 1971. I have also consulted the earlier serialized version from *Tanin* appearing in 1944. See the issue from 17 Birinciteşrin 1944.

105. TNA, FO 800/80, First Lord of the Admiralty Winston Churchill to Enver Pasha, August 15, 1914.

106. M. Şükrü Hanioğlu, *Preparation for a Revolution* (Oxford University Press, 2001), 289–95.

107. "Bu beyânât-ı şifahiyeyi ben tabiî kâfi bulmuyorum," see Cavid, *Meşrutiyet Ruznâmesi*, August 17, 1914, vol. 2, 623; Berlin ordered mobilization on August 1, 1914, and declared war on Russia on August 1 and on France on August 3, 1914. Britain declared war on Germany on August 4, 1914 (and on Austria-Hungary on August 12, the Ottoman Empire on November 5, 1914, and Bulgaria on October 15, 1915).

108. Serge Sazonov, *Fateful Years, 1909–1916* (New York: Frederick A. Stokes, 1928), 50.

109. Sazonov, *Fateful Years*, 63.

110. Sazonov, 49.

111. Sazonov, 72.

112. Giers reported this to Sazonov on August 19, cited in Bobroff, *Roads to Glory*, 106.

113. Bobroff, 106. Bobroff notes that the Ottoman government "unsurprisingly, was dissatisfied with this lackluster Entente offering."

114. Cavid, *Meşrutiyet Ruznâmesi*, August 19, 1914, vol. 2, 625–27.

115. Cavid, vol. 2, 625–26. Cemal added the delivery of the two ships the Ottomans had ordered with British companies as a third demand.

116. Cavid, vol. 2, 628.

117. Sir L. Mallet, no. 24, *Correspondence Respecting Events Leading to the Rupture of Relations with Turkey*, Miscellaneous no. 13, Presented to both Houses of Parliament by Command of His Majesty, November 1914 (London: Printed under the Authority of His Majesty's Stationery Office, 1914), 8; Cemal also requested delivery of the two British ships that had been sequestered.

118. Cavid, *Meşrutiyet Ruznâmesi*, August 20, 1914, vol. 2, 628.

119. Cavid, *Meşrutiyet Ruznâmesi*, August 22, 1914, vol. 2, 630.

120. Cavid, *Meşrutiyet Ruznâmesi*, August 22, 1914, vol. 2, 631.

121. Cavid, *Meşrutiyet Ruznâmesi*, August 22, 1914, vol. 2, 630.

122. Bobroff, *Roads to Glory*, 107 and 112; for a more moderate account of Krivoshein and Russian policy more broadly, albeit beginning in 1915, see Peter Holquist, "The Politics and

Practice of the Russian Occupation of Armenia, 1915–February 1917," in Suny, Göçek, and Naimark, *Question of Genocide*, 151–74.

123. Bobroff, *Roads to Glory*, 106.

124. *Rupture*, no. 64, Sir L. Mallet to Sir Edward Grey, September 6, 1914, received September 7.

125. Bobroff, *Roads to Glory*, 93.

126. Aksakal, *Ottoman Road to War*, 72–77.

127. Grey to Buchanan, March 11, 1915, cited in Wilson, "Grey and the Russian Threat to India," 280.

128. Wilson, "Grey and the Russian Threat to India," 282; Wilson emphasizes that the principal reason for Britain to enter the war was to stand by her allies Russia and France. Grey threatened to resign if Britain did not act, followed by Asquith. Grey made Asquith see King George V and told him, you must stay with Russia. In 1916 Paul Cambon signed the Sykes-Picot-Sazonov agreement for the French side.

129. See Mallet's statement: "I gather from the telegrams from French Minister for Foreign Affairs that he thinks that we should take a stronger line with the Turks. Nothing would give me and my Russian colleague greater pleasure if our Governments are ready to accept the consequences which both of us think would be of the most serious character." See TNA, FO 800/80, September 26, 1914, sent 6:45 p.m., received 10:45 p.m., Mallet to Grey; also Bobroff, *Roads to Glory*, 107 and 112.

130. Cavid, *Meşrutiyet Ruznâmesi*, September 6, 1914, vol. 2, 644.

131. The text was drafted by Hüseyin Cahid, the former editor of *Tanin* newspaper, and was to be submitted to Great Power embassies the following evening, September 7, 1914. See Cavid, *Meşrutiyet Ruznâmesi*, September 20, 1914, vol. 2, 656–58.

132. Kayra, *Hoşça Kal Trabzon, Merhaba İstanbul*, 199. The facsimile of the original diary is given on pages 197–349; see also the chapter by Christoph Herzog, "The Urban Experience of Women's Memoirs: Mediha Kayra's World War I Notebook," in *Women and the City, Women in the City: A Gendered Perspective on Ottoman Urban History*, ed. Nazan Maksudyan (Berghahn, 2014), 146–68; for Ottoman children in the First World War, see Nazan Maksudyan, *Ottoman Children and Youth during World War I* (Syracuse University Press, 2019).

133. Kayra, *Hoşça Kal Trabzon*, 200.

134. Vedat Eldem, *Harp ve Mütareke Yıllarında Osmanlı İmparatorluğu'nun Ekonomisi* (Türk Tarih Kurumu Basımevi, 1994), 29. The decree abolishing these special privileges consisted of a single article: "The financial, economic, judicial, and administrative exemptions (*imtiyazat*) known as Capitulations are terminated by decision of the Council of Ministers; irade-i senniye, Mehmed Reşad."

135. Bobroff, *Roads to Glory*, 112.

136. Bobroff, 112; see also Holquist, "The Politics and Practice of the Russian Occupation," 151–74.

137. TNA, FO 800/80, September 26, 1914, sent 6:45 p.m., received 10:45 p.m., Mallet to Grey.

138. BA-MA, RM40/184, "Kritische Stellungnahme des Admirals Souchon zum türkischen Operationsplan Herbst 1914," 32, folio 68.

139. In the words of the German admiral who led the naval attack on Russia on October 29, 1914, see BA-MA, RM40/184, "Kritische Stellungnahme des Admirals Souchon zum türkischen Operationsplan Herbst 1914," 77, folio 113.

140. BA-MA, RM40/184, "Kritische Stellungnahme des Admirals Souchon zum türkischen Operationsplan Herbst 1914," 53, folio 89.

141. BA-MA, RM 40/454, H[umann] to B[usse], October 25 [1914], folio 306, the note reads: "Enclosed 16 letters provided by the Navy Minister [Cemal]. They are the requested orders for the commanders." Subsequently the letters were ordered to be destroyed, see BA-MA, RM 40/454, folio 196, Souchon to Ships, [November] 4, 1914.

142. BA-MA, RM 40/771, folio 2–20 reverse, Logbook Berk-i Satvet, Oberstleutnant zur See von Mellenthin, October 10, 1914, to December 12, 1914, read and signed by Souchon on December 14, 1914.

143. BA-MA, RM 40/54, 28, Souchon to Etappe, October 29, 1914.

144. BA-MA, RM 40/54, 29, Souchon to Etappe, October 30, 1914, 1:35 a.m.

145. George Abel Schreiner, *From Berlin to Bagdad: Behind the Scenes in the Near East* (New York: Harper & Brothers, 1918), 59. Schreiner spent nine months in the empire during the war as a reporter for the Associated Press.

146. Schreiner, *Berlin to Bagdad*, 60. Entente archives tend to confirm Said Halim's fears. The French foreign minister, Gaston Doumergue, behind closed doors, and, in conversation with the Russian ambassador at Paris, noted as early as August 11 that the Entente could issue the territorial guarantee the Ottomans were demanding to "calm" Ottoman fears. Doing so would not, however, "prevent us from solving the Straits question in line with our thinking at war's end." See Aksakal, *Ottoman Road to War*, 3; Bobroff, *Roads to Glory*, 103, citing Izvolskii to Sazonov, August 10, 1914.

147. Schreiner, *From Berlin to Bagdad*, 60.

148. "Turkey Distrusted Allies, Says Halim," *New York Times*, February 22, 1915.

149. Schreiner, *Berlin to Bagdad*, 62.

150. *Meclis-i Ayan'ın Zabıt Ceridesi*, 15 Şubat 1331 (February 28, 1916).

Chapter 2. An Empire's Domestic Revolution

1. MAE, Serie Guerre 867, September 9, 1914, no. 152, Cipher, Defrance to Ministère des Affaires Étrangeres, and November 12, 1914, no. 158, Cipher, Defrance to Ministère des Affaires Étrangeres.

2. Quoted in Najwa al-Qattan, "When Mothers Ate Their Children: Wartime Memory and the Language of Food in Syria and Lebanon," *International Journal of Middle East Studies* 46 (2014): 727.

3. Edward W. Said, *Out of Place: A Memoir* (Knopf, 1999), 8–10. Said's father had left Jerusalem for the United States in 1912 or 1913, during the Balkan Wars, to escape being conscripted by Ottoman authorities. For emigration, see Stacy D. Fahrenthold, *Between the Ottomans and the Entente: The First World War in the Syrian and Lebanese Diaspora, 1908–1925* (Oxford University Press, 2019); Akram Fouad Khater, *Inventing Home: Emigration, Gender, and the Middle Class in Lebanon, 1870–1920* (University of California Press, 2001).

4. This expression, connoting "internal enemy," originated in the Spanish civil war of the 1930s.

5. For the origins of the 1908 Constitutional Revolution, see the definitive work by M. Şükrü Hanioğlu, *Preparation for a Revolution: The Young Turks 1902–1908* (Oxford University Press, 2001), and idem, *The Young Turks in Opposition* (Oxford University Press, 1995). See also the crucial publications by Erik Jan Zürcher, "Macedonians in Anatolia: The Importance of the Macedonian Roots of the Unionists for Their Policies in Anatolia after 1914," *Middle Eastern Studies* 50 (2014): 960–75, and idem, "The Young Turk Revolution: Comparisons and Connections," *Middle Eastern Studies* 55 (2019): 481–98.

6. That parliament was shut down and the constitution suspended by Sultan Abdülhamid II because of the Ottoman-Russian war of 1877–78. See Christoph Herzog and Malik Sharif, *The First Ottoman Experiment in Democracy* (Ergon, 2010).

7. Ali Abdullatif Ahmida, *The Making of Modern Libya: State Formation, Colonization, and Resistance*, 2nd ed. (State University of New York Press, 2009), 103–40; Stefan Hock, "'Waking Us from This Endless Slumber': The Ottoman-Italian War and North Africa in the Ottoman Twentieth Century," *War in History* 26 (2019): 204–26; Eileen Ryan, *Religion as Resistance: Negotiating Authority in Italian Libya* (Oxford University Press, 2019).

8. Ali Birinci, *Hürriyet ve İtilâf Fırkası: II. Meşrutiyet Devrinde İttihat ve Terakki'ye Karşı Çıkanlar* (Dergâh Yayınları, 2012; 1990), 56–57.

9. This event is known as the *Bab-ı Âli Baskını*—The Raid (or March) on the Sublime Porte.

10. Şehbenderzade Filibeli Ahmet Hilmi, *Muhalefetin İflası* (Kostantiniyye: Hikmet Matbaa-i İslamiyesi, 1331 [1915]), 6.

11. Birinci, *Hürriyet ve İtilâf Fırkası*, 46 and 64; Ilham Khuri-Makdisi, *The Eastern Mediterranean and the Making of Global Radicalism, 1860–1914* (University of California Press, 2010). See also Nobuyoshi Fujinami, "Decentralizing Centralists, or the Political Language on Provincial Administration in the Second Ottoman Constitutional Period," *Middle Eastern Studies* 49 (2013): 880–900; and Cenk Reyhan, *Türkiye'de Liberalizm Kökenleri: Prens Sabahaddin (1877–1948)* (İmge Kitabevi, 2008).

12. Ahmet Emin Yalman, *Turkey in the World War* (Yale University Press, 1930), 50.

13. Yalman, *Turkey in the World War*, 50.

14. Yalman, 50.

15. Yalman, 44–45. See also Christine Philliou, *Turkey: A Past against History* (University of California Press, 2021).

16. Hüseyin Cahit Yalçın, *Siyasal Anılar*, ed. Rauf Mutluay (Türkiye İş Bankası Kültür Yayınları, 1976), 150–51.

17. Yalçın, *Siyasî Anılar*, 166.

18. Because of a fire in 1910, the Assembly had moved from Çırağan Palace to Nazime Palace, also known as Cemile Palace, adjacent to Çırağan.

19. At the time parliament was meeting in a special session in the summer to complete unfinished business. The parliament's regular session ran from October to March.

20. *Meclis-i Mebusan'ın Zabıt Ceridesi*, 20 Temmuz 1330 (August 2, 1914).

21. *Meclis-i Ayan'ın Zabıt Ceridesi*, 20 Temmuz 1330 (August 2, 1914).

22. See Hanioğlu, *Young Turks in Opposition*.

23. See Bedross Der Matossian, *Shattered Dreams of Revolution* (Stanford University Press, 2014); Nader Sohrabi, *Revolution and Constitutionalism in the Ottoman Empire and Iran* (Cambridge University Press, 2011), 224–83; on the effects of parliamentary politics in Palestine, see Michelle U. Campos, *Ottoman Brothers: Muslims, Christians, and Jews in Early Twentieth-Century Palestine* (Stanford University Press, 2011); on the making of the revolution itself, see Hanioğlu, *Preparation for a Revolution*. For historians, the minutes of the parliament are an invaluable if imperfect source for understanding the stakes of political debate during the war years. The records also reveal the extent to which information about wartime events were known in the capital.

24. George Abel Schreiner, *From Berlin to Bagdad: Behind the Scenes in the Near East* (New York: Harper & Brothers, 1918), 62.

25. BOA, DH.ŞFR, 437/120, Cevdet to Interior Ministry, 7 Ağustos 1330 (August 20, 1914).

26. BOA, DH.EUM 4. Şube 1/4, Governorate of Syria to Interior Ministry, 13 Ağustos 1330 (August 26, 1914).

27. BOA, DH.EUM 4. Şube 1/4, Governorate of Syria to Interior Ministry, 19 Ağustos 1330 (September 1, 1914).

28. BOA, DH.EUM 4. Şube 1/4, Governor Hulusi to Interior Ministry, 20 Ağustos 1330 (September 2, 1914).

29. BOA, DH.EUM 4. Şube 1/4, Governor Hulusi to Interior Ministry, 23 Ağustos 1330 (September 5, 1914).

30. BOA, DH.EUM 4. Şube 1/4, *Urgent* (Müstaceldir), Governor Bekir Sami to Interior Ministry, 20 Ağustos 1330 (September 2, 1914).

31. On Bekir Sami, see Dimitry R. Zhantiev, "Making Opinion at the Summit: A Northern Caucasian Nobleman in the Ottoman-Turkish Ruling Elite: Bekir Sami-Bey Kundukh (1865–1933)," *Archiv Orientální* 80 (2012): 273–76.

32. Engin Deniz Akarlı, *The Long Peace: Ottoman Lebanon, 1861–1920* (University of California Press, 1993), 71–81, 121–31. The following are percentages of a total population of 414,800 (for 1913/1914): Maronite 58.4; Druze 11.4; Greek Orthodox 12.6; Greek Catholic 7.7; Shiite 5.7; Sunni 3.5; Other 0.7, see Akarlı, 106.

33. Sabine Prätor, *Der arabische Faktor in der jungtürkischen Politik: eine Studie zum osmanischen Parlament der II. Konstitution (1908–1918)* (Klaus Schwarz, 1993), 14; Abdulrahim Abuhusayn, "An Ottoman against the Constitution: The Maronites of Mount Lebanon and the Question of Representation in the Ottoman Parliament," in *Religion, Ethnicity and Contested Nationhood in the Former Ottoman Space*, ed. Jørgen Nielsen (Brill, 2012), 89–113.

34. Greater Syria's population stood around 4 million in 1914; Beirut's around 185,000. See Melanie S. Tanielian, *Charity of War: Famine, Humanitarian Aid, and World War I in the Middle East* (Stanford University Press, 2017). On the naval blockade, see Heather Jones, "A Forgotten Front? The Mediterranean Blockade in the First World War," *International History Review* 46 (2024): 426–43.

35. BOA, DH.EUM 4. Şube 1/4, *Urgent* (Müstaceldir), Governor Bekir Sami to Interior Ministry, 20 Ağustos 1330 (September 2, 1914). See also Tamara Chalaba, *The Shi'is of Jabal 'Amil and the New Lebanon: Community and Nation, 1918–1943* (Palgrave, 2006).

36. MAE, Série Guerre 867, December 1, 1914. Despite the date on the document, these discussions took place prior to September 5, 1914.

37. MAE, Série Guerre 867, September 5, 1914.

38. MAE, Série Guerre 867, September 9, 1914.

39. BOA, DH.EUM 4. Şube 1/4, *Coded Telegram* (Şifre), Governor Bekir Sami to Interior Ministry, 30 Ağustos 1330 (September 12, 1914); Ohannes Pasha's telling of the episode differs somewhat from that of the archival account, adding that Shoufati was the owner of a liquor store from Beirut and a Christian who had a personal dispute with the Druze police officer. In Ohannes's account, the flag touching the ground was only a secondary circumstance, not the actual cause of the disagreement, 80–81: "J'avais déjà mes informations personnelles à ce sujet. Il s'agissait tout simplement d'une dispute entre l'individu incriminé, Nedjib Chouéfati, chrétien de Beyrouth, tenancier d'un débit de vins et liqueurs et un gendarme druze. Celui-ci avait voulu empêcher le liquoriste de déplacer un pavois attaché au-dessus de l'entrée de sa boutique et qui en gênait l'accès. La querelle devint d'autant plus vive que les relations personnelles entre l'agent de l'autorité et le boutiquier étaient déjà, paraît-il, très peu amicales. Ce dernier s'étant saisi du drapeau, il y eut une lutte pendant laquelle l'emblème national toucha forcément la terre. À cela se réduisait l'‘horrible crime' dont on voulait accabler le Liban et son gouverneur."

40. BOA, DH.EUM 4. Şube 1/4, *Coded Telegram* (Şifre), Governor Bekir Sami to Interior Ministry, 30 Ağustos 1330 (September 12, 1914).

41. MAE, Série Guerre 867, November 27, 1914.

42. MAE, Série Guerre 867, December 23, 1914.

43. Cemal Paşa, *Hatırât: 1913–1922* (Dersaadet: n.p., 1922). Eşref was one of the agents searching the consulates, see Benjamin C. Fortna, *The Circassian: A Life of Eşref Bey, Late Ottoman Insurgent and Special Agent* (Oxford University Press, 2016), 172–73, and M. Talha Çiçek, *War and State Formation in Syria: Cemal Pasha's Governorate during World War I, 1914–1917* (Routledge, 2014), especially 43–47.

44. Special Collection, Princeton University, Sir John Maxwell Papers, box 4, folder 5, Sir John Maxwell, Cairo, to Kitchener, October 21, 1914.

45. Ronald Bobroff, *Roads to Glory: Late Imperial Russia and the Turkish Straits* (I. B. Tauris, 2006), 110, citing Vvedenskii to Sazonov, August 3, 1914.

46. Quoted in Donald Bloxham, *The Great Game of Genocide: Imperialism, Nationalism, and the Destruction of the Ottoman Armenians* (Oxford University Press, 2005), 72. See the same source for an August 5, 1914, letter from Catholikos Kevork V to Vorontsov-Dashkov assuring Vorontsov-Dashkov and the tsar of the loyalty of both Russian and Ottoman Armenians.

47. Bobroff, *Roads to Glory*, 110–11, citing Sazonov to Sukhomlinov, August 15, 1914.

48. Hilmar Kaiser, *The Extermination of Armenians in the Diarbekir Region* (Istanbul Bilgi University Press, 2015), 124.

49. Bobroff, *Roads to Glory*, 111, citing Vorontsov-Dashkov to Sazonov, September 6, 1914.

50. Bobroff, 111.

51. ATASE, BDH, Klasör 577, Yeni Dosya 3, Fihrist 13, *İstihbarât* (Intelligence), 2–3 Ağustos 330 (August 15–16, 1914).

52. BOA, DH.EUM 2. Şube 1/31, *Şifre* (Coded Telegram), Governor Tahsin to Directorate of General Security, 12 Ağustos 330 (August 25, 1914).

53. BOA, DH.EUM 2. Şube 2/32, Governor Azmi to Interior Ministry, *Şifre* (Coded Telegram), 9 Teşrin-i evvel 1330 (October 22, 1914). This document is also cited in Taner Akçam,

The Young Turks' Crime against Humanity: The Armenian Genocide and Ethnic Cleansing in the Ottoman Empire (Princeton University Press, 2011), 150n84, where translation and interpretation differ from mine.

54. See the preface by Zalman Shazar in Izhak Ben-Zvi, *The Hebrew Battalions: Letters*, trans. Taffi Baker and Margalit Benaya (Jerusalem: Yad Izhak Ben-Zvi, 1969), 9; Martin Watts, *The Jewish Legion and the First World War* (Palgrave Macmillan, 2004), 21.

55. Quoted in Abigail Jacobson, *From Empire to Empire: Jerusalem between Ottoman and British Rule* (Syracuse University Press, 2011), 27.

56. Louis A. Fishman, *Jews and Palestinians in the Late Ottoman Era, 1908–1914: Claiming the Homeland* (Edinburgh University Press, 2020), 138, 160–62, 157–66.

57. On imperial citizenship in Palestine during this period, see especially Campos, *Ottoman Brothers.*

58. Mehmet Beşikçi, *The Ottoman Mobilization of Manpower in the First World War: Between Voluntarism and Resistance* (Brill, 2012); Yücel Yanıkdağ, *Healing the Nation: Prisoners of War, Medicine and Nationalism in Turkey, 1914–1939* (Edinburgh University Press, 2013); Akın, *When the War Came Home.*

59. Glenda Abramson, *Hebrew Writing of the First World War* (Vallentine Mitchell, 2008), 335 and 340–46.

60. Mark Levene, "The Balfour Declaration: A Case of Mistaken Identity," *English Historical Review* 107 (1992): 54–77; Susan Pedersen, "Writing the Balfour Declaration into the Mandate for Palestine," *International History Review* 45 (2023): 279–91.

61. Watts, *Jewish Legion*, 3–4. Watts's analysis is based on some 637 individual testimonials by members of the Jewish Legion.

62. Watts, 21–29.

63. Johann Büssow, "Ottoman Reform and Urban Government in the District of Jerusalem, 1867–1917," in *Urban Governance under the Ottomans: Between Cosmopolitanism and Conflict*, ed. Ulrike Freitag and Nora Lafi (Routledge, 2014), 97–141, here 100.

64. Campos, *Ottoman Brothers*; Jacobson, *From Empire to Empire*; Julia Phillips Cohen, *Becoming Ottomans: Sephardi Jews and Imperial Citizenship in the Modern Era* (Oxford University Press, 2014).

65. Kristen Alff, "Changing Capitalist Structures and Settler-Colonial Land Purchases in Northern Palestine, 1897–1922," *International Journal of Middle East Studies* 55 (2023): 675–92; Fishman, *Jews and Palestinians*, 46–48 and 80.

66. Fishman, 84.

67. Fujinami, "Decentralizing Centralists."

68. Quoted in Dmitry Shumsky, *Beyond the Nation-State: The Zionist Political Imagination from Pinsker to Ben Gurion* (Yale University Press, 2018), 119.

69. Shumsky, *Beyond the Nation-State*, 120. Italics in Shumsky. Ahad Ha'am was the Hebrew pen name of Asher Zvi Hirsch Ginsberg.

70. Quoted in Shumsky, 90.

71. Shumsky, 50–89.

72. Shumsky, 133–34, citing Vladimir Jabotinsky, "O federatsii," in *Radikal*, January 15, 1906, and 138.

73. Orit Bashkin, "The Colonized Semites and the Infectious Disease: Theorizing and Narrativizing Anti-Semitism in the Levant, 1870–1914," *Critical Inquiry* 47 (2021): 189–217.

74. Quoted in Campos, *Ottoman Brothers*, 213.

75. Çiçek, *War and State Formation in Syria*, 79.

76. Hasan Kayalı, *Arabs and Young Turks: Ottomanism, Arabism, and Islamism in the Ottoman Empire, 1908–1918* (University of California Press, 1997), 146–48; Michael Christopher Low, *Imperial Mecca: Ottoman Arabia and the Indian Ocean Hajj* (Columbia University Press, 2020).

77. Kayalı, *Arabs and Young Turks*, 160–65.

78. Kayalı, 170, though Idrisi rejected the government's offer of this amnesty.

79. Kayalı, 172. By the final decades of the nineteenth century, "the Hijaz and the steamship hajj already had emerged as deeply contested imperial spaces." See Low, *Imperial Mecca*, 21.

80. DH.KMS, 2/2-1, *Şifre* (Coded Telegram), Governor Vehib to Interior Ministry, 22 Nisan 1330 (May 5, 1914).

81. BOA, DH.KMS 2/2-1, *Şifre* (Coded Telegram), Governor Vehib to Interior Ministry, 8 Haziran 1330 (June 21, 1914).

82. Quoted from the governor's report in Kayalı, *Arabs and Young Turks*, 184.

83. BOA, DH.KMS 2/2-1, *Şifre* (Coded Telegram), Governor Vehib to Interior Ministry, 3 Ağustos 1330 (August 16, 1914).

84. "The 1916 Arab rising can be traced to contacts established between the British and Sharif Husain of Mecca, head of the house of Hashem, in September 1914." Bloxham, *Great Game of Genocide*, 134–35, citing TNA, FO 371/2768, 69301, "Correspondence with the Grand Sherif of Mecca," April 12, 1916.

Chapter 3. An Empire's Bloody War: Sarıkamış, Suez, Gallipoli

1. Michael Francis Laffan, *Islamic Nationhood and Colonial Indonesia: The Umma below the Winds* (Routledge Curzon, 2003); Julia A. Clancy-Smith, *Rebel and Saint: Muslim Notables, Populist Protest, Colonial Encounters (Algeria and Tunisia, 1800–1904)* (University of California Press, 1994); Cheikh Anta Babou, *Fighting the Greater Jihad: Amadu Bamba and the Founding of the Muridiyya of Senegal, 1853–1913* (Ohio University Press, 2007); Cemil Aydın, *The Idea of the Muslim World: A Global Intellectual History* (Harvard University Press, 2019).

2. Michael Bonner, *Jihad in Islamic History: Doctrines and Practice* (Princeton University Press, 2006), 1–2.

3. Bonner, *Jihad in Islamic History*, 12.

4. Mustafa Aksakal, "'Holy War Made in Germany'? Ottoman Origins of the 1914 Jihad," *War in History* 18 (2011): 184–99.

5. Enver Pascha, *Um Tripolis* (Munich: Hugo Bruckmann, 1918); İpek Yosmaoğlu, *Blood Ties: Religion, Blood Ties, and the Politics of Nationhood in Ottoman Macedonia, 1878–1908* (Cornell University Press, 2013).

6. Sohail H. Hashmi, ed., *Just Wars, Holy Wars, and Jihads: Christian, Jewish, and Muslim Encounters and Exchanges* (Oxford University Press, 2012); Lothar Brock and Hendrik Simon, eds., *The Justification of War and International Order: From Past to Present* (Oxford University Press, 2021).

7. Rachel Simon, *Libya between Ottomanism and Nationalism* (Klaus Schwarz, 1987), 87.

8. Annette Becker, *War and Faith: The Religious Imagination in France, 1914–1930* (Berg, 1998).

9. For the play, see Mehmed Sezai, *Cihad-ı mukaddes yahud Trablusgarb'da Osmanlı-İtalya Cengi* (Izmir: Keşişyan Matbaası, 1327/1911) ["The Holy War, or, The Ottoman-Italian War in Tripolitania"].

10. Hasan Kayalı, *Arabs and Young Turks: Ottomanism, Arabism, and Islamism in the Ottoman Empire, 1908–1918* (University of California Press, 1997), 189. See the book's cover illustration for the stamp; Michael A. Reynolds, *Shattering Empires: The Clash and Collapse of the Ottoman Empires, 1908–1918* (Cambridge University Press, 2011), 220–22.

11. "Seni ve bütün alemi kim yaratdı?"

12. Harbiye Dairesi Piyade Şubesi, *1330 Senesi Seferberliğinde Piyade İkmal Efradının Ders Kitabı* (Istanbul, 1330/1914), 3–7.

13. Responses were written down by the instructing officer and those records that survive are now kept in the archives of the Turkish Defense Ministry, an invaluable collection awaiting its historians.

14. Mehmed Şükrü, *Heyet-i İhtiyariye* (Istanbul, 1332/1916), 44–45.

15. ATASE, BDH, Klasör 68, Yeni Dosya 337, Fihrist 1 and 1–1, Enver to Cavid, 24/25 Temmuz 330 (August 6, 1914).

16. ATASE, BDH, Klasör 68, Yeni Dosya 337, Fihrist 3–2, Enver to Talib, 28 Temmuz 333 [*sic*, 330] (August 10, 1914). On Talib Bey, see Aline Schläpfer, "Between Ruler and Rogue: Sayyid Talib al-Naqib and the British in Early Twentieth-Century Basra," in *Age of Rogues: Rebels, Revolutionaries and Racketeers at the Frontiers of Empires*, ed. Ramazan Hakkı Öztan and Alp Yenen (Edinburgh University Press, 2021), 235–57.

17. M. Şükrü Hanioğlu, "Ottoman Jihad or Jihads: The Ottoman Shīʿī Jihad, the Successful One," in *Jihad and Islam in World War I: Studies on the Ottoman Jihad on the Centenary of Snouck Hurgronje's "Holy War Made in Germany,"* ed. Erik-Jan Zürcher (Leiden University Press, 2016), 117–34.

18. Şükrü, *Heyet-i İhtiyariye*, 45–46. See also the works by Mevlanzâde Rifaat.

19. A significant number of these refugees eventually returned to Russia because of difficulties resettling in the Ottoman Empire. See Candan Badem, "'Forty Years of Black Days'? The Russian Administration of Kars, Ardahan, and Batum, 1878–1918," in *Russian-Ottoman Borderlands: The Eastern Question Reconsidered*, ed. Lucien J. Frary and Mara Kozelsky (University of Wisconsin Press, 2014), 221–50; Sonya Mirzoyan and Candan Badem, *The Construction of the Tiflis-Aleksandropol-Kars Railway (1895–1899)* (The Institute for Historical Justice and Reconciliation, 2013), 4–15.

20. Dominic Lieven, *The End of Tsarist Russia: The March to World War I and Revolution* (Penguin, 2015).

21. BA-MA, RH 61/1088, Telegramm des Botschafters, December 6, 1914.

22. Reynolds, *Shattering Empires*, 144, and Eric Lohr, *Nationalizing the Russian Empire: The Campaign against Enemy Aliens during World War I* (Harvard University Press, 2003); Timothy Snyder, *Bloodlands: Europe between Hitler and Stalin* (Basic Books, 2010); Joshua A. Sanborn, *Imperial Collapse: The Great War and the Destruction of the Russian Empire* (Oxford University Press, 2015).

23. BOA, DH.ŞFR 435/40, *Urgent*, Governor Reşid to Interior Ministry, 21 Temmuz 1330 (August 3, 1914), and BOA, DH.EUM.VRK 12/60, Foreign Ministry Political Director Ahmed Reşid to Interior Ministry, 23 Temmuz 1330 (August 5, 1914), and Enclosure, Petrograd Embassy to Foreign Ministry, August 4, 1914.

24. BOA, DH.ŞFR 437/83, Tahsin to Interior Ministry, 4 Ağustos 1330 (August 17, 1914).

25. BOA, DH.EUM 2Sb 1/40, Governor Cemal Azmi to Interior Ministry, arrived 24 Ağustos 1330 (September 6, 1914.)

26. Ottoman military intelligence produced voluminous reports from the Russian front. See Somer Alp Şimşeker, *Birinci Dünya Savaşı'nda Osmanlı İstihbaratı: İkinci Şube Tarihi* (Kronik, 2022), 242, 287–89.

27. BA-MA, RH 61/1088, "Telegramm des Botschafters Pera v. 6. Dezember 1914," Wangenheim to Foreign Office, December 6, 1914.

28. ATASE, BDH, Klasör 1726, Yeni Dosya 72, Fihrist 1–21, Enver to Talat, *To Be Decoded Personally*, 4/10/30 [4 Kanun-u evvel 1330; December 17, 1914].

29. BOA, DH.ŞFR 455/81, For the Interior Minister Only (*bizzat halli*), Governor Tahsin to Interior Minister Talat, 14 Kanun-u evvel 1330 (December 27, 1914).

30. BOA, DH.ŞFR 455/124, Very Secret (*Gayet Mahremdir*), Governor Cemal Azmi to Interior Ministry, 15/16 Kanun-u evvel 1330 (December 28/29, 1914).

31. BOA, DH.EUM 2. Şube 3/62, intercepted Russian telegram of December 31, 1914, Sefa Bey (Bucharest) to Interior Ministry, January 2, 1915.

32. Armen Garo, *Bank Ottoman: Memoirs of Armen Garo, the Armenian Ambassador to America from the Independent Republic of Armenia*, trans. Haig T. Paritzian, ed. and intro Simon Vratzian (Detroit: Armen Topouzian, 1990), 198ff; where he speculates about the following scenario: "Had the Armenians cast their lot in 1914 on the German-Turkish side, as did the Bulgarians in 1915, how would the course of events be affected in the Near East?" He notes, "First of all, the horrible massacre of the Armenians would not take place. On the contrary, the Turks and the Germans would try in every way possible to placate the Armenians to the end of the war. Secondly, since the Georgians and the Tartars were extremely desirous of collaborating with the Turks and the Germans, as proven by the events of 1918, and if the Armenians had joined them in 1914, cutting the railways behind the Russian army, the entire territory of the Caucasus would be wrested away from the Russians, and the Turks and the Germans would have reached Baku the autumn of the same year. The Armenians, the Georgians and the Tartars of the Caucasus could easily mobilize an army of 700,000 men able to defend the Caucasus Mountain range against the Russians. Then the entire Turkish army would be in a position immediately to advance into the interior of Asia and join forces with the seventeen million Moslems of Asiatic Russia. Obviously, neither Persia nor Afghanistan would be able to remain neutral, in the face of such great Turkish success. In that eventuality, Russia would be compelled to transfer the larger part of her armed forces from the West to the East, thus being unable to defend her Western front as well as she had done. Consequently, the disintegration of Russia would most probably take place in the summer of 1915, when the Germans occupied Russian Poland. Furthermore, Great Britain would be forced to reassign the greater part of her newly organized land forces to the defense of India and therefore she would not be able to send as large a force as she did to the defense of heroic France. Again, most probably, neither Italy nor Romania would, under such circumstances, break their neutrality. Thus, the war could have

ended in the victory of the Central Powers, at least on land, in 1915 or 1916." See also idem, *Why Armenia Should Be Free: Armenia's Role in the Present War* (Hairenik, 1918).

33. BOA, DH.ŞFR 48/260-1, Interior Minister Talat to Governor of Trabzon, 21 Kanun-u evvel 1330 (January 3, 1915).

34. BOA, DH.ŞFR 456/112, Urgent (*Müstaceldir*), Governor of Erzurum Tahsin to Interior Minister Talat, 25 Kanun-u evvel 1330 (January 7, 1915).

35. BOA, HR.SYS 2255/26, "Sarıkamış'da esir edilüb Rusya'da mevaki-yi muhtelifede bulunan Osmanlı harb esirleri," *Osmanlı Hilal-i Ahmeri*, the file is dated August 4, 1915.

36. BOA, DH.ŞFR 456/100, To Be Decoded Personally (*Bizzat Hallolunacakdır*), Fourth Army Commander and Navy Minister Ahmed Cemal to Interior Minister Talat, 24 Kanun-u evvel 1330 (January 6, 1915).

37. BOA, HR.SYS 2348/5, Reports from Athens and Rome, January 22, 1915.

38. BOA, HR.SYS 2348/5, Reports from Athens and Rome, February 6, 1915.

39. BOA, HR.SYS 2348/5, Reports from Athens and Rome, February 15, 1915.

40. Friedrich Kress von Kressenstein, *Mit den Türken zum Suezkanal* (Berlin: Otto Schlegel, 1938), 78.

41. *The Memoirs and Diaries of Muhammad Farid, an Egyptian Nationalist Leader (1868–1919)*, ed. Arthur Goldschmidt Jr. (Mellen University Research Press, 1992), 6–7.

42. William Ochsenwald, *The Hijaz Railroad* (University of Virginia Press, 1980).

43. BOA, DH.EUM 7. Şube 3/4, Commander of the Mount Lebanon Volunteer Detachment Shakib Arslan to Interior Ministry, 8 Kanun-u sani 1330 (January 21, 1915).

44. Conde de Ballobar [Antonio de la Cierva y Lewita], *Jerusalem in World War I: The Palestine Diary of a European Diplomat*, ed. Eduardo Manzano Moreno and Roberto Mazza (London: I. B. Tauris, 1996), 47, entry on January 22, 1915.

45. Kress, *Mit den Türken*, 88.

46. Kress, 92–93 and 98.

47. BOA, DH.ŞFR 460/69, Urgent (*Müstaceldir*), Mutasarrıf of Jerusalem Midhat to Interior Ministry, 25 Kanun-u sani 1330 (February 7, 1915).

48. BOA, DH.KMS 30/67, Fourth Army Commander and Navy Minister Cemal to Interior Ministry, 28/30 Kanun-u sani 1330 (February 10/12, 1915).

49. BOA, DH.KMS 30/67, Jerusalem Headquarters to Interior Ministry, 16 Şubat 1330 (March 1, 1915).

50. BOA, DH.ŞFR 49/270, coded telegram, Minister Talat to Fourth Army Commander and Navy Minister Cemal, 31 Kanun-u sani 1330 (February 13, 1915).

51. Ballobar, *Jerusalem in World War I*, 51.

52. Siham Tergeman, *Daughter of Damascus*, trans. Andrea Rugh (Center for Middle Eastern Studies, University of Texas at Austin, 1994), 178.

53. Tergeman, *Daughter of Damascus*, 180–81.

54. Kress, *Mit den Türken*, 103.

55. Kress, 105.

56. Kress, 109; for the environmental mobilization of the Sinai as a military base, see Önder Eren Akgül, "War on the Desert: The Militarization of the Sinai and Its Greater Syrian Sacrificial Frontier during World War I," *International Journal of Middle East Studies* 56 (2024): 91–113.

57. Klaus Wolf, *Gallipoli 1915: Das deutsch-türkische Militärbündnis im Ersten Weltkrieg* (Report Verlag, 2008), 86–87.

58. Sabahaddin's letter was dated February 28, 1915, and was sent from Athens. See BOA, HR.SYS 2264/2, Ambassador at Athens Galib to Foreign Minister and Grand Vizier Said Halim, *mahremdir* (secret), 1 Mart 1915 (March 1, 1915); and in the same source, Hariciye Nezareti Şifre Kalemi, "Huzur-u Ali-yi Nezaretpenahiye Atina sefiri Galib Bey'den takdim edildiği 2 Mart 915 tarihli ve 206 numerolu telgrafname-i hallidir." According to Galib Bey [Söylemezoğlu], there was talk of Sabahaddin Bey attempting to contact Ottoman forces in Thrace to lead them on Istanbul and topple the government.

59. "Télégrame adressé par le Prince Sabaheddine Bey à Sa Majestè Impériale Le Sultan Mohammed V, Constantinople, Athènes, le 28 février 1915," in BOA, HR.SYS 2264/2.

60. ATASE, BDH Klasör 323, Yeni Dosya 1304, Fihrist 1 and 1–1, To the Commander of the Fourth Army Corps, 27/28 Şubat 1330 [March 12/13, 1915]

61. Enver to Falkenhayn, quoted in Wolf, *Gallipoli 1915*, 89.

62. Wolf, 90–94.

63. Wolf, 88 and 96.

64. Wolf, 97–98.

65. *Meclis-i Ayan'ın Zabıt Ceridesi*, 28 Kanun-u evvel 1331 (January 10, 1916).

Chapter 4. Empire of Hunger

1. Comments by Hamdullah Emin Pasha (Antalya), *Meclis-i Mebusan'ın Zabıt Ceridesi*, 21 Kanun-u evvel 1331 (January 3, 1916).

2. See the comments of Cemil Zehavi (Jamil Zahawi) Bey (Baghdad), *Meclis-i Mebusan'ın Zabıt Ceridesi*, 21 Kanun-u evvel 1331 (January 3, 1916). On locusts see Samuel Dolbee, *Locusts of Power: Borders, Empire, and Environment in the Modern Middle East* (Cambridge University Press, 2023), 135–90; Zachary J. Foster, "The 1915 Locust Attack in Syria and Palestine and Its Role in the Famine during the First World War," *Middle Eastern Studies* 51 (2014): 371; on the harrowing conditions of famine, see especially Tylor Brand, *Famine Worlds: Life at the Edge of Suffering in Lebanon's Great War* (Stanford University Press, 2023); Leila Tarazi Fawaz, *A Land of Aching Hearts: The Middle East in the Great War* (Harvard University Press, 2014); Selim Deringil, *The Ottoman Twilight in the Arab Lands: Turkish Memoirs and Testimonies of the Great War* (Academic Studies Press, 2019); Melanie S. Tanielian, *Charity of War: Famine, Humanitarian Aid, and World War I in the Middle East* (Stanford University Press, 2017); Najwa al-Qattan, "When Mothers Ate Their Children: Wartime Memory and the Language of Food in Syria and Lebanon," *International Journal of Middle East Studies* 46 (2014): 719–36.

3. Heather Jones, "A Forgotten Front? The Mediterranean Blockade in the First World War," *International History Review* 46 (2024): 426–43.

4. Quoted in Jones, "Forgotten Front?," 436. Kitchener drowned at sea; his ship sunk by a German submarine.

5. Jones, 426.

6. Comments by the assistant director of the Agricultural Bank (*Ziraat Bankası*), *Meclis-i Ayan'ın Zabıt Ceridesi*, 16 Teşrin-i sani 1331 (November 29, 1915).

7. *Meclis-i Ayan'ın Zabıt Ceridesi*, 28 Kanun-u evvel 1331 (January 10, 1916).

8. On this theme, see Akın, *When the War Came Home*.

9. BOA, DH.EUM.MTK 54/26, 6 Teşrin-i evvel 1330 (October 19, 1914); the regulation also appeared in the Interior Ministry's gazette, *Dahiliye Nezareti Muharrerat-ı Umumiye Mecmuası*, 4 Teşrin-i evvel 1330 [October 17, 1914], see A. Gündüz Ökçün, *Tarımda Ekme ve Çalışma Yükümlülüğü (Mükellefiyyet-i Ziraiyye), Belgeler 1914–1922* (Ankara Üniversitesi, 1983), 3–4.

10. Ökçün, *Tarımda Ekme ve Çalışma Yükümlülüğü.*

11. Yavuz Selim Karakışla, *Women, War and Work in the Ottoman Empire: Society for the Employment of Ottoman Muslim Women (1916–1923)* (Ottoman Bank and Research Center, 2005), and idem, "Osmanlı Ordusunda Kadın Askerler," *Tarih ve Toplum* (June 1999): 14–24.

12. Vedat Eldem, *Harp ve Mütareke Yıllarında Osmanlı İmparatorluğu'nun Ekonomisi* (Türk Tarih Kurumu Basımevi, 1994), 35–36.

13. Measures of one *dönüm* of land varied across the empire and over time. In 1881 state authorities set the "new dönüm" at twenty-five hundred square meters, but in most places the old usage of the measurement of roughly one thousand square meters prevailed. Using the 1881 figure, forty-five *dönüm* would equal about twenty-eight acres. Using the older standard (which is also the standard measure still in use in the Middle East today), forty-five *dönüm* comprise some eleven acres, or about four *dönüm* per one acre.

14. Nicola Ziadeh, "A First-Person Account of the First World War in Greater Syria," in *The First World War as Remembered in the Countries of the Eastern Mediterranean*, ed. Olaf Farschid, Manfred Kropp, and Stephan Dähne (Würzburg: Ergon, 2006), 266–69. The family was from Jerusalem, but Nicola's father, because of his knowledge of German, had found work with the Hejaz Railway line in Damascus.

15. BOA, DH.SYS 123-9/21-8, Bekir Sami to Interior Ministry, 28 Teşrin-i evvel 1330 (November 10, 1914), and 30 Teşrin-i evvel 1330 (November 12, 1914).

16. BOA, DH.SYS 123-9/21-8, Bekir Sami to Interior Ministry, 11 Teşrin-i sani 1330 (November 24, 1914).

17. BOA, DH.SYS 123-9/21-8, Bekir Sami to Interior Ministry, 23 Teşrin-i sani 1330 (December 6, 1914), and ibid., 27 Teşrin-i sani 1330 (December 10, 1914).

18. BOA, DH.SYS 123-9/21-8, Bekir Sami to Interior Ministry, 1 Kanun-u evvel 1330 (December 14, 1914).

19. BOA, DH.SYS 123-9/21-8, Commerce and Agriculture Ministry to Interior Ministry, 4 Kanun-u evvel 1330 (December 17, 1914).

20. *Meclis-i Ayan'ın Zabıt Ceridesi*, 11 Şubat 1330 (February 24, 1915).

21. BOA, MV 195/38. 19 Teşrin-i sani 1330/December 2, 1914. The cabinet debated an Interior Ministry memorandum dated November 29, 1914.

22. Eldem, *Harp ve Mütareke Yıllarında*, 131.

23. BOA, MV 195/38. 19 Teşrin-i sani 1330 (December 2, 1914).

24. Eldem, *Harp ve Mütareke Yıllarında*, 38. These figures do not include yields from Basra, Baghdad, Bitlis, Erzurum, Hijaz, Jerusalem, or Yemen.

25. Eldem, *Harp ve Mütareke Yıllarında*, 30–33, citing *Memalik-i Osmaniye'nin 1329 ve 1330 senelerine mahsus ziraat istatistikleri* (Istanbul: Ticaret ve Ziraat Nezareti, 1916 and 1917).

26. *Meclis-i Mebusan'ın Zabıt Ceridesi*, 16 Subat 1330 (March 1, 1915). The delegate was the Armenian deputy from Muş, Kegham Efendi (Der Garabedian).

27. Foster, "The 1915 Locust Attack in Syria and Palestine," 371.

28. *Meclis-i Mebusan'ın Zabıt Ceridesi*, 17 Kanun-u sani 330, 2 Şubat 1330 (February 15, 1915)

29. *Meclis-i Mebusan'ın Zabıt Ceridesi*, 17 Kanun-u sani 330, 2 Şubat 1330 (February 15, 1915). Special funds were made available from the Finance Ministry by February 10, 1915, and the parliament was informed on February 15, 1915.

30. BOA, DH.İ.UM.Ek 7/50, Governor Bekir Sami to Interior Ministry, 8 Mart 1331 (March 21, 1915).

31. Jones, "Forgotten Front?" 438.

32. Conde de Ballobar [Antonio de la Cierva y Lewita], *Jerusalem in World War I: The Palestine Diary of a European Diplomat*, ed. Eduardo Manzano Moreno and Roberto Mazza (London: I. B. Tauris, 1996), 55–56, entry for March 23, 1915.

33. Ballobar, *Jerusalem in World War I*, 57, entry for March 30, 1915. Locusts are grasshoppers that pass through a "Jekyll-to-Hyde transformation." Abundant rainfall causes grasshopper populations to increase; physical contact with other grasshoppers (the touching of the hindlegs) activates a hormonal switch that eventually renders the insects "gregarious," at which point they can morph into swarming seas of locusts. In this state, locusts begin "coordinating their growth, behavior and egg laying." Keith Cressman, Senior Locust Forecasting Officer at the Food and Agriculture Organization of the United Nations, see *New York Times*, "When Weather Changes, Grasshopper Turns Locust," April 8, 2013.

34. Ballobar, *Jerusalem in World War I*, 67.

35. Ballobar, 68, entry for June 15, 1915.

36. Nafi 'Utref, "Nema-yı Bedenî," 1 Haziran 1333 [June 1, 1917] *Muallim* (1): 348–51; see also Olcay Neyzi, Hatice Nurçin Saka, and Selim Kurtoğlu, "Anthropometric Studies on the Turkish Population—A Historical Review," *Journal of Clinical Research in Pediatric Endocrinology* 5 (2013): 1–12. For Germany, see Mary E. Cox, *Hunger in War and Peace: Women and Children in Germany, 1914–1924* (Oxford University Press, 2019).

37. BOA, DH.ŞFR 476/118, coded telegram, Fourth Army Commander and Navy Minister Cemal to Interior Ministry, 9 Haziran 1331 (June 22, 1915).

38. Akram Fouad Khater, *Inventing Home: Emigration, Gender, and the Middle Class in Lebanon, 1870–1920* (University of California Press, 2001).

39. There is a vast literature on land reform, including the Land Code of 1858, in the nineteenth and twentieth centuries.

40. Elizabeth R. Williams, *States of Cultivation: Imperial Transition and Scientific Agriculture in the Eastern Mediterranean* (Stanford University Press, 2023), 68–72. Williams presents a lively portrait of Hüseyin Kâzım's travails in taking on the local elite's abuses in their ownership of agricultural land. Hüseyin Kâzım was the governor of Aleppo province in 1910.

41. Kristen Alff, "Levantine Joint-Stock Companies, Trans-Mediterranean Partnerships, and Nineteenth Century Capitalist Development," *Comparative Studies in Society and History* 60 (2018): 150–77, here 157.

42. Graham Aumann Pitts, "A Hungry Population Stops Thinking about Resistance: Class, Famine, and Lebanon's World War I Legacy," *Journal of Ottoman and Turkish Studies* 7 (2020): 220. In May 1915 the governor of Syria province, Hulusi, warned that powerful business leaders in Beirut opposed his shipping of aid. He believed that local elites, for commercial reasons, were keeping grain prices intentionally high. See Pitts, 228.

43. See Pitts. Sursock died under mysterious circumstances, see especially "Entrepreneurs and Profiteers," in Fawaz, *Land of Aching Hearts*, 121–60.

44. Graham Aumann Pitts, "The Ecology of Migration: Remittances in World War I Mount Lebanon," *Arab Studies Journal* 26 (2018): 108.

45. Pitts, "Ecology of Migration," 103–4.

46. Pitts, "Hungry Population Stops Thinking about Resistance," 222 and 224.

47. BOA, DH.İ.UM.Ek 10/21, coded telegram, Governor Azmi to Interior Ministry, 22 Ağustos 1331 (September 4, 1915).

48. Elizabeth F. Thompson, *Colonial Citizens: Republican Rights, Paternal Privilege and Gender in French Syria and Lebanon* (Columbia University Press, 2000), 19–23, for quotes see 22. For the original French document, see Série Guerre 873, June 6, 1916.

49. Pitts, "Hungry Population Stops Thinking about Resistance," 225, citing the diary of a Christian priest, Yusuf al-Sayigh.

50. Quoted in Jones, "Forgotten Front?" 437.

51. Simon Jackson, "Transformative Relief: Imperial Humanitarianism and Mandatory Development in Syria-Lebanon," *Humanity* (2017): 247–68.

52. Fritz Grobba, *Die Getreidewirtschaft Syriens und Palästinas seit Beginn des Weltkrieges* (Hannover: Orient-Buchhandlung Heinz Lafaire, 1923), 13.

53. *Meclis-i Mebusan'ın Zabıt Ceridesi*, 26 Teşrin-i evvel 1331 [November 8, 1915].

54. BOA, DH.ŞFR 467/32, Governor Mahmud Nedim to Interior Ministry, 26 Mart 1331 (April 8, 1915).

55. BOA, DH.ŞFR 487/50, Governor Mahmud Nedim to Interior Ministry, 22 Ağustos 1331 (September 4, 1915).

56. BOA, DH.İD 219/9, Mahmud Nedim to Interior Ministry, 20 Kanun-u evvel 1330 (January 2, 1915). Specifically, the document inquired into conscripting those men in Yemen not born of a Yemeni father, as those born of Yemeni parents were exempt. More broadly on Yemen in the late Ottoman period, see Thomas Kühn, "Shaping and Reshaping Colonial Ottomanism."

57. *Meclis-i Mebusan'ın Zabıt Ceridesi*, 16 Teşrin-i sani 1331 (November 29, 1915). Ali Galip Efendi was the deputy from Karesi in the Assembly.

58. Eldem, *Harp ve Mütareke Yıllarında*, 56.

59. Eldem, 56.

60. *Meclis-i Ayan'ın Zabıt Ceridesi*, 21 Eylül 1331 (October 4, 1915).

61. BOA, DH.İ.UM 59-1/1-58, Mutasarrıf of Kale-yi Sultaniye to Commerce and Agriculture Ministry, 5 Eylül 331 (September 18, 1915).

62. BOA, DH.İ.UM 59-1/1-58, Finance Ministry to Interior Ministry, 27 Eylül 1331 (October 10, 1915).

63. BOA, DH.İ.UM 59-1/1-58, Mutasarrıf of Kale-yi Sultaniye to Commerce and Agriculture Ministry, 5 Eylül 1331 (September 18, 1915).

64. BOA, DH.SYS 123-9/21-8, Commerce and Agriculture Minister to Interior Ministry, 3 Mart 1331 (March 16, 1915).

65. BOA, DH.İ.UM 93-1/1-4, Sub-Governor of Karahisar-ı Sahib Celaleddin to Interior Ministry, 12 Şubat 1330 (February 25, 1915).

66. Ticaret ve Ziraat Nezareti, İstatistik İdare-i Umumiyesi Müdüriyeti, *Memalik-i Osmaniye 1329 senesine Mahsus Ziraat İstatistiğidir* (Dersaadet: Matbaa-i Aliye, 1332 [1916]), pages

unnumbered. On the Ottoman Empire's joining the International Institute of Agriculture and collection of agricultural statistics in the early twentieth century, see Elizabeth R. Williams, "'The Agriculture Ministry of the Whole World': The International Institute of Agriculture and the Politics of Ottoman Statistics Collection," *Comparative Studies of South Asia, Africa and the Middle East* 43 (2023): 224–41.

67. Ticaret ve Ziraat Nezareti, *Memalik'i Osmaniye 1329 senesine Mahsus Ziraat İstatiğidir.*

68. BOA, DH.İ.UM 93-1/1-4, Governor of Istanbul Province to Interior Ministry, 14 Şubat 1330 (February 27, 1915).

69. BOA, MV 196/137, 15 Şubat 1330 (February 28, 1915).

70. BOA, MV 196/137, 15 Şubat 1330 (February 28, 1915).

71. BOA, DH.SYS 123-9/21-8, Commerce and Agriculture Minister to Interior Ministry, 3 Mart 1331 (March 16, 1915). Italy would enter the war in May 1915 on the side of the Entente.

72. Şevket Pamuk, *Uneven Centuries: Economic Development of Turkey since 1820* (Princeton University Press, 2018), 165–66.

73. *Meclis-i Ayan'ın Zabıt Ceridesi*, 21 Kanun-u evvel 1331 (January 3, 1916). The locusts were described as being "uçkun bir halde," that is, in a flying or gregarious state. Locusts had come from Sudan, across the desert (Sinai), and were to be fought with an "arsenic compound." Tests were to be carried out to confirm that animals and the soil would not be contaminated or harmed.

74. BA-MA, RM 40/216, Folio 160–62, Chemin de Fer Ottoman d'Anatolie to Souchon, Anpflanzung von Baumwolle, April 1, 1916; also see Gratien, *Unsettled Plain*, 96–107.

75. *Meclis-i Ayan'ın Zabıt Ceridesi*, 7 Kanun-u sani 1331 (January 20, 1916).

76. *Meclis-i Ayan'ın Zabıt Ceridesi*, 14 Kanun-u sani 1331 (January 27, 1916).

77. *Meclis-i Mebusan'ın Zabıt Ceridesi*, 2 Şubat 1331 (February 15, 1916).

78. BOA, DH.İ.UM.Ek 16/73, *Çekirge Kanunu* [Locust Law], 7 Mart 1332 (March 20, 1916); debated in the Assembly, see *Meclis-i Mebusan'ın Zabıt Ceridesi*, 6 Şubat 1331 (February 19, 1916).

79. BOA, DH.İ.UM 22-1/52, *Çekirgelerin Yumurta Bırakdıkları Mahallerin Tayin ve İraesine Dair Nizamnamedir*, 30 Haziran 1332 (July 13, 1916).

80. BOA, DH.İ.UM 22-1/52, Commerce and Agriculture Ministry to Interior Ministry, 13 Temmuz 1334 (July 13, 1918).

81. BOA, DH.SYS 123-9/21-8, Commerce and Agriculture Minister to Interior Ministry, 3 Mart 1331 (March 16, 1915).

82. Males born in 1898 were ordered to "have completed all [required medical] exams by the end of August 1332 [falling on September 12, 1916]," see BOA, İ.DUİT 76/65, 7 Mart 1332 (March 20, 1916); see also Mehmet Beşikçi, *The Ottoman Mobilization of Manpower in the First World War: Between Voluntarism and Resistance* (Brill, 2012), 108, citing *Düstur*, Second Series, vol. 7, 589–90, and vol. 8, 730, respectively. The official state gazette, the *Takvim-i Vekayi*, published the new regulation raising the military age to fifty on March 24, 1916.

83. *Meclis-i Ayan'ın Zabıt Ceridesi*, 25 Şubat 1331 (March 9, 1916).

84. BOA, DH.UMVM 148/53, June 9, 1917.

85. *Meclis-i Mebusan'ın Zabıt Ceridesi*, 21 Kanun-u evvel 1331 (January 3, 1916).

86. *Meclis-i Mebusan'ın Zabıt Ceridesi*, 21 Kanun-u evvel 1331 (January 3, 1916).

87. *Meclis-i Mebusan'ın Zabıt Ceridesi*, 21 Kanun-u evvel 1331 (January 3, 1916).

88. *Meclis-i Mebusan'ın Zabıt Ceridesi*, 21 Kanun-u evvel 1331 (January 3, 1916).

89. Friedrich Kress von Kressenstein, *Mit den Türken zum Suezkanal* (Berlin: Otto Schlegel, 1938), 148–49.

90. *Meclis-i Mebusan'ın Zabıt Ceridesi*, 21 Kanun-u evvel 1331 (January 3, 1916).

91. BOA, DH.İ.UM 94-4/1-48, War Ministry to Interior Ministry, 29 Şubat 1331 (March 13, 1916).

92. BOA, DH.İ.UM 94-4/1-48, War Ministry to Interior Ministry, 2 Mart 1332 (March 15, 1916); the projected need was for the year 1332 of the Ottoman Rumi calendar, which ran from March 1916 to February 1917.

93. BOA, DH.İ.UM 94-4/1-48, War Ministry to Interior Ministry, 29 Şubat 1331 (March 13, 1916).

94. BOA, DH.İ.UM 94-4/1-48, War Ministry to Interior Ministry, 16 Mart 1332 (March 29, 1916).

95. Kress, *Mit den Türken*, 119–24.

96. BOA, DH.İ.UM 93-4/1-48, War Ministry to Interior Ministry, March 20, 1916. Estimating the Ottoman army at eight hundred thousand men in 1916, the proposed amount of meat would yield about 1.6 kilograms of meat per person per week, or about 230 grams per person per day.

97. BOA, DH.İ.UM 94-4/1-48, War Ministry to Interior Ministry, 25 March 1332 (April 7, 1916).

98. BOA, DH.İ.UM 94-4/1-48, Governor Haydar to Interior Ministry, 3 Nisan 1332 (April 16, 1916).

99. BOA, DH.İ.UM.Ek 24/91, Telegram from Emrudabad to Interior Ministry, 18 Teşrin-i sani 1332 (December 1, 1916).

100. al-Qattan, "When Mothers Ate Their Children"; Brands, *Famine Worlds.*

Chapter 5. Empire of Atrocity

1. Ronald Grigor Suny, *"They Can Live in the Desert but Nowhere Else": A History of the Armenian Genocide* (Princeton University Press, 2015); Yaşar Tolga Cora, Dzovinar Derderian, and Ali Sipahi, eds., *The Ottoman East in the Nineteenth Century: Societies, Identities and Politics* (I. B. Tauris, 2016).

2. *Meclis-i Mebusan'ın Zabıt Ceridesi*, 7 Kanun-u sani 1330 (January 20, 1915).

3. Recent scholarship puts the number of Armenians killed at around seven hundred thousand, with half perishing in the camps of Deir Zor. See Matthias Bjørnlund, who put the number of Armenian deportees reaching Deir Zor at around four hundred thousand, with two hundred thousand massacred in the camps, while another two hundred thousand died of hunger and disease, in Bjørnlund, "'A Fate Worse than Dying': Sexual Violence during the Armenian Genocide," in *Brutality and Desire: War and Sexuality in Europe's Twentieth Century*, ed. Dagmar Herzog (Palgrave Macmillan, 2009), 32; Fuat Dündar, *Crime of Numbers: The Role of Statistics in the Armenian Question (1878–1918)* (Transaction Publishers, 2010), 150–51, puts the total number of Armenians perished at 664,000, out of a total Armenian population of 1.5 million. Raymond Kévorkian estimates the number of those who

perished possibly as high as 1.5 million, in *The Armenian Genocide: A Complete History* (I. B. Tauris, 2011).

4. Caroline Elkins, *Legacy of Violence: A History of the British Empire* (Alfred A. Knopf, 2022); A. Dirk Moses, *The Problems of Genocide: Permanent Security and the Language of Transgression* (Cambridge University Press, 2021); Dierk Walter, *Colonial Violence: European Empires and the Use of Force*, trans. Peter Lewis (Oxford University Press, 2017).

5. Elkins, *Legacy of Violence*, 79.

6. Priya Satia, "The Defense of Inhumanity: Air Control and the British Idea of Arabia," *American Historical Review* 111 (2006): 16–51.

7. Benjamin Madley, *An American Genocide: The United States and the California Indian Catastrophe* (Yale University Press, 2016), 142, 144, 179, 185, 198, 268, 275.

8. Fuat Balkan, *Komitacı: BJK'nin Kurucusu Fuat Balkan'ın Anıları*, ed. Turgut Gürer (Istanbul: Gürer, 2006), 43 and 45.

9. Philip Spencer, "Imperialism, Anti-Imperialism and the Problem of Genocide: Past and Present," *History* 98 (2013): 620.

10. Spencer, "Imperialism, Anti-Imperialism and the Problem of Genocide," 620.

11. Spencer, 620.

12. Klaus Richter, "'A Mass Which You Could Form into Whatever You Wanted': Refugees and State Building in Lithuania and Courland, 1914–21," in *Europe on the Move: Refugees in the Era of the Great War*, ed. Peter Gatrell and Liubov Zhvanko (Manchester University Press, 2017), 47. "In 1914, the imperial Russian army deported up to one million Jews living in its western borderlands because they were suspected of disloyalty and potential espionage for the Germans." See A. Dirk Moses, "Empire, Colony, Genocide: Keywords and Philosophy of History," in *Empire, Colony, Genocide: Conquest, Occupation, and Subaltern Resistance in World History*, ed. A. Dirk Moses (Berghahn, 2008), 28.

13. Ruth Leiserowitz, "Population Displacement in East Prussia during the First World War," in Gatrell and Zhvanko, *Europe on the Move*, 26.

14. Mark Levene, "Deadly Geopolitics, Ethnic Mobilisations, and the Vulnerability of Peoples, 1914–1918," in *The First World War as a Caesura? Demographic Concepts, Population Policy, and Genocide in the Late Ottoman, Russian, and Habsburg Spheres*, ed. Christin Pschischholz (Duncker and Humblot, 2020), 22. See also Eric Lohr, *Nationalizing the Russian Empire: The Campaign against Enemy Aliens during World War I* (Harvard University Press, 2003), and Michael A. Reynolds, *Shattering Empires: The Clash and Collapse of the Ottoman Empires, 1908–1918* (Cambridge University Press, 2011), 220–22.

15. Richard J. Evans, *The Pursuit of Power: Europe, 1815–1914* (Penguin, 2016), 637.

16. Evans, *Pursuit of Power*, 636.

17. *Der Prozeß Talaat Pascha: Stenographischer Bericht über die Verhandlung gegen den des Mordes an Talaat Pascha angeklagten armeniaschen Studenten Salomon Teilirian vor dem Schwurgericht des Landgerichts III zu Berlin, Aktenzeichen: C.J. 22/21, am 2. und 3. Juni 1921, Mit einem Vorwort von Armin T. Wegner und einem Anhang* (Berlin: Deutsche Verlagsgesellschaft für Politik und Geschichte, 1921), 57.

18. *Der Prozeß Talaat Pascha*, 56.

19. *Der Prozeß Talaat Pascha*, 59.

20. The number of published memoirs and recorded oral testimonies range in the hundreds. Oral testimonies are housed at the University of Southern California.

21. Hagop S. Der-Garabedian, *Jail to Jail: Autobiography of a Survivor of the 1915 Armenian Genocide*, trans. Aghop H. Der-Karabetian (iUniverse, 2004), x–xi.

22. For the most complete analysis of this argument, see Yektan Türkyılmaz, "Rethinking Genocide: Violence and Victimhood in Eastern Anatolia, 1913–1915," PhD diss., Duke University, 2011.

23. Ussama Makdisi, *Age of Coexistence: The Ecumenical Frame and the Making of the Modern Arab World* (California University Press, 2019)

24. Yervant N. Alexanian, *Forced into Genocide: Memoirs of an Armenian Soldier in the Ottoman Turkish Army*, ed. Adrienne G. Alexanian, intro. Sergio La Porta (Transaction, 2017); Kalusd Sürmenyan, *Harbiyeli bir Osmanlı Ermenisi: Mülâzim-ı Sânî Sürmenyan'ın Savaş ve Tehcir Anıları*, ed. and trans. Yaşar Tolga Cora (Tarih Vakfı Yurt Yayınları, 2015).

25. Alexanian, *Forced into Genocide*, 29–30.

26. Sürmenyan, *Harbiyeli bir Osmanlı Ermenisi*, 40–41.

27. Sürmenyan, 42.

28. Sürmenyan, 45.

29. Der-Garabedian, *Jail to Jail*. Der-Garabedian tells the story of his conscription in Maraş.

30. Nicholas Doumanis, *Before the Nation: Muslim-Christian Coexistence and Its Destruction in Late Ottoman Anatolia* (Oxford University Press, 2013), 3; see also Erik Jan Zürcher, "The Young Turks—Children of the Borderlands," in *Turkology Update Leiden Project Working Papers Archive* (2002): 1–9 and idem, "How Europeans Adopted Anatolia and Created Turkey," *European Review* 13 (2005): 379–94.

31. Uğur Ümit Üngör, *The Making of Modern Turkey: Nation and State in Eastern Anatolia, 1913–1950* (Oxford University Press, 2011), 103–4.

32. Letter of Vicar of Bayazid to Patriarch Zaven, August 19, 1914, quoted in Zaven Der Yeghiayan, *My Patriarchal Memoirs: Zaven Der Yeghiayan, Armenian Patriarch of Constantinople, 1913–1922*, trans. Ared Misirliyan, annotated by Vatche Ghazarian (Mayreni, 2002), 40–41.

33. Letter of Prelate of Erzurum/Garin to Patriarch Zaven, September 17, 1914, quoted in Der Yeghiayan, *My Patriarchal Memoirs*, 40.

34. Der Yeghiayan, 41.

35. Der Yeghiayan, 38.

36. Letter from the Prelate of Diyarbekir Chëlghadian Vartabed to Patriarch Zaven, September 27, 1914, quoted in Der Yeghiyan, 36.

37. Letter from the Prelate of Diyarbekir to Patriarch Zaven, in Der Yeghiayan, 37, brackets in original.

38. Letter from the Prelate of Diyarbekir to Patriarch Zaven, in Der Yeghiayan, 37, parentheses and brackets in original.

39. Der Yeghiayan,36.

40. Der Yeghiayan, 35.

41. Letter of Vicar of Bayazid to Patriarch Zaven, August 19, 1914, in Der Yeghiayan, 40–41.

42. Letter of Vicar of Bayazid to Patriarch Zaven, in Der Yeghiayan, 41.

43. Aram Arkun, "Zeytun and the Commencement of the Armenian Genocide," in *A Question of Genocide: Armenians and Turks at the End of the Ottoman Empire*, ed. Ronald Grigor Suny, Fatma Müge Göçek, and Norman M. Naimark (Oxford University Press, 2011), 225.

44. Hilmar Kaiser, "Regional Resistance to Central Government Policies: Ahmed Djemal Pasha, the Governors of Aleppo, and Armenian Deportees in the Spring and Summer of 1915," *Journal of Genocide Research* 12 (2010): 177–78.

45. Der Yeghiayan, *My Patriarchal Memoirs*, 50–52.

46. Ronald Grigor Suny, "Imperial Choices: Perceiving Threats and the Descent to Genocide," in *The First World War as a Caesura? Demographic Concepts, Population Policy, and Genocide in the Late Ottoman, Russian, and Habsburg Spheres*, ed. Christin Pschischholz (Duncker and Humblot, 2020), 55. Bloxham has shown how the public action of the volunteers was meant to serve as a signal to their "compatriots" to take up arms "in a common action" and fight "to acquire the rights of autonomy." See Donald Bloxham, *The Great Game of Genocide: Imperialism, Nationalism, and the Destruction of the Ottoman Armenians* (Oxford University Press, 2005), 39, citing Bibliothèque Nubar, Paris, Archives de la delegation nationale arménienne, Correspondence Arménie 1915, I, Nubar to Kouchakian, October 26, 1915.

47. BOA, DH.EUM 2Sb 3/62, Foreign Ministry's Political Director Ahmed Reşid to Interior Ministry, 4 Kanun-u evvel 1330 (December 17, 1914). Carries note that "War Ministry has been notified."

48. Donald Bloxham, "The First World War and the Development of the Armenian Genocide," in Suny, Göçek, and Naimark, *A Question of Genocide*, 263.

49. Bloxham, *Great Game of Genocide*, 80; see also Arkun, "Zeytun and the Commencement of the Armenian Genocide," 223.

50. Princeton University Special Collections, Sir John Maxwell Papers C0583, Box 1a, Folder 3, folio 1–13 (pages 10–13 misnumbered as 11–14).

51. Der Yeghiayan, *My Patriarchal Memoirs*, 34.

52. Erik Jan Zürcher, "Ottoman Labour Battalions in World War I," in *Der Völkermord an den Armeniern und die Shoah*, ed. Hans-Lukas Kieser and Dominik J. Schaller (Chronos, 2002), 187 and 193.

53. *Meclis-i Ayan'ın Zabıt Ceridesi*, 16 Şubat 1330 (March 1, 1915).

54. Kaiser, "Regional Resistance to Central Government Policies," 177.

55. Der Yeghiayan, *My Patriarchal Memoirs*, 53.

56. Quoted in Kaiser, "Regional Resistance to Central Government Policies," 179.

57. Der Yeghiayan, *My Patriarchal Memoirs*, 52.

58. Princeton Special Collections, Sir John Maxwell Papers C0583, box 1a, folder 3, folio 1–13 (pages 10–13 misnumbered as 11–14), especially 8: "I hold very strongly to the opinion, and I think Lord Kitchener shared it that had the Alexandretta scheme been adopted in February 1915, Turkey would have been beaten and detached from the Central Aliance [*sic*]." The plan was reconsidered in October 1915 and discussed in the British War Council, see *The Present and Prospective Situation in Syria and Mesopotamia*, Secret, October 19, 1915, in Princeton Special Collections, Sir John Maxwell Papers C0583, box 22, folder 3.

59. *Meclis-i Mebusan'ın Zabıt Ceridesi*, 4 Şubat 1330 (February 17, 1915).

60. *Meclis-i Mebusan'ın Zabıt Ceridesi*, 7 Şubat 1330 (February 20, 1915).

61. *Meclis-i Mebusan'ın Zabıt Ceridesi*, 9 Şubat 1330 (February 22, 1915).

62. Quoted in Friedrich Kress von Kressenstein, *Mit den Türken zum Suezkanal* (Berlin: Otto Schlegel, 1938), 249.

63. BOA, DH.EUM 2. Şube 5/34, Enver to Interior Ministry, 17 Şubat 1330 (March 2, 1915), and Istanbul Police Director to Interior Ministry, 21 Şubat 1330 (March 6, 1915).

64. Entente declaration, May 24, 1915 (in Suny, "*They Can Live in the Desert*", 308.

65. Taner Akçam and Ümit Kurt, *The Spirit of the Laws: The Plunder of Wealth in the Armenian Genocide*, trans. Aram Arkun (Berghahn, 2015), 19–33; and Taner Akçam, *The Young Turks' Crime against Humanity: The Armenian Genocide and Ethnic Cleansing in the Ottoman Empire* (Princeton University Press, 2011).

66. *Meclis-i Ayan'ın Zabıt Ceridesi*, 15 Eylül 1331 (September 28, 1915).

67. *Meclis-i Ayan'ın Zabıt Ceridesi*, 21 Eylül 1331 (October 4, 1915). "Bundan başka, bugün ve dağlarında sefil ve sergerdân bir halde sürünüyor. Mevsim-i şita hulûl etmeden evvel bunların, ya yurtlarına iade edilmesini veyahut menfaatları nereleri ise oralarda iskan olunmasını Hükumetin nasaafet [nısfet] ve adaletinden beklerim. Heyet-i Muhteremenin bu arzuma iştiraki halinde Reis Beyefendinin Hükumete bu ciheti tebliğ etmelerini rica ederim. (hay hay sesleri)."

68. *Meclis-i Ayan'ın Zabıt Ceridesi*, 28 Eylül 1331 (October 11, 1915).

69. *Meclis-i Ayan'ın Zabıt Ceridesi*, 30 Teşrin-i sani 1331 (December 13, 1915).

70. Üngor, *Making of Modern Turkey*, 118, citing DH.SFR 54/39.

71. BA-MA, RM 40/456, folio 256 and reverse, Confidential (*Zur vertraulichen Kenntnisnahme*), H[umann] to Berlin, June 15, 1915.

72. DE/PA-AA/R14086, Ambassador Wangenheim to Chancellor Bethmann Hollweg, no. 372, June 17, 1915, found at Wolfgang Gust et al., www.armenocide.net.

73. *Talât Paşa'nin Hâtıraları*, ed. Enver Bolayır (Istanbul: Güven Yayınevi, 1946), 64.

74. Kress, *Mit den Türken*, 132.

75. Kress, 133.

76. Kress, 140.

77. BA-MA, RM 40/208, folio 29 (original in Ottoman Turkish), Enver to ministries and military commands, 1/10/331 (December 14, 1915).

78. Kress, *Mit den Türken*, 138. This was a view contrary to that of many of his German colleagues; the majority disavowed responsibility. General Liman von Sanders maintained that German officers had no direct knowledge of events.

79. BA-MA, RM 40/212, Folio 257–65, Reisebericht von Korv. Kapt. Busse von 16. Bis 27. Dezember 1915, Beirut, December 27, 1915.

80. Ali Rıza Eti, *Bir Onbaşının Doğu Cephesi Günlüğü, 1914–1915*, ed. Gönül Eti (Istanbul: Türkiye İş Bankası Kültür Yayınları, 2009), 26 and 46. There is a significant range for the casualty figures of the Third Army at Sarıkamış, as well as for its original strength. Reynolds gives the strength of the Third Army as ninety-five thousand men, see Reynolds, *Shattering Empires*, 125.

81. For a thorough treatment of the topic, based on research in the Archives of the Turkish General Staff, see Mehmet Beşikçi, *The Ottoman Mobilization of Manpower in the First World War: Between Voluntarism and Resistance* (Brill, 2012), 249–309.

82. Eti, *Bir Onbaşının Doğu Dephesi Günlüğü*, 135.

83. Der Yeghiayan, *My Patriarchal Memoirs*, 34.

84. Der Yeghiayan, 34.

85. Alexanian, *Forced into Genocide*, 33–34; Sürmenyan, *Harbiyeli bir Osmanlı Ermenisi*, 50–51.

86. Sürmenyan, *Harbiyeli bir Osmanlı Ermenisi*, 57–61.

87. Alexanian, *Forced into Genocide*, 43.

88. Alexanian, 49.

89. Alexanian, 51.

90. Alexanian, 52.

91. Alexanian, 54.

92. Sürmenyan, *Harbiyeli bir Osmanlı Ermenisi*, 52.

93. *Mareşal Fevzi Çakmak ve Günlüküleri*, ed. Nilüfer Hatemi (Yapı Kredi Yayınları, 2002), I: 309, diary entry for March 16, 1915/2 Mart 1331.

94. Sürmenyan, *Harbiyeli bir Osmanlı Ermenisi*, 62.

95. Sürmenyan, 70–71.

96. Alexanian, *Forced into Genocide*, 65.

97. Alexanian, 66 and 70–72.

98. Sürmenyan, *Harbiyeli bir Osmanlı Ermenisi*, 64.

99. Sürmenyan, 65.

100. Sürmenyan, 66.

101. Sürmenyan, 66–67.

102. Sürmenyan, 74.

103. Sürmenyan, 80–82; the deported members of his family were his wife, mother, sister, brother-in-law, and nephews.

104. Sürmenyan, 84–91.

105. Alexanian, *Forced into Genocide*, 76.

106. Sürmenyan, *Harbiyeli bir Osmanlı Ermenisi*, 72.

107. *Meclis-i Mebusan'ın Zabıt Ceridesi*, 4 Subat 1331 (February 17, 1916).

108. *Meclis-i Ayan'ın Zabıt Ceridesi*, 28 Subat 1331 (March 12, 1916).

109. *Meclis-i Ayan'ın Zabıt Ceridesi*, 28 Subat 1331 (March 12, 1916).

110. *Meclis-i Ayan'ın Zabıt Ceridesi*, 28 Subat 1331 (March 12, 1916).

111. *Meclis-i Ayan'ın Zabıt Ceridesi*, 28 Subat 1331 (March 12, 1916).

112. *Meclis-i Ayan'ın Zabıt Ceridesi*, 28 Subat 1331 (March 12, 1916).

113. BOA, DH.ŞFR 54A/10, coded telegram, Interior Minister Talat to Commander of the Third Army, 2 Temmuz 1331 (July 15, 1915).

114. BOA, DH.ŞFR 54A/10, coded telegram, Interior Minister Talat to Commander of the Third Army, 2 Temmuz 1331 (July 15, 1915).

115. BOA, DH.ŞFR 54A/10, coded telegram, Interior Minister Talat to Commander of the Third Army, 2 Temmuz 1331 (July 15, 1915).

116. BOA, DH.İ.UM 59-1/1-38, coded telegram, Mahmud Kâmil to Interior Ministry, 3 Temmuz 1331 (July 16, 1915).

117. Kaiser, "Regional Resistance to Central Government Policies," 210.

Chapter 6. Resistance, Rebellion, and Revolution: The End of the Ottoman Empire

1. Elizabeth F. Thompson, *Justice Interrupted: The Struggle for Constitutional Government in the Middle East* (Harvard University Press, 2013), 118.

2. Salim Tamari, ed., *Year of the Locust: A Soldier's Diary and the Erasure of Palestine's Ottoman Past* (University of California Press, 2011), 143.

3. Nazik Ali Jawdat, "Pictures from the Past," in *Remembering Childhood in the Middle East: Memoirs from a Century of Change*, ed. Elizabeth Warnock Fernea, 19–32 (Austin: University of Texas Press, 2002), quote from 29–30, also partially quoted in Leila Tarazi Fawaz, *A Land of Aching Hearts: The Middle East in the Great War* (Harvard University Press, 2014), 239–40.

4. Jawdat, "Pictures from the Past," 28–29.

5. The book appeared in English, *The Forty Days of Musa Dagh*, in 1933. A second translation appeared in 2012. Film studio MGM planned a feature in the 1930s, but the project was shut down over objections by the Turkish government. Several attempts later, a film based on the novel appeared in 1982.

6. Mehmet Beşikçi, *The Ottoman Mobilization of Manpower in the First World War: Between Voluntarism and Resistance* (Brill, 2012).

7. Elif Maḥir Metinsoy, *Ottoman Women during World War I: Everyday Experiences, Politics and Conflict* (Cambridge University Press, 2017); Kate Dannies, "'A Pensioned Gentleman': Women's Agency and the Political Economy of Marriage in Istanbul during World War I," *Journal of the Ottoman and Turkish Studies Association* 6 (2019): 13–31; Yiğit Akın, "War, Women, and the State: The Politics of Sacrifice in the Ottoman Empire during the First World War," *Journal of Women's History* 26 (2014): 12–35.

8. Christoph Herzog, "The Ottoman Politics of War in Mesopotamia, 1914–1918, and Popular Reactions: The Example of Hilla," in *Popular Protest and Political Participation in the Ottoman Empire*, Studies in Honor of Suraiya Faroqhi, ed. Eleni Gara, M. Erdem Kabadayı, and Christoph K. Neumann (Istanbul Bilgi University Press, 2011), 311–12.

9. Quoted in Herzog, "Ottoman Politics of War in Mesopotamia," 307: "Irak ahalisi cebr ve şiddet görmezlerse tuğyan ederler. Bunda tarih şahiddir." The report appears to be from late 1914 or early 1915, see the same work at 306.

10. BOA, DH.EUM 4. Şube 24/7, Şefik (for the governor) to Interior Ministry, 31 Temmuz 331 (August 13, 1915).

11. BOA, DH.EUM 4. Şube 24/7, War Ministry to Interior Ministry, 23 Ağustos 331 (September 5, 1915).

12. Herzog, "Ottoman Politics of War in Mesopotamia," 313–18; for Herzog's reference to "massacre," see 316.

13. Herzog, "Ottoman Politics of War in Mesopotamia," 317.

14. BA-MA, N131/2, folio 4, Yusuf Ziya to Sixth Army, 15-11-331 (January 28, 1916).

15. BA-MA, N131/3, folio 33, Goltz to Enver, *Geheim*, 28-12-1331 and 12-3-1916.

16. BA-MA, N131/3, folios 81–85, Colmar von der Goltz, "Bericht über die Lage der 6. osmanischen Armee," March 23, 1916, quote from folio 85.

17. For mutual respect and bonds among officers, see Michael Provence, *The Last Ottoman Generation and the Making of the Modern Middle East* (Cambridge University Press, 2017),

32–48. For a mixed assessment, see Laila Parsons, *The Commander: Fawzi al-Qawuqji and Fight for Arab Independence, 1914–1948* (Hill and Wang, 2016), 3–37. For examples of contempt, see Selim Deringil, *The Ottoman Twilight in the Arab Lands: Turkish Memoirs and Testimonies of the Great War* (Academic Studies Press, 2019), xvii–lix and 187–94.

18. *Meclis Ayan'ın Zabıt Ceridesi*, 22 Şubat, 1331 (March 6, 1916).

19. *Meclis Ayan'ın Zabıt Ceridesi*, 22 Şubat, 1331 (March 6, 1916).

20. Hasan Kayalı, *Arabs and Young Turks: Ottomanism, Arabism, and Islamism in the Ottoman Empire, 1908–1918* (University of California Press, 1997), 197.

21. Conde de Ballobar [Antonio de la Cierva y Lewita], *Jerusalem in World War I: The Palestine Diary of a European Diplomat*, ed. Eduardo Manzano Moreno and Roberto Mazza (London: I. B. Tauris, 1996), 109–10. Entry for September 9, 1916.

22. King Constantine I (1868–1923) was replaced by his young son, Alexander, who died in 1920 of infection from a macaque ape bite. After his death, Constantine returned to the throne.

23. BOA, HR.SYS 2264/2, Ambassador at Athens Galib to Foreign Minister and Grand Vizier Said Halim, coded telegram, *mahremdir* (secret), 14 Kanun-u evvel 1915 (December 14, 1915).

24. Janet Klein, "Kurdish Nationalists and Non-Nationalist Kurdists: Rethinking Minority Nationalism and the Dissolution of the Ottoman Empire, 1908–1909," *Nations and Nationalism* 13 (2007): 135–53.

25. BOA, HR.SYS 2264/2, Ambassador at Athens Galib to Foreign Minister and Grand Vizier Said Halim, coded telegram, *mahremdir* (secret), 14 Kanun-u evvel 1915 (December 14, 1915).

26. BOA, HR.SYS 2264/2, Ambassador at Bern Fuad Selim to Foreign Ministry, *mahremdir* (secret), 17 Mayıs 1916 (May 17, 1916). For the letter, see Midhat Bey, *Lettre ouverte à Son Altesse Saïd Pacha, Grand Vézir*, in the same file. The letter is printed but bears no publisher. The last page is signed Genève, May 1, 1916.

27. BOA, HR.SYS 2264/2, Bucharest Ambassador Ahmed Tevfik to Foreign Minister Halil Bey, *mahremdir* (secret), 30 Haziran 1916 (June 30, 1916).

28. BOA, HR.SYS 2264/2, Bern Ambassador Fuad Selim to Foreign Ministry, *mahremdir* (secret), 11 Temmuz 1916 (July 11, 1916). İzzet had been a close advisor to Sultan Abdülhamid II, and he belonged to a group of former leaders the Unionists targeted after coming to power. See also Mostafa Minawi, *Losing Istanbul: Ottoman-Arab Imperialists and the End of Empire* (Stanford University Press, 2022), 8.

29. BOA, HR SYS 2264/2, Consul at Geneva Yusuf to Foreign Ministry, *mahremdir* (secret), 11 Temmuz 1916 (July 11, 1916).

30. BOA, HR.SYS 2316/7, Consul at Geneva Yusuf to Foreign Ministry, *mahremdir* (secret), 19 Temmuz 1916 (July 19, 1916). A "Special Desk" had been set up for "The Proclamation of Hüseyin Pasha as Caliph."

31. HR.SYS 2316/8, Consul-General at Geneva Yusuf to Foreign Ministry, *mahremdir* (secret), 21 Temmuz 1916 (July 21, 1916).

32. BOA, HR.SYS 2316/7, Consul at Geneva Yusuf to Foreign Ministry, *mahremdir* (secret), 24 Temmuz 1916 (July 24, 1916). It is unclear if Sabahaddin participated in the meeting. Cf on French caliphate; also Landolin Müller.

33. BOA, HR.SYS 2264/2, Foreign Ministry to Bern Embassy, *mahremdir* (secret), 10 Eylül 1332 (September 23, 1916).

34. BOA, HR.SYS 2264/2, Ambassador Fuad Selim (Bern) to Foreign Ministry, *mahremdir* [secret], 29 Eylül 1916 (September 29, 1916).

35. BOA, HR.SYS 2264/2, Ambassador at Vienna to Foreign Minister Halil Bey, 30 Teşrin-i evvel 1916 (October 30, 1916).

36. BOA, HR SYS.2264/2, Interior Minister Talat to Foreign Ministry, *mahremdir* [secret], 14 Teşrin-i sani 1332 (November 27, 1916).

37. BOA, DH.EUM 2 Sb 26 50, Karargah-i Umumi İkinci İstihbarat Şubesi Müdiriyeti'ne 15 Ağustos 1332 (August 28, 1916); *Ermeni komiteleri amal ve harekat-i ihtilaliyesi: Ilan-i mesrutiyetten evvel ve sonra* (Istanbul: Matbaa-i Amire, 1332).

38. *Aleyh Divan-ı Harb-i Örfisinde Tedkik Olunan Mesele-yi Siyasiye Hakkında İzahat*, Dördüncü Ordu-yu Hümayun Tarafından Neşr Edilmişdir (Dersaadet: Tanin Matbaası, 1332 [1916]).

39. BA-MA, N 523/13, 1–11, *Streng Vertraulich* [Strictly Confidential] Konstantinopel, August 7, 1916.

40. *Meclis-i Ayan'ın Zabıt Ceridesi*, 7 Teşrin-i sani 1332 (November 20, 1916).

41. *Meclis-i Ayan'ın Zabıt Ceridesi*, 14 Teşrin-i sani 1332 (November 27, 1916).

42. BOA, HR.SYS 2316/12, Sharif Husayn statement for revolt, in Arabic, dated 11 Zilkaade 334 (September 9, 1916). With a Turkish translation, dated 1961.

43. BOA, HR.SYS 2316/12, in Arabic, dated 11 Zilkaade 334 (September 9, 1916).

44. al-Amīr Shākib Arslān, *Sīrah Zātiyyah* (Beirut: Dār al-Tāl'iyya lil'taba'a wa al-nashr, 1969), 171; given Shākib Arslān's many other actions and statements for Ottoman coexistence, his account, written many years later, seems plausible.

45. For example, see Jafar al-Askari, *A Soldier's Story: From Ottoman Rule to Independent Iraq: The Memoirs of Jafar Pasha Al-Askari (1885–1936)*, ed. William Facey, trans. Mustafa Tariq al-Askari (Arabian Publishing, 2003), 30. Also George Antonius, cited in Deringil, *Ottoman Twilight*, xxxv.

46. Tamari, *Year of the Locust*, 155.

47. Elizabeth F. Thompson, *How the West Stole Democracy from the Arabs: The Syrian Congress of 1920 and the Destruction of its Historic Liberal-Islamic Alliance* (Atlantic Monthly, 2021); Jonathan Wyrtzen, *Worldmaking in the Long Great War: How Local and Colonial Struggles Shaped the Modern Middle East* (Columbia University Press, 2022); Laura Robson, *The Politics of Mass Violence in the Middle East* (Oxford University Press, 2020).

48. BOA, DH.EUM 4. Şube 7/39, Governor of Beirut Azmi to Interior Ministry, *coded* (şifre), 30 Temmuz 1332 (August 12, 1916).

49. N131/5, folio 1–7, Mustafa Kemal (Aleppo) to Jildirim, September 1, 1917. Promoted to "mirliva," or brigadier general, Mustafa Kemal was granted the title of "pasha" on April 1, 1916. See M. Şükrü Hanioğlu, *Atatürk: Entelektüel Biyografi* (Bağlam, 2023), 248–49.

50. Hanioğlu, *Atatürk*, 249, citing letter dated September 20, 1917, Mustafa Kemal to Enver, with copies to Cemal and Talat.

51. On the British commander General Allenby's dramatic entry into the city, see Eugene Rogan, *The Fall of the Ottomans: The Great War in the Middle East* (Basic Books, 2015), 311–53.

52. Heather Jones, "A Forgotten Front? The Mediterranean Blockade in the First World War," *International History Review* 46 (2024): 426–43.

53. Nicola Ziadeh, "A First-Person Account of the First World War in Greater Syria," in *The First World War as Remembered in the Countries of the Eastern Mediterranean*, ed. Olaf Farschid, Manfred Kropp, and Stephan Dähne (Würzburg: Ergon, 2006), 271–77, for quotes 271.

54. Simon Jackson, "Transformative Relief: Imperial Humanitarianism and Mandatory Development in Syria-Lebanon," *Humanity* (2017): 247–68.

55. A copy can be found in "Baghdad," March 19, 1917, British Library, India Office Records and Private Papers, IOR/L/PS/18/B253, in Qatar Digital Library.

56. In a final campaign in 1918, German armies nearly succeeded in changing the outcome of the war. See Holger Afflerbach, *Auf Messers Schneide: Wie das Deutsche Reich den Ersten Weltkrieg veror* (C. H. Beck, 2018).

57. Ömer Seyfeddin, *Yarınki Turan Devleti*, Türk Yurdu Kütüphanesi (Kader Matbaası, 1330 [November 24, 1914]), 3–20.

Conclusion: Dismembered Empire, Remembered Past

1. *Meclis-i Mebusan'ın Zabıt Ceridesi*, 23 Haziran 1330 (July 6, 1914).

2. "Memorandum, Presented by the Greek Members of the Turkish Parliament, to the American Commission on Mandates over Turkey" (The American Hellenic Society, Columbia University, 1919).

3. "Memorandum, Presented by the Greek Members of the Turkish Parliament," 3.

4. "Memorandum, Presented by the Greek Members of the Turkish Parliament," 4; and Vangelis Kechriotis, "On the Margins of National Historiography: The Greek *İttahtçı* Emmanouil Emmanouilidis—Opportunist or Ottoman Patriot?" in *Untold Histories of the Middle East: Recovering Voices from the 19th and 20th Centuries*, ed. Amy Singer, Christopher K. Neumann, and Akşin Somel (Routledge, 2011), 125–42, here especially 128–32.

5. In his comparative study of nationalist movements in the Habsburg, Ottoman, and Russian empires in the First World War, Aviel Roshwald underscored the critical role of "extraordinary and short-lived circumstances" produced by "regional or global crisis" that "suddenly and unexpectedly" placed "the trappings of political sovereignty . . . within the reach of nationalists." See Aviel Roshwald, *Ethnic Nationalism and the Fall of Empires: Central Europe, Russia, and the Middle East, 1914–1923* (Routledge, 2001), 2.

6. Eleutherios Venizelos, "Greece before the Peace Congress of 1919: A Memorandum Dealing with the Rights of Greece" (American Hellenic Society, 1919).

7. Venizelos, "Greece before the Peace Conference," 25.

8. Venizelos, 25.

9. Venizelos, 11 and 26.

10. Avetis Aharonian and Boghos Nubar, *The Armenian Question before the Peace Conference: A Memorandum Presented Officially by the Representatives of Armenia to the Peace Conference at Versailles, on February 26th, 1919* (New York: Press Bureau, the Armenian National Union of America, 1919), 23.

11. Aharonian and Nubar, *Armenian Question before the Peace Conference*, 9.

12. Aharonian and Nubar, 23.

13. Aharonian and Nubar, 20.

14. Aharonian and Nubar, 12.

15. Avetis Aharonian, "A Memorandum Presented by the President of the Delegation of the Armenian Republic to the President of the Peace Conference," in Aharonian and Nubar, *Armenian Question before the Peace Conference*, 65–69, quotation on 65.

16. Shérif Pasha, "Memorandum on the Claims of the Kurd People," March 22, 1919 (Imprimerie A.-G. L'Hoir, 1919), 3.

17. Shérif Pasha, "Memorandum on the Claims of the Kurd People," 3.

18. Shérif Pasha, 14.

19. Shérif Pasha, 4–14, quotation on Wilson on 14.

20. Article 22, Covenant of the League of Nations.

21. Resolution of the Syrian General Congress, July 2, 1919, available at Wilson Center, Digital Archive. See especially Elizabeth F. Thompson, *How the West Stole Democracy from the Arabs: The Syrian Congress of 1920 and the Destruction of Its Historic Liberal-Islamic Alliance* (Atlantic Monthly, 2021); Jonathan Wyrtzen, *Worldmaking in the Long Great War: How Local and Colonial Struggles Shaped the Modern Middle East* (Columbia University Press, 2022); Laura Robson, *The Politics of Mass Violence in the Middle East* (Oxford University Press, 2020). For the treaties, see Leonard V. Smith, *Sovereignty at the Paris Peace Conference of 1919* (Oxford University Press, 2018); Aimee Genell, "The End of Egypt's Occupation: Ottoman Sovereignty and the End of the British Declaration of Protection," in *Beyond Versailles: Sovereignty, Legitimacy, and Formation of New Politics after the Great War*, ed. Marcus M. Payk and Roberta Pergher (Indiana University Press, 2019), 77–98; and Aimee M. Genell, "Autonomous Provinces and the Problem of 'Semi-Sovereignty' in European International Law," *Journal of Balkan and Near Eastern Studies* 18 (2016): 533–49; Jörn Leonhard, *Der überforderte Frieden: Versailles und die Welt, 1918–1923* (C. H. Beck, 2018), 503–21, 708–17, 746–58; and also Jörn Leonhard, *Die Büchse der Pandora: Geschichte des Ersten Weltkriegs* (C. H. Beck, 2014), 939–1014.

22. Resolution of the Syrian General Congress, July 2, 1919.

23. Resolution of the Syrian General Congress, July 2, 1919.

24. On the French bombardment of Damascus in 1925, see Susan Pedersen, *The Guardians: The League of Nations and the Crisis of Empire* (Oxford University Press, 2015), 142–68; on the indiscriminate use of airpower in Iraq, see Priya Satia, "The Defense of Inhumanity: Air Control and the British Idea of Arabia," *American Historical Review* 111 (2006): 16–51; also Robson, *Mass Violence*.

25. Ahmet Rıza, *The Moral Bankruptcy of Western Policy towards the East* (Ankara: Ministry of Culture and Tourism, 1988), 6–7, originally published as Ahmed Rıza, *La Faillite morale de la politique occidentale en Orient* (Paris: Libraire Picart, 1922), 10–11: "Que rest-t-il, matériellement et moralement, de l'œuvre coloniale des siècles précédents? Un bouleversement gigantesque du monde entier; des races humaines presque complètement anéanties; d'autres transplantées d'un continent sur l'autre par les flottes des Nègriers, des territoires immenses dévastés, hier, l'esclavage, la misère aujourd'hui. La civilisation n'a pas supprimé la barbarie, elle l'a tout simplement raffinée."

26. Ahmed Rıza, *Moral Bankrutpcy*, 14.

27. Cemil Koçak, *Umûmî Müfettişikler (1927–1952)*, 3rd ed. (İletişim Yayınları, 2016; 2010; 2003); Uğur Ümit Üngör, *The Making of Modern Turkey: Nation and State in Eastern Anatolia,*

1913–1950 (Oxford University Press, 2011). Furthermore, all throughout the 1920s, the new government in Ankara carried out environmental and ethnographic studies across Asia Minor/Anatolia, laying physical claim to its new political boundaries.

28. Mahmood Mamdani has argued that modernity itself is colonial and that the modern state, originating in 1492, is inherently colonial. See Mahmood Mamdani, *Neither Settler nor Native: The Making and Unmaking of Permanent Minorities* (Harvard University Press, 2020); Senem Aslan, "Everyday Forms of State Power and the Kurds in the Early Turkish Republic," *International Journal of Middle East Studies* 43 (2011): 75–93.

29. Friedrich Kress von Kressenstein, *Mit den Türken zum Suezkanal* (Berlin: Otto Schlegel, 1938), 73.

30. Kress, *Mit den Türken*, 75.

31. Muhammad Kurd Ali, *Memoirs: A Selection* (Washington, DC: American Council of Learned Societies, 1954), 47.

32. Demetra Vaka, *The Unveiled Ladies of Stamboul* (Books for Libraries Press, 1923), v–vi.

BIBLIOGRAPHY

Primary Sources

Archives

TURKEY

ATASE, Archive of the Turkish General Staff, Ankara

BDH	Birinci Dünya Harbi

BOA, Cumhurbaşkanlığı Osmanlı Arşivi, Presidential Ottoman Archives, Istanbul

A.AMD	Sadâret Evrakı, Âmedî Kalemi
DH.EUM	Dahiliye Nezareti, Emniyet-i Umumiye
DH.EUM.AYŞ	Dahiliye Nezareti, Emniyet-i Umumiye, Asayiş
DH.EUM.MTK	Dahiliye Nezareti, Emniyet-i Umumiye, Muhaberât ve Tensîkât
DH.EUM.VRK	Dahiliye Nezareti, Emniyet-i Umumiye, Evrak Odası
DH.İD	Dahiliye Nezareti, İdarî
DH.İ.UM	Dahiliye Nezareti, İdâre-i Umumiye
DH.KMS	Dahiliye Nezareti, Kalem-i Mahsûs
DH.ŞFR	Dahiliye Nezareti, Şifre Kalemi
DH.UMVM	Dahiliye Nezareti, Umûr-ı Mahallıye-i Vilayât Müdüriyeti
HR.SYS	Hariciye Nezareti, Siyasî
İ.DUİT	İrâde, Dosya Usulü
MV	Meclis-i Vükelâ

GERMANY

BA-MA, Bundesarchiv-Militärarchiv, Freiburg, i.Br.

N	Nachlässe
RM	Kaiserliche Marine
RH	Reichsheer und Heer

PA-AA, Politisches Archiv, Auswärtiges Amt (PA-AA), Berlin

R	Reich

FRANCE

MAE, Ministère des Affaires Étrangères, La Courneuve

Série Guerre

UNITED KINGDOM

TNA, The National Archives, London

FO Foreign Office

UNITED STATES

Princeton University Special Collections, Princeton

Sir John Maxwell Papers

Georgetown University, Booth Family Center for Special Collections, Washington, DC

Cornelius Van H. Engert Papers

Contemporary Publications

Aharonian, Avetis. "A Memorandum Presented by the President of the Delegation of the Armenian Republic to the President of the Peace Conference." In Aharonian and Nubar, *Armenian Question before the Peace Conference* , 65–69.

Aharonian, Avetis, and Boghos Nubar. *The Armenian Question before the Peace Conference: A Memorandum Presented Officially by the Representatives of Armenia to the Peace Conference at Versailles, on February 26th, 1919*. New York: Press Bureau, the Armenian National Union of America, 1919.

Ahmed Rıza. *La faillite morale de la politique occidentale en Orient*. Paris: Libraire Picart, 1922.

Ahmed Selahaddin. *Berlin Kongresi'nin diplomasi tarihine bir nazar: Külliyati hukuk ve siyasiyat'dan birinci kitab*. 1327 [1911/1912].

Ahmed Selahaddin. *Hukuk-i Beyneldüvvelin Mukaddimat-ı Nazariye ve Safahatı Tekamüliyesi*. Dersaadet: Kanaat Matbaası, 1331 [1915].

Ahmed Selahaddin. *Makedonya Meselesi ve Balkan Harb-ı Âhiri*. Dersaadet: Kanaat Matbaası, 1331 [1915].

Ahmet Rıza. *The Moral Bankruptcy of Western Policy towards the East*. Ankara: Ministry of Culture and Tourism, 1988.

Aleyh Divan-ı Harb-i Örfisinde Tedkik Olunan Mesele-yi Siyasiye Hakkında İzahat. Dördüncü Ordu-yu Hümayun Tarafından Neşr Edilmişdir. Dersaadet: Tanin Matbaası, 1332 [1916].

Enver Pascha. *Um Tripolis*. Munich: Hugo Bruckmann, 1918.

Grobba, Fritz. *Die Getreidewirtschaft Syriens und Palästinas seit Beginn des Weltkrieges*. Hanover: Orient-Buchhandlung Heinz Lafaire, 1923.

Harbiye Dairesi Piyade Şubesi. *1330 Senesi Seferberliğinde Piyade İkmal Efradının Ders Kitabı* Istanbul, 1330 [1914].

İbnürrefet Mehmed Memduh. *Kapitülasyon-Capitulations: Yahud, memalik-i osmaniye'de ecnebilerin haiz olduğu imtiyazat.* Dersaadet: Matbaa-i Ahmet İhsan, 1327 [1911/12].

Kress von Kressenstein, Friedrich. *Mit den Türken zum Suezkanal.* Berlin: Otto Schlegel, 1938.

Meclis-i Ayan'ın Zabıt Ceridesi. 1914–1918.

Meclis-i Mebusan'ın Zabıt Ceridesi. 1914–1918.

Mehmed Sezai. *Cihad-ı mukaddes yahud Trablusgarb'da Osmanlı-İtalya Cengi.* Izmir: Keşişyan Matbaası, 1327 [1911].

Mehmed Şükrü. *Heyet-i İhtiyariye.* Istanbul, 1332 [1916].

"Memorandum, Presented by the Greek Members of the Turkish Parliament, to the American Commission on Mandates over Turkey." American Hellenic Society, Columbia University, 1919.

Nafi 'Utref. "Nema-yı Bedenî." 1 Haziran 1333 [June 1, 1917] *Muallim* (1): 348–51.

Ömer Seyfeddin. *Yarınki Turan Devleti,* Türk Yurdu Kütüphanesi. Kader Matbaası, 1330 [November 24, 1914].

Schreiner, George Abel. *From Berlin to Bagdad: Behind the Scenes in the Near East.* New York: Harper & Brothers, 1918.

Şehbenderzade Filibeli Ahmet Hilmi. *Muhalefetin İflası.* Kostantiniyye: Hikmet Matbaa-i İslamiyesi, 1331 [1915].

Shérif Pasha. "Memorandum on the Claims of the Kurd People." March 22, 1919. Imprimerie A.-G. L'Hoir, 1919.

Ticaret ve Ziraat Nezareti, İstatistik İdare-i Umumiyesi Müdiriyeti: Memalik-i Osmaniye 1329 senesine Mahsus Ziraat İstatistiğidir. Dersaadet: Matbaa-i Aliye, 1332 [1916].

"Turkey Distrusted Allies, Says Halim." *New York Times,* February 22, 1915.

Venizelos, Eleutherios. "Greece before the Peace Congress of 1919: A Memorandum Dealing with the Rights of Greece." American Hellenic Society, 1919.

Yalçın, Hüseyin Cahit. *Siyasal Anılar.* Edited by Rauf Mutluay. Türkiye İş Bankası Kültür Yayınları, 1976.

Yalman, Ahmet Emin. *Turkey in the World War.* New Haven: Yale University Press, 1930.

Published Primary Sources

BOGHOS NUBAR PAPERS

Correspondence Respecting Events Leading to the Rupture of Relations with Turkey. Miscellaneous no. 13, Presented to both Houses of Parliament by Command of His Majesty, November 1914. London: Printed under the Authority of His Majesty's Stationery Office, 1914.

Der Prozeß Talaat Pascha: Stenographischer Bericht über die Verhandlung gegen den des Mordes an Talaat Pascha angeklagten armeniaschen Studenten Salomon Teilirian vor dem Schwurgericht des Landgerichts III zu Berlin, Aktenzeichen: C.J. 22/21, am 2. und 3. Juni 1921, Mit einem Vorwort von Armin T. Wegner und einem Anhang. Berlin: Deutsche Verlagsgesellschaft für Politik und Geschichte, 1921.

Ermeni komiteleri amal ve harekat-i ihtilaliyesi: Ilan-i mesrutiyetten evvel ve sonra. Istanbul: Matbaa-i Amire, 1332.

Gooch, G. P., and Harold William Vazeille Temperley, eds. *The Near and Middle East on the Eve of the World War*. Vol. 10, part 1. *British Documents on the Origins of the War, 1898–1914*. London: H.M.S.O., 1927.

Ökçün, A. Gündüz. *Tarımda Ekme ve Çalışma Yükümlülüğü (Mükellefiyyet-i Ziraiyye), Belgeler 1914–1922*. Ankara Üniversitesi, 1983.

Trotsky, Leon. *The Balkan Wars, 1912–13: The War Correspondence of Leon Trotsky*. Translated by Brian Pearce, edited by George Weissman and Duncan Williams. Monad Press, 1980.

DIARIES, MEMOIRS, AND LETTERS

al-Askari, Jafar. *A Soldier's Story: From Ottoman Rule to Independent Iraq: The Memoirs of Jafar Pasha Al-Askari (1885–1936)*. Edited by William Facey. Translated by Mustafa Tariq al-Askari. N.p.: Arabian Publishing, 2003.

Alexanian, Yervant N. *Forced into Genocide: Memoirs of an Armenian Soldier in the Ottoman Turkish Army*. Edited by Adrienne G. Alexanian. Introduced by Sergio La Porta. New York: Transaction, 2017.

Balkan, Fuat. *Komitacı: BJK'nin Kurucusu Fuat Balkan'ın Anıları*. Edited by Turgut Gürer. Istanbul: Gürer, 2006.

Ballobar, de Conde [Antonio de la Cierva y Lewita]. *Jerusalem in World War I: The Palestine Diary of a European Diplomat*. Edited by Eduardo Manzano Moreno and Roberto Mazza. London: I. B. Tauris, 1996.

Behar, Cem, ed. *Osmanlı İmparatorluğu'nun ve Türkiye'nin Nüfusu, 1500–1927*. Ankara: Devlet İstatistik Enstitüsü Matbaası, 1996.

Ben-Zvi, Izhak. *The Hebrew Battalions: Letters*. Translated by Taffi Baker and Margalit Benaya. Jerusalem: Yad Izhak Ben-Zvi, 1969.

Bolayır, Enver, ed. *Talât Paşa'nin Hâtıraları*. Istanbul: Güven Yayınevi, 1946.

Cavid Bey. *Meşrutiyet Ruznâmesi*. Volumes 1–4. Edited by Hasan Babacan and Servet Avşar. Ankara: Türk Tarih Kurumu, 2014.

Cemal Paşa. *Hatırât: 1913–1922*. Dersaadet: n.p., 1922.

Der-Garabedian, Hagop S. *Jail to Jail: Autobiography of a Survivor of the 1915 Armenian Genocide*. Translated by Aghop H. Der-Karabetian. New York: iUniverse, 2004.

Der Yeghiayan, Zaven. *My Patriarchal Memoirs: Zaven Der Yeghiayan, Armenian Patriarch of Constantinople, 1913–1922*. Translated by Ared Misirliyan. Annotated by Vatche Ghazarian. Barrington, RI: Mayreni, 2002.

Eti, Ali Rıza. *Bir Onbaşının Doğu Cephesi Günlüğü, 1914–1915*. Edited by Gönül Eti. Istanbul: Türkiye İş Bankası Kültür Yayınları, 2009.

Garo, Armen. *Bank Ottoman: Memoirs of Armen Garo, the Armenian Ambassador to America from the Independent Republic of Armenia*. Translated by Haig T. Partizian, edited and introduction by Simon Vratzian. Detroit: Armen Topouzian, 1990.

Goldschmidt, Arthur, Jr., ed. *The Memoirs and Diaries of Muhammad Farid, an Egyptian Nationalist Leader (1868–1919)*. San Francisco: Mellen University Research Press, 1992.

Hatemi, Nilüfer, ed. *Mareşal Fevzi Çakmak ve Günlüküleri*. 2 volumes. Istanbul: Yapı Kredi Yayınları, 2002.

Jawdat, Nazik Ali. "Pictures from the Past." In *Remembering Childhood in the Middle East: Memoirs from a Century of Change*, edited by Elizabeth Warnock Fernea, 19–32. Austin: University of Texas Press, 2002.

Kayra, Mediha. *Hoşça Kal Trabzon, Merhaba İstanbul: Bir Kız Çocuğunun Günlüğünden I. Dünya Savaşı'nda Anadolu.* Edited by Cahit Kayra. Istanbul: Tarihçi Kitabevi, 2013.

Muhammad Kurd Ali. *Memoirs: A Selection.* Washington, DC: American Council of Learned Societies, 1954.

Pomiankowski, Joseph. *Der Zusammenbruch des Ottomanischen Reiches: Erinnerungen an die Türkei aus der Zeit des Weltkrieges.* Vienna: Amalthea-Verlag, 1928.

Sazonov, Serge. *Fateful Years, 1909–1916.* New York: Frederick A. Stokes, 1928.

Shākib Arslān, al-Amīr. *Sīrah Zātiyyah.* Beirut: Dār al-Tāl'iyya lil'taba'a wa al-nashr, 1969.

Sürmenyan, Kalusd. *Harbiyeli bir Osmanlı Ermenisi: Mülâzım ı Sânî Sürmenyan'ın Savaş ve Tehcir Anıları.* Edited and translated by Yaşar Tolga Cora. İstanbul: Tarih Vakfı Yurt Yayınları, 2015.

Tergeman, Siham. *Daughter of Damascus.* Translated by Andrea Rugh. Austin: Center for Middle Eastern Studies University of Texas at Austin, 1994.

Theodore, D[emetrios] E. *The Sacrificials: Part of an Autobiography Depicting the Life of Minorities in a War Torn Country.* N.p., 1970.

Tamari, Salim, ed. *Year of the Locust: A Soldier's Diary and the Erasure of Palestine's Ottoman Past.* Berkeley: University of California Press, 2011.

Ziadeh, Nicola. "A First-Person Account of the First World War in Greater Syria." In *The First World War as Remembered in the Countries of the Eastern Mediterranean*, edited by Olaf Farschid, Manfred Kropp, and Stephan Dähne, 265–77. Würzburg: Ergon, 2006.

Secondary Sources

Abramson, Glenda. *Hebrew Writing of the First World War.* Vallentine Mitchell, 2008.

Abuhusayn, Abdulrahim. "An Ottoman against the Constitution: The Maronites of Mount Lebanon and the Question of Representation in the Ottoman Parliament." In *Religion, Ethnicity and Contested Nationhood in the Former Ottoman Space*, edited by Jørgen Nielsen, 89–113. Brill, 2012.

Adanır, Fikret. "Non-Ottomans in the Ottoman Army and the Ottoman Defeat in the Balkan War of 1912–1913." In Suny, Göçek, and Naimark, *Question of Genocide*, 136–48.

Afflerbach, Holger. *Auf Messers Schneide: Wie das Deutsche Reich den Ersten Weltkrieg verlor.* C. H. Beck, 2018.

Ahmad, Feroz. "Unionist Failure to Stay Out of the War in October–November 1914." *Perceptions* 20 (2015): 23–38.

Ahmed, Faiz. *Afghanistan Rising: Islamic Law and Statecraft between the Ottoman and British Empires.* Harvard University Press, 2017.

Ahmida, Ali Abdullatif. *The Making of Modern Libya: State Formation, Colonization, and Resistance.* 2nd ed. State University of New York Press, 2009.

Akarlı, Engin Deniz. *The Long Peace: Ottoman Lebanon, 1861–1920.* University of California Press, 1993.

Akçam, Taner. *The Young Turks' Crime against Humanity: The Armenian Genocide and Ethnic Cleansing in the Ottoman Empire.* Princeton University Press, 2011.

Akçam, Taner, and Ümit Kurt, *The Spirit of the Laws: The Plunder of Wealth in the Armenian Genocide.* Translated by Aram Arkun. Berghahn, 2015.

Akgül, Önder Eren. "War on the Desert: The Militarization of the Sinai and Its Greater Syrian Sacrificial Frontier during World War I." *International Journal of Middle East Studies* 56 (2024): 91–113.

Akın, Yiğit. "War, Women, and the State: The Politics of Sacrifice in the Ottoman Empire during the First World War." *Journal of Women's History* 26 (2014): 12–35.

Akın, Yiğit. *When the War Came Home: The Ottomans' Great War and the Devastation of an Empire.* Stanford University Press, 2018.

Aksakal, Mustafa. "'Holy War Made in Germany'? Ottoman Origins of the 1914 Jihad." *War in History* 18 (2011): 184–99.

Aksakal, Mustafa. *The Ottoman Road to War in 1914: The Ottoman Empire and the First World War.* Cambridge University Press, 2008.

Alff, Kristen. "Changing Capitalist Structures and Settler-Colonial Land Purchases in Northern Palestine, 1897–1922." *International Journal of Middle East Studies* 55 (2023): 675–92.

al-Qattan, Najwa. "When Mothers Ate Their Children: Wartime Memory and the Language of Food in Syria and Lebanon." *International Journal of Middle East Studies* 46 (2014): 719–36.

Amzi-Erdoğdular, Leyla. *The Afterlife of Ottoman Europe: Muslims in Habsburg Bosnia Herzegovina.* Stanford University Press, 2024.

Anscombe, Frederick F. *The Ottoman Gulf: The Creation of Kuwait, Saudi Arabia, and Qatar.* Columbia University Press, 1997.

Antaramian, Richard E. *Brokers of Empire, Brokers of Faith: Armenians and the Politics of Reform in the Ottoman Empire.* Stanford University Press, 2020.

Arıkan, Zeki. "Balkan Savaşı ve Kamuoyu." In *Bildiriler: Dördüncü Askeri Tarih Semineri.* Genelkurmay Basımevi, 1989.

Arkun, Aram. "Zeytun and the Commencement of the Armenian Genocide." In Suny, Göçek, and Naimark, *Question of Genocide,* 221–43.

Aslan, Senem. "Everyday Forms of State Power and the Kurds in the Early Turkish Republic." *International Journal of Middle East Studies* 43 (2011): 75–93.

Aydın, Cemil. *The Idea of the Muslim World: A Global Intellectual History.* Harvard University Press, 2019.

Babou, Cheikh Anta. *Fighting the Greater Jihad: Amadu Bamba and the Founding of the Muridiyya of Senegal, 1853–1913.* Ohio University Press, 2007.

Badem, Candan, "'Forty Years of Black Days'? The Russian Administration of Kars, Ardahan, and Batum, 1878–1918." In *Russian-Ottoman Borderlands: The Eastern Question Reconsidered,* edited by Lucien J. Frary and Mara Kozelsky, 221–50. University of Wisconsin Press, 2014.

Bashkin, Orit. "The Colonized Semites and the Infectious Disease: Theorizing and Narrativizing Anti-Semitism in the Levant, 1870–1914." *Critical Inquiry* 47 (2021): 189–217.

Bast, Oliver. "Les 'Buts de guerre' de la Perse neutre pendant la Première Guerre mondiale." *Relations Internationales* 160 (2015): 95–110.

Bayly, C. A. *The Birth of the Modern World, 1780–1914: Global Connections and Comparisons.* Blackwell, 2003.

Becker, Annette. *War and Faith: The Religious Imagination in France, 1914–1930.* Berg, 1998.

Ben-Bassat, Yuval, and Eyal Ginio. "Introduction: The Case Study of Palestine during the Young Turk Era." In *Late Ottoman Palestine*, edited by Yuval Ben-Bassat and Eyal Ginio, 1–14. I. B. Tauris, 2011.

Benton, Lauren. *They Called It Peace: Worlds of Imperial Violence*. Princeton University Press, 2024.

Benton, Lauren, and Lisa Ford. *Rage for Order: The British Empire and the Origins of International Law, 1800–1850*. Harvard University Press, 2017.

Beşikçi, Mehmet. *The Ottoman Mobilization of Manpower in the First World War: Between Voluntarism and Resistance*. Brill, 2012.

Birdal, Murat. *The Political Economy of Ottoman Public Debt: Insolvency and European Financial Control in the Late Nineteenth Century*. I. B. Tauris, 2010.

Birinci, Ali. *Hürriyet ve İtilâf Fırkası: II. Meşrutiyet Devrinde İttihat ve Terakki'ye Karşı Çıkanlar*. 1990. Repr., Dergâh Yayınları, 2012.

Bjørnlund, Matthias. "'A Fate Worse than Dying': Sexual Violence during the Armenian Genocide." In *Brutality and Desire: War and Sexuality in Europe's Twentieth Century*, edited by Dagmar Herzog, 16–58. Palgrave Macmillan, 2009.

Bloxham, Donald. "The First World War and the Development of the Armenian Genocide." In Suny, Göçek, and Naimark, *Question of Genocide*, 260–75.

Bloxham, Donald. *The Great Game of Genocide: Imperialism, Nationalism, and the Destruction of the Ottoman Armenians*. Oxford University Press, 2005.

Bobroff, Ronald. *Roads to Glory: Late Imperial Russia and the Turkish Straits*. I. B. Tauris, 2006.

Bonner, Michael. *Jihad in Islamic History: Doctrines and Practice*. Princeton University Press, 2006.

Brand, Tylor. *Famine Worlds: Life at the Edge of Suffering in Lebanon's Great War*. Stanford University Press, 2023.

Brock, Lothar, and Hendrik Simon, eds. *The Justification of War and International Order: From Past to Present*. Oxford University Press, 2021.

Büssow, Johann. "Ottoman Reform and Urban Government in the District of Jerusalem, 1867–1917." In *Urban Governance under the Ottomans: Between Cosmopolitanism and Conflict*, edited by Ulrike Freitag and Nora Lafi, 97–141. Routledge, 2014.

Campos, Michelle U. *Ottoman Brothers: Muslims, Christians, and Jews in Early Twentieth-Century Palestine*. Stanford University Press, 2011.

Cân, Lale. *Spiritual Subjects: Central Asian Pilgrims and the Ottoman Hajj at the End of Empire*. Stanford University Press, 2020.

Çetinkaya, Y. Doğan. *The Young Turks and the Boycott Movement: Nationalism, Protest and the Working Classes in the Formation of Modern Turkey*. I. B. Tauris, 2014.

Çetinkaya, Y. Doğan. "1908 Devrimi ve Toplumsal Seferberlik." In *II. Meşrutiyet'i Yeniden Düşünmek*, edited by Ferdan Ergut, 13–27. Tarih Vakfı, 2010.

Chalaba, Tamara. *The Shi'is of Jabal 'Amil and the New Lebanon: Community and Nation, 1918–1943*.

Chehabi, H. E., and Ali Gheissari. "Extraterritoriality and Capitulations in Qajar Iran." In *Unconquered States: Non-European Powers in the Imperial Age*, edited by H. E. Chehabi and David Motadel, 190–204. Oxford University Press, 2024.

Çiçek, M. Talha. *War and State Formation in Syria: Cemal Pasha's Governorate during World War I, 1914–1917*. Routledge, 2014.

Clancy-Smith, Julia A. *Rebel and Saint: Muslim Notables, Populist Protest, Colonial Encounters (Algeria and Tunisia, 1800–1904)*. University of California Press, 1994.

Cohen, Julia Phillips. *Becoming Ottomans: Sephardi Jews and Imperial Citizenship in the Modern Era*. Oxford University Press, 2014.

Cole, Juan R. I. *Colonialism and Revolution in the Middle East: Social and Cultural Origins of Egypt's 'Urabi Movement*. Princeton University Press, 1993.

Conte, Giampaolo. "Unholy Alliances: Disentangling the Economic Relations between Italy, the Holy See and the Ottoman Empire." *International History Review* 43 (2021): 1142–59.

Conte, Giampaolo, and Gaetano Sabatini. "Debt and Imperialism in Pre-Protectorate Tunisia, 1867–1870: A Political and Economic Analysis." *Journal of European Economic History* 47 (2018): 9–32.

Conte, Giampaolo, and Gaetano Sabatini. "The Ottoman External Debt and Its Features under European Financial Control (1881–1914)." *Journal of European Economic History* 43 (2014): 69–96.

Cora, Yaşar Tolga, Dzovinar Derderian, and Ali Sipahi, eds. *The Ottoman East in the Nineteenth Century: Societies, Identities and Politics*. I. B. Tauris, 2016.

Cox, Mary E. *Hunger in War and Peace: Women and Children in Germany, 1914–1924*. Oxford University Press, 2019.

Dannies, Kate. "'A Pensioned Gentleman': Women's Agency and the Political Economy of Marriage in Istanbul during World War I." *Journal of the Ottoman and Turkish Studies Association* 6 (2019): 13–31.

Der Matossian, Bedross. *Shattered Dreams of Revolution: From Liberty to Violence in the Late Ottoman Empire*. Stanford University Press, 2014.

Deringil, Selim. *The Ottoman Twilight in the Arab Lands: Turkish Memoirs and Testimonies of the Great War*. Academic Studies Press, 2019.

Deringil, Selim. "'They Live in a State of Nomadism and Savagery': The Late Ottoman Empire and the Post-Colonial Debate." *Comparative Studies in Society and History* 45 (2003): 311–42.

Dockter, A. Warren. "'A Great Turkish Policy': Winston Churchill, the Ottoman Empire and the Origins of the Dardanelles Campaign." *History: The Journal of the Historical Association* 102 (2017): 68–91.

Dolbee, Samuel. *Locusts of Power: Borders, Empire, and Environment in the Modern Middle East*. Cambridge University Press, 2023.

Doumanis, Nicholas. *Before the Nation: Muslim-Christian Coexistence and Its Destruction in Late Ottoman Anatolia*. Oxford University Press, 2013.

Dündar, Fuat. *Crime of Numbers: The Role of Statistics in the Armenian Question (1878–1918)*. Transaction Publishers, 2010.

Dündar, Fuat. *İttihat ve Terakki'nin Müslümanları İskân Politikası (1913–1918)*. İletişim, 2001.

El Shakry, Omnia S. *The Great Social Laboratory: Subjects of Knowledge in Colonial and Postcolonial Egypt*. Stanford University Press, 2007.

Eldem, Edhem. "Ottoman Financial Integration with Europe: Foreign Loans, the Ottoman Bank, and the Ottoman Public Debt." *European Review* 13 (2005): 431–45

Eldem, Vedat. *Harp ve Mütareke Yıllarında Osmanlı İmparatorluğu'nun Ekonomisi.* Türk Tarih Kurumu Basımevi, 1994.

Elkins, Caroline. *Legacy of Violence: A History of the British Empire.* Alfred A. Knopf, 2022.

Erol, Emre. *The Ottoman Crisis in Western Anatolia: Turkey's Belle Époque and the Transition to a Modern Nation State.* I. B. Tauris, 2016.

Evans, Richard J. *The Pursuit of Power: Europe, 1815–1914.* Penguin, 2016.

Fahrenthold, Stacy D. *Between the Ottomans and the Entente: The First World War in the Syrian and Lebanese Diaspora, 1908–1925.* Oxford University Press, 2019.

Fawaz, Leila Tarazi. *A Land of Aching Hearts: The Middle East in the Great War.* Harvard University Press, 2014.

Fishman, Louis A. *Jews and Palestinians in the Late Ottoman Era, 1908–1914: Claiming the Homeland.* Edinburgh University Press, 2020.

Fortna, Benjamin C. *The Circassian: A Life of Eşref Bey, Late Ottoman Insurgent and Special Agent.* Oxford University Press, 2016.

Foster, Zachary J. "The 1915 Locust Attack in Syria and Palestine and Its Role in the Famine during the First World War." *Middle Eastern Studies* 51 (2014): 370–94.

Fratantuono, Ella. *Governing Migration in the Late Ottoman Empire.* Edinburgh University Press, 2024.

Fujinami, Nobuyoshi. "Decentralizing Centralists, or the Political Language on Provincial Administration in the Second Ottoman Constitutional Period." *Middle Eastern Studies* 49 (2013): 880–900.

Fulton, L. Bruce. "France and the Ottoman Empire." In *The Ottoman Empire and the Great Powers,* edited by Marian Kent, 138–64. Frank Cass, 1996; 1984.

Garo, Armen. *Why Armenia Should Be Free: Armenia's Role in the Present War.* Hairenik, 1918.

Gatrell, Peter, and Liubov Zhvanko, eds. *Europe on the Move: Refugees in the Era of the Great War.* Manchester University Press, 2017.

Genell, Aimee. "The End of Egypt's Occupation: Ottoman Sovereignty and the End of the British Declaration of Protection." In *Beyond Versailles: Sovereignty, Legitimacy, and Formation of New Politics after the Great War,* edited by Marcus M. Payk and Roberta Pergher, 77–98. Indiana University Press, 2019.

Genell, Aimee M. "Autonomous Provinces and the Problem of 'Semi-Sovereignty' in European International Law." *Journal of Balkan and Near Eastern Studies* 18 (2016): 533–49.

Georgeon, François. "Religion, Politics and Society in the Wake of the Young Turk Revolution: The 'Ramadan of Freedom' in Istanbul." In *The Young Turk Revolution and the Ottoman Empire: The Aftermath of 1908,* edited by Noémi Lévy-Aksu and François Georgeon, 175–95. I. B. Tauris, 2017.

Ginio, Eyal. *The Ottoman Culture of Defeat: The Balkan Wars and Their Aftermath.* Oxford University Press, 2016.

Gökatalay, Semih. "Economic Nationalism of the Committee of Union and Progress Revisited: The Case of the Society for the Ottoman Navy." *Nationalities Papers* 48 (2020): 942–56.

Grant, Jonathan. "The Sword of the Sultan: Ottoman Arms Imports, 1854–1914." *Journal of Military History* 66 (2002): 9–36.

Gratien, Chris. *The Unsettled Plain: An Environmental History of the Late Ottoman Frontier.* Stanford University Press, 2022.

Greble, Emily. *Muslims and the Making of Modern Europe*. Oxford University Press, 2021.

Güvenç, Serhat. *Birinci Dünya Savaşına Giden Yol: Osmanlıların Drednot Düşleri*. İş Bankası, 2009.

Haddad, Mahmoud. "Syria and Iraq as Proxy Colonies before Colonization: The Ottoman Vali versus the Western Consul in the Era of Capitulations." *Die Welt des Islams* 60 (2020): 3–30.

Hajdarpasic, Edin. *Whose Bosnia? Nationalism and Political Imagination in the Balkans, 1840–1914*. Cornell University Press, 2014.

Halpern, Paul G. *The Naval War in the Mediterranean, 1914–1918*. Naval Institute Press, 1987.

Hamed-Troyansky, Vladimir. *Empire of Refugees: North Caucasian Muslims and the Late Ottoman State*. Stanford University Press, 2024.

Hanioğlu, M. Şükrü. *Atatürk: Entelektüel Biyografi*. Bağlam, 2023.

Hanioğlu, M. Şükrü. *A Brief History of the Late Ottoman Empire*. Princeton University Press, 2008.

Hanioğlu, M. Şükrü. "Ottoman Jihad or Jihads: The Ottoman Shīʿī Jihad, the Successful One." In *Jihad and Islam in World War I: Studies on the Ottoman Jihad on the Centenary of Snouck Hurgronje's "Holy War Made in Germany,"* edited by Erik-Jan Zürcher, 117–34. Leiden University Press, 2016.

Hanioğlu, M. Şükrü. *Preparation for a Revolution: The Young Turks 1902–1908*. Oxford University Press, 2001.

Hanioğlu, M. Şükrü. *The Young Turks in Opposition*. Oxford University Press, 1995.

Hashmi, Sohail H., ed. *Just Wars, Holy Wars, and Jihads: Christian, Jewish, and Muslim Encounters and Exchanges*. Oxford University Press, 2012.

Herzog, Christoph. "The Ottoman Politics of War in Mesopotamia, 1914–1918, and Popular Reactions: The Example of Hilla." In *Popular Protest and Political Participation in the Ottoman Empire*, Studies in Honor of Suraiya Faroqhi, edited by Eleni Gara, M. Erdem Kabadayı, and Christoph K. Neumann, 303–18. Istanbul Bilgi University Press, 2011.

Herzog, Christoph. "The Urban Experience of Women's Memoirs: Mediha Kayra's World War I Notebook." In *Women and the City, Women in the City: A Gendered Perspective on Ottoman Urban History*, edited by Nazan Maksudyan, 146–68. Berghahn, 2014.

Herzog, Christoph, and Malik Sharif. *The First Ottoman Experiment in Democracy*. Ergon, 2010.

Hock, Stefan. "'Waking Us from This Endless Slumber': The Ottoman-Italian War and North Africa in the Ottoman Twentieth Century." *War in History* 26 (2019): 204–26.

Holquist, Peter. "The Politics and Practice of the Russian Occupation of Armenia, 1915–February 1917." In Suny, Göçek, and Naimark, *Question of Genocide*, 151–74.

Jackson, Simon. "Transformative Relief: Imperial Humanitarianism and Mandatory Development in Syria-Lebanon." *Humanity* (2017): 247–68.

Jacobson, Abigail. *From Empire to Empire: Jerusalem between Ottoman and British Rule*. Syracuse University Press, 2011.

Jones, Heather. "A Forgotten Front? The Mediterranean Blockade in the First World War." *International History Review* 46 (2024): 426–43.

Kaiser, Hilmar. *The Extermination of Armenians in the Diarbekir Region*. Istanbul Bilgi University Press, 2015.

Kaiser, Hilmar. "Regional Resistance to Central Government Policies: Ahmed Djemal Pasha, the Governors of Aleppo, and Armenian Deportees in the Spring and Summer of 1915." *Journal of Genocide Research* 12 (2010): 173–218.

Kaligian, Dikran Mesrob. *Armenian Organization and Ideology under Ottoman Rule, 1908–1914*. Transaction, 2009.

Karakışla, Yavuz Selim. "Osmanlı Ordusunda Kadın Askerler." *Tarih ve Toplum* (June 1999): 14–24.

Karakışla, Yavuz Selim. *Women, War and Work in the Ottoman Empire: Society for the Employment of Ottoman Muslim Women (1916–1923)*. Ottoman Bank and Research Center, 2005.

Karl, Rebecca E. *Staging the World: Chinese Nationalism at the Turn of the Twentieth Century*. Duke University Press, 2002.

Karpat, Kemal. *The Politicization of Islam: Reconstructing Identity, State, Faith, and Community in the Late Ottoman State*. Oxford University Press, 2001.

Kaya, Gökhan. *II. Meşrutiyet Döneminin Demokratları: Osmanlı Demokrat Fırkası (Fırka-i İbad)*. İletişim, 2011.

Kayalı, Hasan. *Arabs and Young Turks: Ottomanism, Arabism, and Islamism in the Ottoman Empire, 1908–1918*. University of California Press, 1997.

Kayaoğlu, Turan. *Legal Imperialism: Sovereignty and Extraterritoriality in Japan, the Ottoman Empire, and China*. Cambridge University Press, 2010.

Kechriotis, Vangelis. "On the Margins of National Historiography: The Greek *İttahtçı* Emmanouil Emmanouilidis—Opportunist or Ottoman Patriot?" In *Untold Histories of the Middle East: Recovering Voices from the 19th and 20th Centuries*, edited by Amy Singer, Christopher K. Neumann, and Akşin Somel, 125–42. Routledge, 2011.

Kechriotis, Vangelis. "Postcolonial Criticism Encounters Late Ottoman Studies." *Historein* 13 (2014): 39–46.

Kévorkian, Raymond. *The Armenian Genocide: A Complete History*. I. B. Tauris, 2011.

Khater, Akram Fouad. *Inventing Home: Emigration, Gender, and the Middle Class in Lebanon, 1870–1920*. University of California Press, 2001.

Kieser, Hans-Lukas. *Talaat Pasha: Father of Modern Turkey, Architect of Genocide*. Princeton University Press, 2018.

Khalidi, Rashid Ismail. *British Policy towards Syria and Palestine, 1906–1914: A Study of the Antecedents of the Hussein-McMahon, the Sykes-Picot Agreement, and the Balfour Declaration*. Middle East Centre, St. Antony's College, 1980.

Khuri-Makdisi, Ilham. *The Eastern Mediterranean and the Making of Global Radicalism, 1860–1914*. University of California Press, 2010.

Kieser, Hans-Lukas, Thomas Schmutz, and Mehmet Polatel. "Reform or Cataclysm? The Agreement of 8 February 1914 Regarding the Ottoman Eastern Provinces." *Journal of Genocide Research* 17 (2015): 285–304.

Kılınçoğlu, Deniz T. *Economics and Capitalism in the Ottoman Empire*. Routledge, 2015.

Klein, Janet. "Kurdish Nationalists and Non-Nationalist Kurdists: Rethinking Minority Nationalism and the Dissolution of the Ottoman Empire, 1908–1909." *Nations and Nationalism* 13 (2007): 135–53.

Koçak, Cemil. *Umûmî Müfettişlikler (1927–1952)*. 3rd ed. İletişim, 2016; 2010; 2003.

Koraltürk, Murat. *Ekonominin Türkleştirilmesi: Erken Cumhuriyet Döneminde.* İletişim, 2011.

Köse, Yavuz. "Between Protest and Envy: Foreign Companies and Ottoman Muslim Society." In *Popular Protest and Political Participation: Studies in Honor of Suraiya Faroqhi*, edited by Eleni Gara, M. Erdem Kabadayı, and Christoph K. Neumann. Istanbul Bilgi University Press, 2011.

Kühn, Thomas. "Shaping and Reshaping Colonial Ottomanism: Contesting Boundaries of Difference and Integration in Ottoman Yemen, 1872–1919." *Comparative Studies of South Asia, Africa, and the Middle East* 27 (2007): 315–31.

Kurzman, Charles. *Democracy Denied, 1905–1915: Intellectuals and the Fate of Democracy.* Harvard University Press, 2008.

Laffan, Michael Francis. *Islamic Nationhood and Colonial Indonesia: The Umma below the Winds.* Routledge Curzon, 2003.

Lambert, Nicholas A. *The War Lords and the Gallipoli Disaster: How Globalized Trade Led Britain to Its Worst Defeat of the First World War.* Oxford University Press, 2021.

Leiserowitz, Ruth. "Population Displacement in East Prussia during the First World War." In Gatrell and Zhvanko, *Europe on the Move*, 23–44.

Leonhard, Jörn. *Der überforderte Frieden: Versailles und die Welt, 1918–1923.* C. H. Beck, 2018.

Leonhard, Jörn. *Die Büchse der Pandora: Geschichte des Ersten Weltkriegs.* C. H. Beck, 2014.

Lessersohn, Nora. "'Provincial Cosmopolitanism' in Late Ottoman Anatolia: An Armenian Shoemaker's Memoir." *Comparative Studies in Society and History* 57 (2015): 528–56.

Levene, Mark. "The Balfour Declaration: A Case of Mistaken Identity." *English Historical Review* 107 (1992): 54–77.

Levene, Mark. "Deadly Geopolitics, Ethnic Mobilisations, and the Vulnerability of Peoples, 1914–1918." In *The First World War as a Caesura? Demographic Concepts, Population Policy, and Genocide in the Late Ottoman, Russian, and Habsburg Spheres*, edited by Christin Pschischholz, 33–48. Duncker and Humblot, 2020.

Lieven, Dominic. *The End of Tsarist Russia: The March to World War I and Revolution.* Penguin, 2015.

Lohr, Eric. *Nationalizing the Russian Empire: The Campaign against Enemy Aliens during World War I.* Harvard University Press, 2003.

Low, Michael Christopher. *Imperial Mecca: Ottoman Arabia and the Indian Ocean Hajj.* Columbia University Press, 2020.

Madley, Benjamin. *An American Genocide: The United States and the California Indian Catastrophe.* Yale University Press, 2016.

Makdisi, Ussama. *Age of Coexistence: The Ecumenical Frame and the Making of the Modern Arab World.* California University Press, 2019.

Makdisi, Ussama. "Ottoman Orientalism." *American Historical Review* 107 (2002): 768–96.

Maksudyan, Nazan. *Ottoman Children and Youth during World War I.* Syracuse University Press, 2019.

Mamdani, Mahmood. *Neither Settler nor Native: The Making and Unmaking of Permanent Minorities.* Harvard University Press, 2020.

McDougall, James. "Sovereignty, Governance, and Political Community in the Ottoman Empire and North Africa." In *Re-imagining Democracy in the Mediterranean, 1780–1860*, edited by Joanna Innes and Mark Philp, 127–52. Oxford University Press, 2018.

Methodieva, Milena B. *Between Empire and Nation: Muslim Reforms in the Balkans*. Stanford University Press, 2021.

Metinsoy, Elif Mahir. *Ottoman Women during World War I: Everyday Experiences, Politics and Conflict*. Cambridge University Press, 2017.

Minawi, Mostafa. *Losing Istanbul: Ottoman-Arab Imperialists and the End of Empire*. Stanford University Press, 2022.

Mirzoyan, Sonya, and Candan Badem. *The Construction of the Tiflis-Aleksandropol-Kars Railway (1895–1899)*. The Institute for Historical Justice and Reconciliation, 2013.

Morawitz, Charles. "Obstacles to Reform in Turkey." *North American Review* 179 (1904): 194–206.

Moses, A. Dirk. "Empire, Colony, Genocide: Keywords and Philosophy of History." In *Empire, Colony, Genocide: Conquest, Occupation, and Subaltern Resistance in World History*, edited by A. Dirk Moses, 3–54. Berghahn, 2008.

Moses, A. Dirk. *The Problems of Genocide: Permanent Security and the Language of Transgression*. Cambridge University Press, 2021.

Motika, Raoul, and Christoph Herzog. "Orientalism Alla Turca: Late 19th/Early 20th Century Ottoman Voyages into the Muslim 'Outback.'" *Die Welt des Islams* 40 (2000): 139–95.

Nacar, Can. *Labor and Power in the Late Ottoman Empire: Tobacco Workers, Managers, and the State, 1872–1912*. Palgrave Macmillan, 2019.

Neyzi, Olcay, Hatice Nurçin Saka, and Selim Kurtoğlu. "Anthropometric Studies on the Turkish Population—A Historical Review." *Journal of Clinical Research in Pediatric Endocrinology* 5 (2013): 1–12.

Ochsenwald, William. *The Hijaz Railroad*. University of Virginia Press, 1980.

Ó Gráda, Cormac. *The Hidden Victims: Civilian Casualties of the Two World Wars*. Princeton University Press, 2024.

Osterhammel, Jürgen. *The Global Transformation of the World: A Global History of the Nineteenth Century*. Translated by Patrick Camiller. Princeton University Press, 2015.

Otte, T. G. *Statesman of Europe: A Life of Sir Edward Grey*. Allen Lane, 2020.

Özbek, Nadir. "Defining the Public Sphere during the Late Ottoman Empire: War, Mass Mobilization and the Young Turk Regime (1908–18)." *Middle Eastern Studies* 43 (2007): 795–805.

Özok-Gündoğan, Nilay. *The Kurdish Nobility in the Ottoman Empire: Loyalty, Autonomy and Privilege*. Edinburgh University Press, 2022.

Öztan, Ramazan Hakkı. "Point of No Return? Prospects of Empire after the Defeat in the Balkan Wars (1912–1913)." *International Journal of Middle East Studies* 50 (2018): 65–84.

Öztan, Ramazan Hakkı, and Alp Yenen, eds. *Age of Rogues: Rebels, Revolutionaries and Racketeers at the Frontiers of Empires*. Edinburgh University Press, 2021.

Pamuk, Şevket. *Uneven Centuries: Economic Development of Turkey since 1820*. Princeton University Press, 2018.

Parsons, Laila. *The Commander: Fawzi al-Qawuqji and the Fight for Arab Independence, 1914–1948*. Hill and Wang, 2016.

Peçe, Uğur Zekeriya. *Island and Empire: How Civil War in Crete Mobilized the Ottoman World.* Stanford University Press, 2024.

Pedersen, Susan. *The Guardians: The League of Nations and the Crisis of Empire.* Oxford University Press, 2015.

Pedersen, Susan. "Writing the Balfour Declaration into the Mandate for Palestine." *International History Review* 45 (2023): 279–91.

Philliou, Christine. *Turkey: A Past against History.* University of California Press, 2021.

Pitts, Graham Auman. "The Ecology of Migration: Remittances in World War I Mount Lebanon." *Arab Studies Journal* 26 (2018): 102–29.

Pitts, Graham Aumann. "A Hungry Population Stops Thinking about Resistance: Class, Famine, and Lebanon's World War I Legacy." *Journal of Ottoman and Turkish Studies* 7 (2020): 217–36.

Pitts, Jennifer. *Boundaries of the International: Law and Empire.* Harvard University Press, 2018.

Polatel, Mehmet. *Armenians and Land Disputes in the Ottoman Empire, 1850–1914.* Edinburgh University Press, 2025.

Prätor, Sabine. *Der arabische Faktor in der jungtürkischen Politik: Eine Studie zum osmanischen Parlament der II. Konstitution (1908–1918).* Klaus Schwarz, 1993.

Provence, Michael. *The Last Ottoman Generation and the Making of the Modern Middle East.* Cambridge University Press, 2017.

Reinhardt, Anne. *Navigating Semi-Colonialism: Shipping, Sovereignty, and Nation-Building in China, 1860–1937.* Harvard University Asia Center, 2018.

Reyhan, Cenk. *Türkiye'de Liberalizm Kökenleri: Prens Sabahaddin (1877–1948).* İmge Kitabevi, 2008.

Reynolds, Michael A. *Shattering Empires: The Clash and Collapse of the Ottoman Empires, 1908–1918.* Cambridge University Press, 2011.

Richter, Klaus. "'A Mass Which You Could Form into Whatever You Wanted': Refugees and State Building in Lithuania and Courland, 1914–21." In Gatrell and Zhvanko, *Europe on the Move,* 45–65.

Robins, Nicholas A., and Adam Jones, eds. *Genocides by the Oppressed: Subaltern Genocide in Theory and Practice.* Indiana University Press, 2009.

Robson, Laura. *The Politics of Mass Violence in the Middle East.* Oxford University Press, 2020.

Rogan, Eugene. *The Fall of the Ottomans: The Great War in the Middle East.* Basic Books, 2015.

Roshwald, Aviel. *Ethnic Nationalism and the Fall of Empires: Central Europe, Russia, and the Middle East, 1914–1923.* Routledge, 2001.

Ryan, Eileen. *Religion as Resistance: Negotiating Authority in Italian Libya.* Oxford University Press, 2019.

Said, Edward W. *Out of Place: A Memoir.* Knopf, 1999.

Sanborn, Joshua A. *Imperial Collapse: The Great War and the Destruction of the Russian Empire.* Oxford University Press, 2015.

Satia, Priya. "The Defense of Inhumanity: Air Control and the British Idea of Arabia." *American Historical Review* 111 (2006): 16–51.

Schläpfer, Aline. "Between Ruler and Rogue: Sayyid Talib al-Naqib and the British in Early Twentieth-Century Basra." In *Age of Rogues: Rebels, Revolutionaries and Racketeers at the*

Frontiers of Empires, edited by Ramazan Hakkı Öztan and Alp Yenen, 235–57. Edinburgh University Press, 2021.

Shenfield, Stephen D. "The Circassians: A Forgotten Genocide?" In *The Massacre in History*, edited by Mark Levene and Penny Roberts, 149–62. Berghahn Books, 1999.

Shumsky, Dmitry. *Beyond the Nation-State: The Zionist Political Imagination from Pinsker to Ben Gurion*. Yale University Press, 2018.

Siegel, Jennifer. *Endgame: Britain, Russia and the Final Struggle for Central Asia*. I. B. Tauris, 2002.

Simon, Rachel. *Libya between Ottomanism and Nationalism*. Klaus Schwarz, 1987.

Şimşeker, Somer Alp. *Birinci Dünya Savaşı'nda Osmanlı İstihbaratı: İkinci Şube Tarihi*. Kronik, 2022.

Smith, Leonard V. *Sovereignty at the Paris Peace Conference of 1919*. Oxford University Press, 2018.

Snyder, Timothy. *Bloodlands: Europe between Hitler and Stalin*. Basic Books, 2010.

Sohrabi, Nader. *Revolution and Constitutionalism in the Ottoman Empire and Iran*. Cambridge University Press, 2011.

Spencer, Philip. "Imperialism, Anti-Imperialism and the Problem of Genocide: Past and Present." *History* 98 (2013): 606–22.

Suny, Ronald Grigor. "Imperial Choices: Perceiving Threats and the Descent to Genocide." In *The First World War as a Caesura? Demographic Concepts, Population Policy, and Genocide in the Late Ottoman, Russian, and Habsburg Spheres*, edited by Christin Pschischholz, 13–31. Duncker and Humblot, 2020.

Suny, Ronald Grigor. *They Can Live in the Desert but Nowhere Else: A History of the Armenian Genocide*. Princeton University Press, 2015.

Suny, Ronald Grigor, Fatma Müge Göçek, and Norman M. Naimark, eds. *A Question of Genocide: Armenians and Turks at the End of the Ottoman Empire*. Oxford University Press, 2011.

Tanielian, Melanie S. *Charity of War: Famine, Humanitarian Aid, and World War I in the Middle East*. Stanford University Press, 2017.

Thompson, Elizabeth F. *Colonial Citizens: Republican Rights, Paternal Privilege and Gender in French Syria and Lebanon*. Columbia University Press, 2000.

Thompson, Elizabeth F. *How the West Stole Democracy from the Arabs: The Syrian Congress of 1920 and the Destruction of Its Historic Liberal-Islamic Alliance*. Atlantic Monthly, 2021.

Thompson, Elizabeth F. *Justice Interrupted: The Struggle for Constitutional Government in the Middle East*. Harvard University Press, 2013.

Thomson, Janice E. *Mercenaries, Pirates, and Sovereigns: State-Building and Extraterritorial Violence in Early Modern Europe*. Princeton University Press, 1994.

Todd, David. *A Velvet Empire: French Informal Imperialism in the Nineteenth Century*. Princeton University Press, 2021.

Toumarkine, Alexandre. *Les migrations des populations musulmanes balkaniques en Anatolie (1876–1913)*. Editions Isis, 1995.

Tunçer, Ali Coşkun. *Sovereign Debt and International Financial Control: The Middle East and the Balkans, 1870–1914*. Palgrave Macmillan, 2015.

Türkyılmaz, Yektan. "Rethinking Genocide: Violence and Victimhood in Eastern Anatolia, 1913–1915." PhD diss., Duke University, 2011.

Üngör, Uğur Ümit. *The Making of Modern Turkey: Nation and State in Eastern Anatolia, 1913–1950*. Oxford University Press, 2011.

Uyar, Mesut. *The Ottoman Army and the First World War*. Routledge, 2020.

Vaka, Demetra. *The Unveiled Ladies of Stamboul*. Books for Libraries Press, 1923.

van den Boogert, Maurits. *The Capitulations and the Ottoman Legal System: Qadis, Consuls and the Beratlıs in the 18th Century*. Brill, 2005.

van der Dussen, W. J. "The Question of Armenian Reforms." *Armenian Review* 39 (1986): 11–28.

Walter, Dierk. *Colonial Violence: European Empires and the Use of Force*. Translated by Peter Lewis. Oxford University Press, 2017.

Watts, Martin. *The Jewish Legion and the First World War*. Palgrave Macmillan, 2004.

Williams, Elizabeth R. "'The Agriculture Ministry of the Whole World': The International Institute of Agriculture and the Politics of Ottoman Statistics Collection." *Comparative Studies of South Asia, Africa and the Middle East* 43 (2023): 224–41.

Williams, Elizabeth R. *States of Cultivation: Imperial Transition and Scientific Agriculture in the Eastern Mediterranean*. Stanford University Press, 2023.

Wilson, Keith. "Grey and the Russian Threat to India, 1892–1915." *International History Review* 38 (2016): 275–84.

Wolf, Klaus. *Gallipoli 1915: Das deutsch-türkische Militärbündnis im Ersten Weltkrieg*. Report Verlag, 2008.

Wyrtzen, Jonathan. *Making Morocco: Colonial Intervention and the Politics of Identity*. Cornell University Press, 2015.

Wyrtzen, Jonathan. *Worldmaking in the Long Great War: How Local and Colonial Struggles Shaped the Modern Middle East*. Columbia University Press, 2022.

Yanıkdağ, Yücel. *Healing the Nation: Prisoners of War, Medicine and Nationalism in Turkey, 1914–1939*. Edinburgh University Press, 2013.

Yıldırım, Onur. *Diplomacy and Displacement: Reconsidering the Turco-Greek Exchange of Populations, 1922–1934*. Routledge, 2006.

Yilmaz, Huseyin. "The Eastern Question and the Ottoman Empire: The Genesis of the Near and Middle East in the Nineteenth Century." In *Is There a Middle East? The Evolution of a Geopolitical Concept*. Edited by Michael E. Bonine, Abbas Amanat, and Michael Ezekiel Gasper, 11–35. Stanford University Press, 2012.

Yosmaoğlu, İpek. *Blood Ties: Religion, Blood Ties, and the Politics of Nationhood in Ottoman Macedonia, 1878–1908*. Cornell University Press, 2013.

Zhantiev, Dimitry R. "Making Opinion at the Summit: A Northern Caucasian Nobleman in the Ottoman-Turkish Ruling Elite: Bekir Sami-Bey Kundukh (1865–1933)." *Archiv Orientální* 80 (2012): 273–76.

Zürcher, Erik Jan. "How Europeans Adopted Anatolia and Created Turkey." *European Review* 13 (2005): 379–94.

Zürcher, Erik Jan. "Macedonians in Anatolia: The Importance of the Macedonian Roots of the Unionists for Their Policies in Anatolia after 1914." *Middle Eastern Studies* 50 (2014): 960–75.

Zürcher, Erik Jan. "Ottoman Labour Battalions in World War I." In *Der Völkermord an den Armeniern und die Shoah*, 187–95, edited by Hans-Lukas Kieser and Dominik J. Schaller. Chronos, 2002.

Zürcher, Erik Jan. *The Young Turk Legacy and National Building: From the Ottoman Empire to Atatürk's Turkey*. I. B. Tauris, 2010.

Zürcher, Erik Jan. "The Young Turk Revolution: Comparisons and Connections." *Middle Eastern Studies* 55 (2019): 481–98.

Zürcher, Erik Jan. "The Young Turks—Children of the Borderlands." in *Turkology Update Leiden Project Working Papers Archive* (2002): 1–9.

INDEX

Pages indicating maps, figures, and tables are shown in italics.